Graphic Classics:
OSCAR WILDE

Graphic Classics® Volume Sixteen

2009

Edited by Tom Pomplun

EUREKA PRODUCTIONS
8778 Oak Grove Road, Mount Horeb, Wisconsin 53572
www.graphicclassics.com

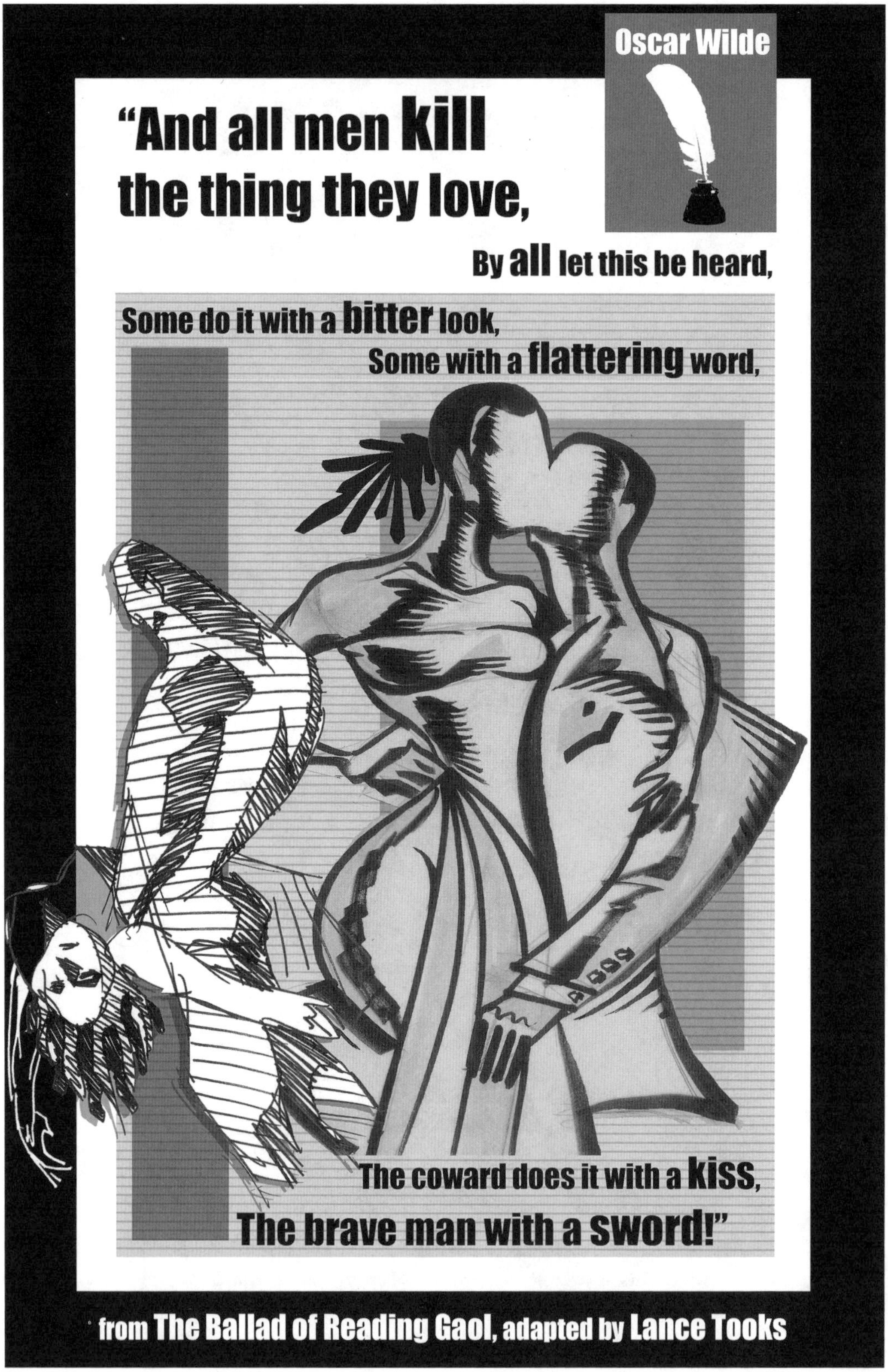
Oscar Wilde
"And all men kill
the thing they love,
By all let this be heard,
Some do it with a bitter look,
Some with a flattering word,
The coward does it with a kiss,
The brave man with a sword!"
from The Ballad of Reading Gaol, adapted by Lance Tooks

CONTENTS

PHRASES AND PHILOSOPHIES FOR THE USE OF THE YOUNG

- The first duty in life is to be as artificial as possible. What the second duty is no one has as yet discovered.
- No great artist ever sees things as they really are. If he did, he would cease to be an artist.
- Experience is the name everyone gives to their mistakes.
- Always forgive your enemies; nothing annoys them so much.
- Of course America had often been discovered before Columbus, but it had always been hushed up.
- I sometimes think that God in creating man somewhat over-estimated his ability.
- As long as war is regarded as wicked, it will always have its fascination. When it is looked upon as vulgar, it will cease to be popular.
- One should always play fairly when one has the winning cards.
- Some cause happiness wherever they go; others whenever they go.
- The difference between journalism and literature is that journalism is unreadable and literature is not read.
- The old believe everything: the middle-aged suspect everything: the young know everything.
- Wickedness is a myth invented by good people to account for the curious attractiveness of others.
- People fashion their God after their own understanding. They make their God first and worship him afterwards.
- The basis of optimism is sheer terror.
- I always pass on good advice. It is the only thing to do with it. It is never of any use to oneself.
- To love oneself is the beginning of a lifelong romance.

— Oscar Wilde

Graphic Classics:
OSCAR WILDE

ILLUSTRATION ©2009 STEPHEN SILVER

The Ballad of Reading Gaol *(excerpt)*
illustrated by Lance Tooks 2

The Picture of Dorian Gray
adapted by Alex Burrows,
illustrated by Lisa K. Weber 4

The Canterville Ghost
adapted by Antonella Caputo,
illustrated by Nick Miller 50

Lord Arthur Savile's Crime
adapted by Rich Rainey,
illustrated by Stan Shaw 80

Salomé
adapted by Tom Pomplun,
illustrated by Molly Kiely 110

Graphic Classics: Oscar Wilde / ISBN 978-0-9787919-6-4 is published by Eureka Productions. Price US $11.95, CAN $13.50. Available from Eureka Productions, 8778 Oak Grove Road, Mount Horeb, WI 53572. Tom Pomplun, publisher, tom@graphicclassics.com. Eileen Fitzgerald, editorial assistant. Compilation and all original works ©2009 Eureka Productions. Graphic Classics is a registered trademark of Eureka Productions. For ordering information and previews of upcoming volumes visit the Graphic Classics website at http://www.graphicclassics.com. Printed in Canada.

3

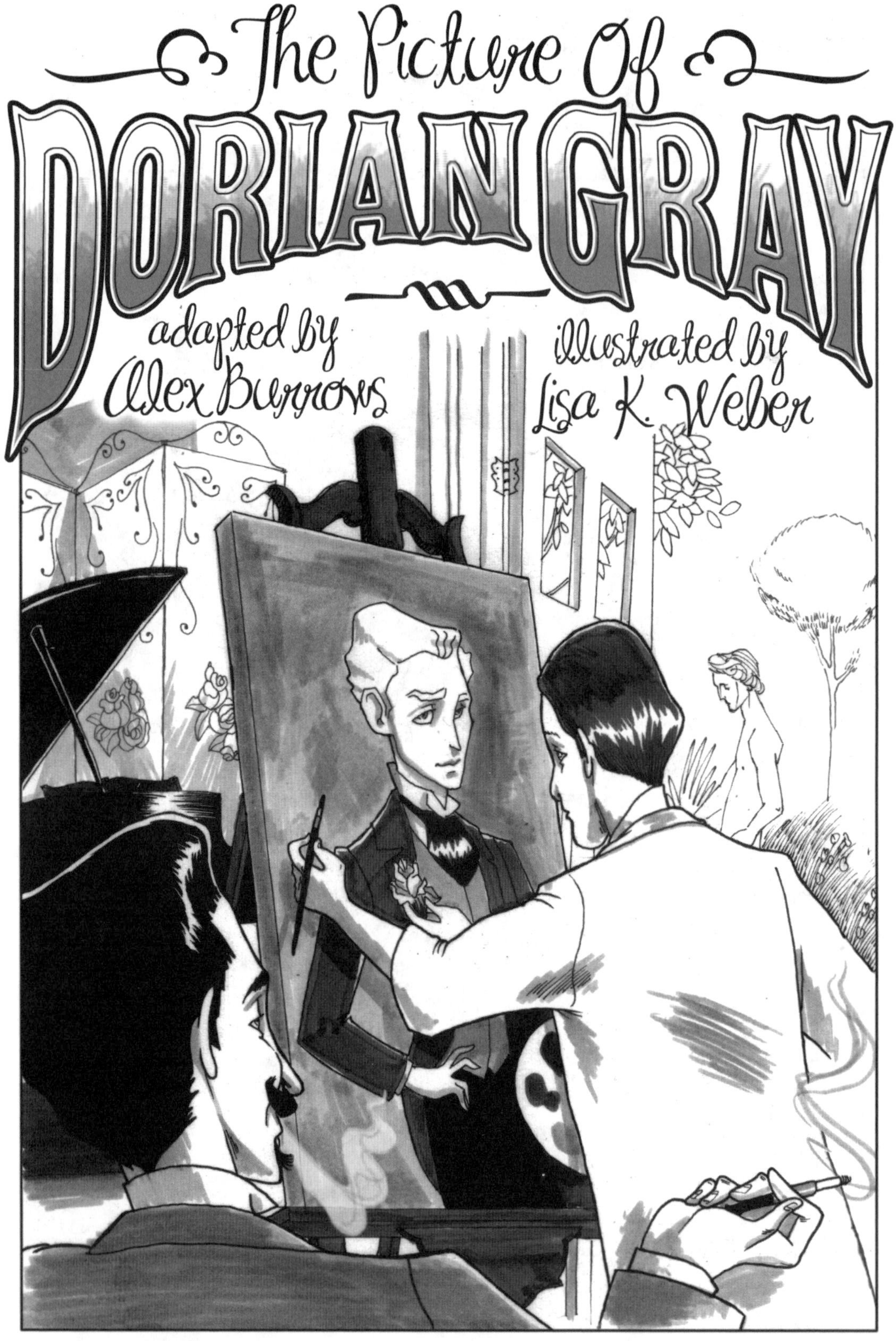
The Picture Of
DORIAN GRAY
adapted by
Alex Burrows
illustrated by
Lisa K. Weber

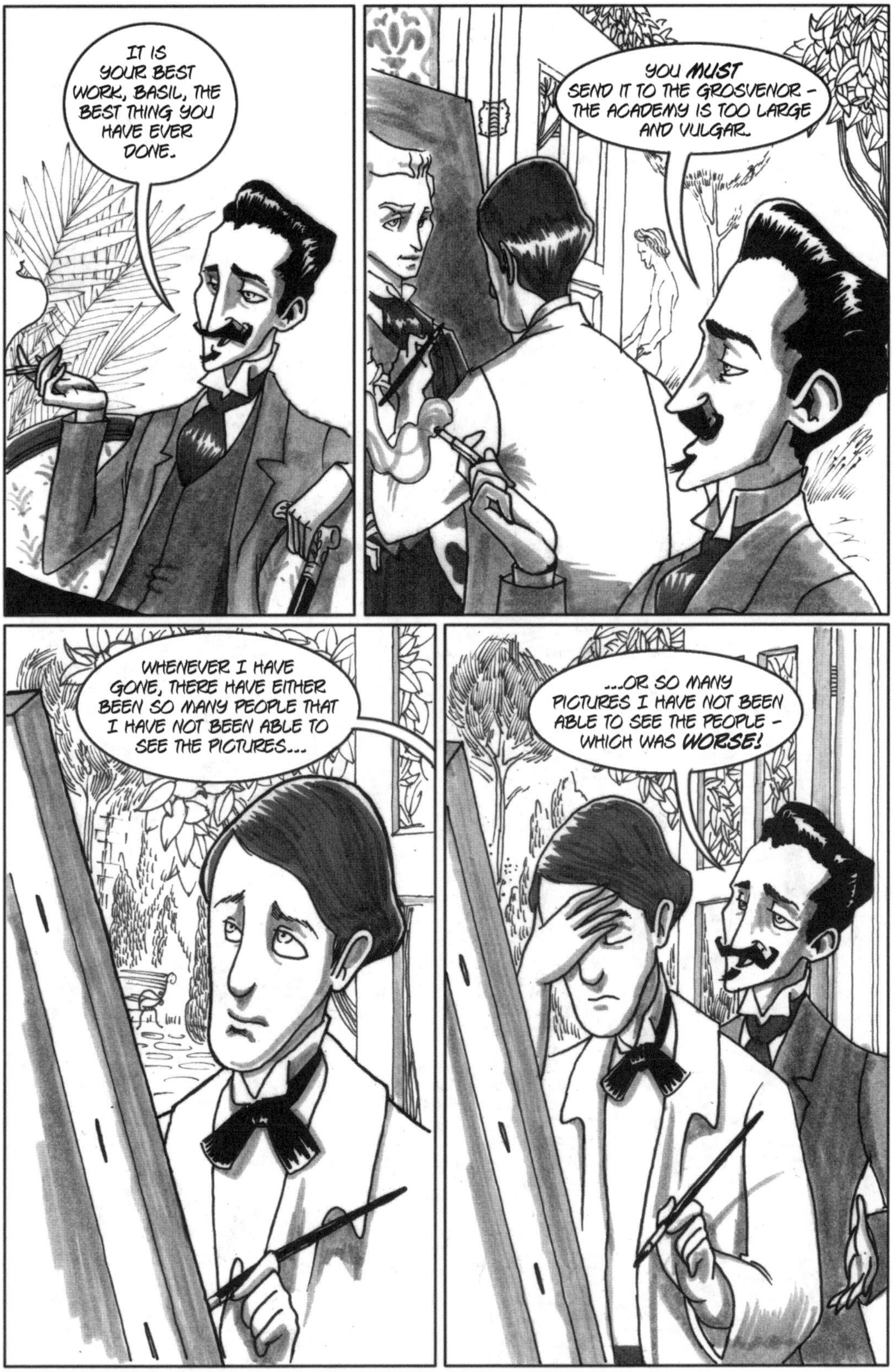
IT IS YOUR BEST WORK, BASIL, THE BEST THING YOU HAVE EVER DONE.
YOU MUST SEND IT TO THE GROSVENOR - THE ACADEMY IS TOO LARGE AND VULGAR.
WHENEVER I HAVE GONE, THERE HAVE EITHER BEEN SO MANY PEOPLE THAT I HAVE NOT BEEN ABLE TO SEE THE PICTURES...
...OR SO MANY PICTURES I HAVE NOT BEEN ABLE TO SEE THE PEOPLE - WHICH WAS WORSE!

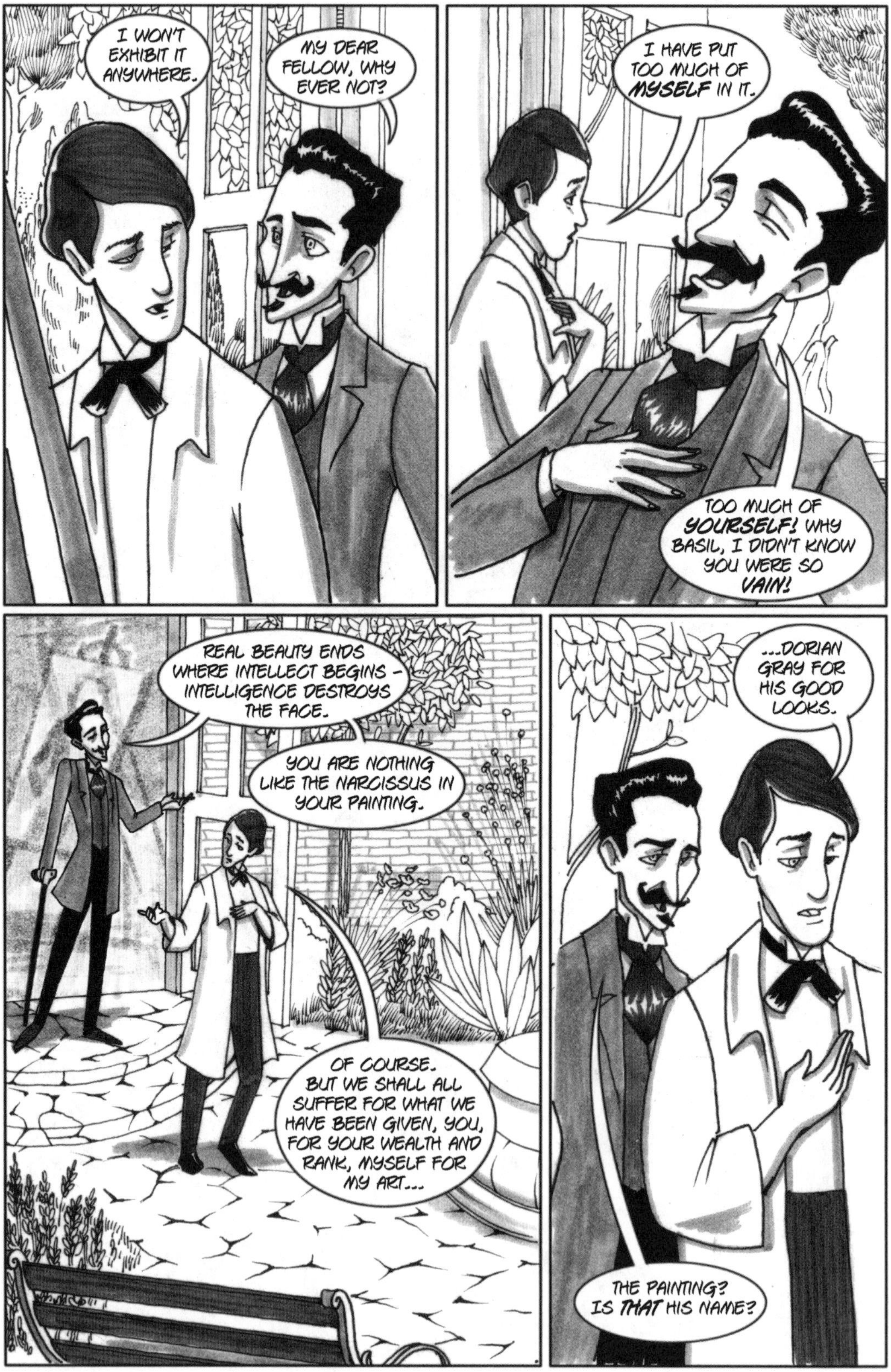
I WON'T EXHIBIT IT ANYWHERE.
MY DEAR FELLOW, WHY EVER NOT?
I HAVE PUT TOO MUCH OF MYSELF IN IT.
TOO MUCH OF YOURSELF! WHY BASIL, I DIDN'T KNOW YOU WERE SO VAIN!
REAL BEAUTY ENDS WHERE INTELLECT BEGINS - INTELLIGENCE DESTROYS THE FACE.
YOU ARE NOTHING LIKE THE NARCISSUS IN YOUR PAINTING.
OF COURSE. BUT WE SHALL ALL SUFFER FOR WHAT WE HAVE BEEN GIVEN, YOU, FOR YOUR WEALTH AND RANK, MYSELF FOR MY ART...
...DORIAN GRAY FOR HIS GOOD LOOKS.
THE PAINTING? IS THAT HIS NAME?

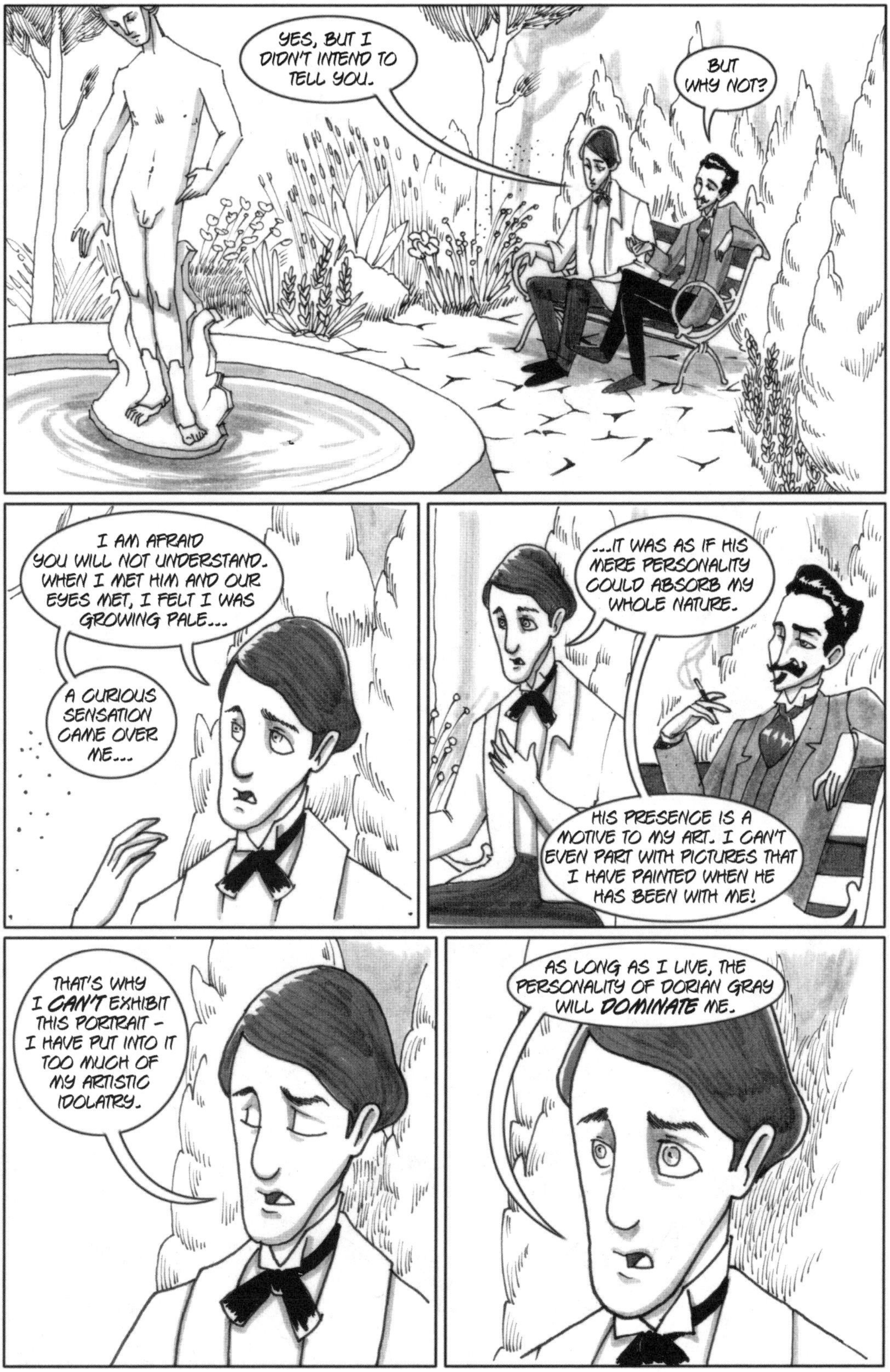
YES, BUT I DIDN'T INTEND TO TELL YOU.
BUT WHY NOT?
I AM AFRAID YOU WILL NOT UNDERSTAND. WHEN I MET HIM AND OUR EYES MET, I FELT I WAS GROWING PALE...
A CURIOUS SENSATION CAME OVER ME...
...IT WAS AS IF HIS MERE PERSONALITY COULD ABSORB MY WHOLE NATURE.
HIS PRESENCE IS A MOTIVE TO MY ART. I CAN'T EVEN PART WITH PICTURES THAT I HAVE PAINTED WHEN HE HAS BEEN WITH ME!
THAT'S WHY I **CAN'T** EXHIBIT THIS PORTRAIT - I HAVE PUT INTO IT TOO MUCH OF MY ARTISTIC IDOLATRY.
AS LONG AS I LIVE, THE PERSONALITY OF DORIAN GRAY WILL **DOMINATE** ME.

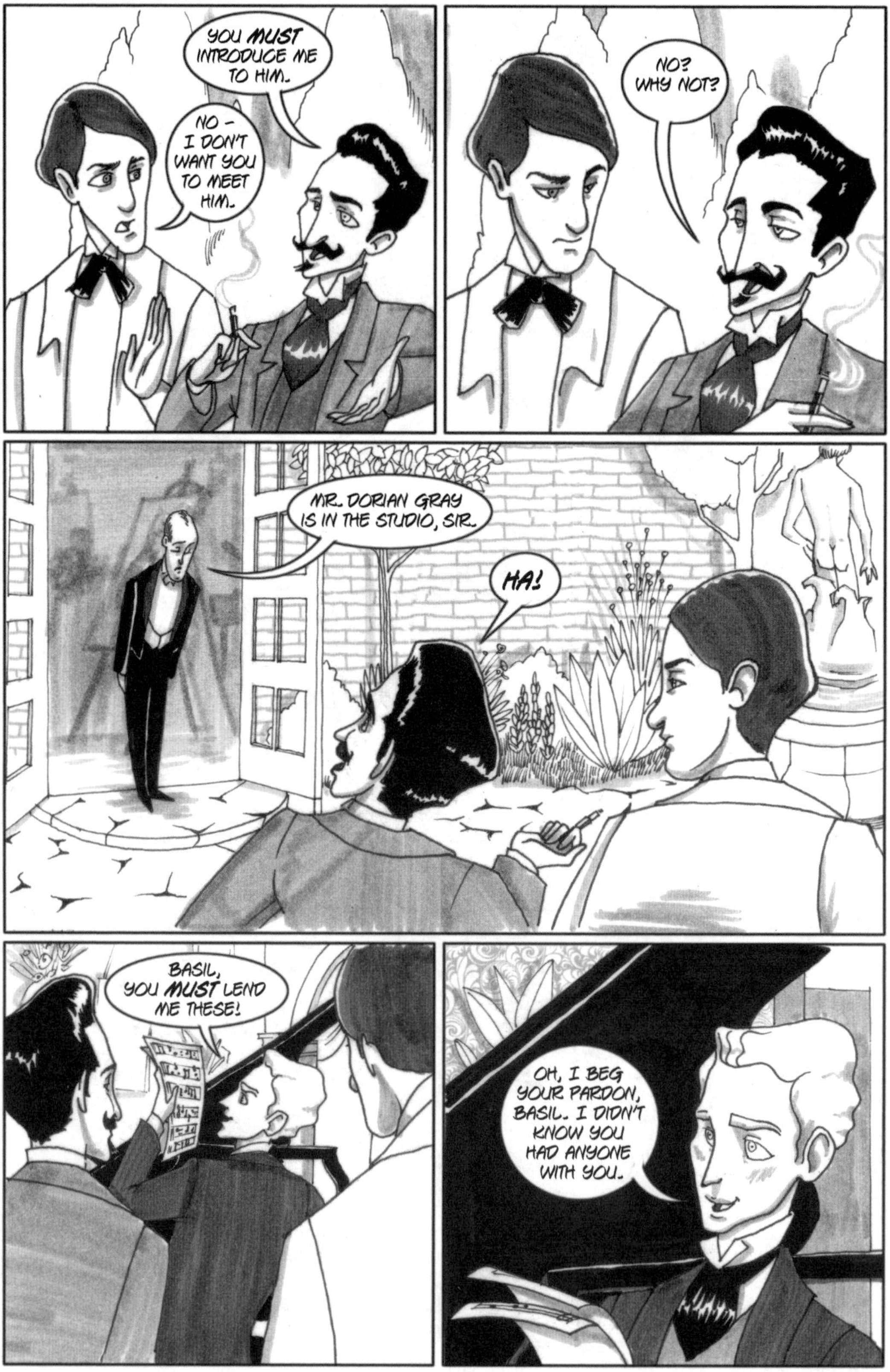
YOU MUST INTRODUCE ME TO HIM.
NO - I DON'T WANT YOU TO MEET HIM.
NO? WHY NOT?
MR. DORIAN GRAY IS IN THE STUDIO, SIR.
HA!
BASIL, YOU MUST LEND ME THESE!
OH, I BEG YOUR PARDON, BASIL. I DIDN'T KNOW YOU HAD ANYONE WITH YOU.

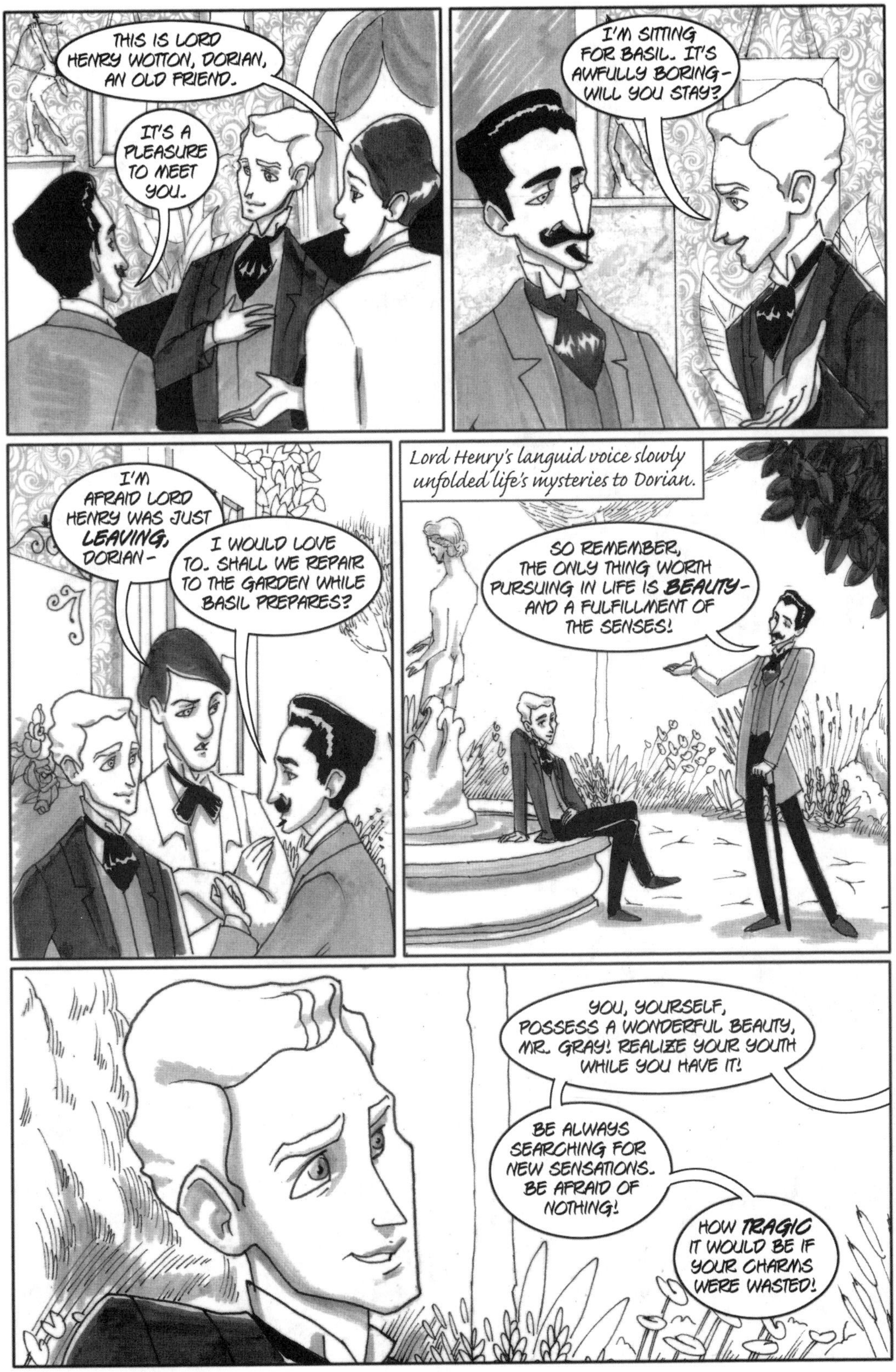
THIS IS LORD HENRY WOTTON, DORIAN, AN OLD FRIEND.
IT'S A PLEASURE TO MEET YOU.
I'M SITTING FOR BASIL. IT'S AWFULLY BORING- WILL YOU STAY?
I'M AFRAID LORD HENRY WAS JUST LEAVING, DORIAN-
I WOULD LOVE TO. SHALL WE REPAIR TO THE GARDEN WHILE BASIL PREPARES?
Lord Henry's languid voice slowly unfolded life's mysteries to Dorian.
SO REMEMBER, THE ONLY THING WORTH PURSUING IN LIFE IS BEAUTY- AND A FULFILLMENT OF THE SENSES!
YOU, YOURSELF, POSSESS A WONDERFUL BEAUTY, MR. GRAY! REALIZE YOUR YOUTH WHILE YOU HAVE IT!
BE ALWAYS SEARCHING FOR NEW SENSATIONS. BE AFRAID OF NOTHING!
HOW TRAGIC IT WOULD BE IF YOUR CHARMS WERE WASTED!

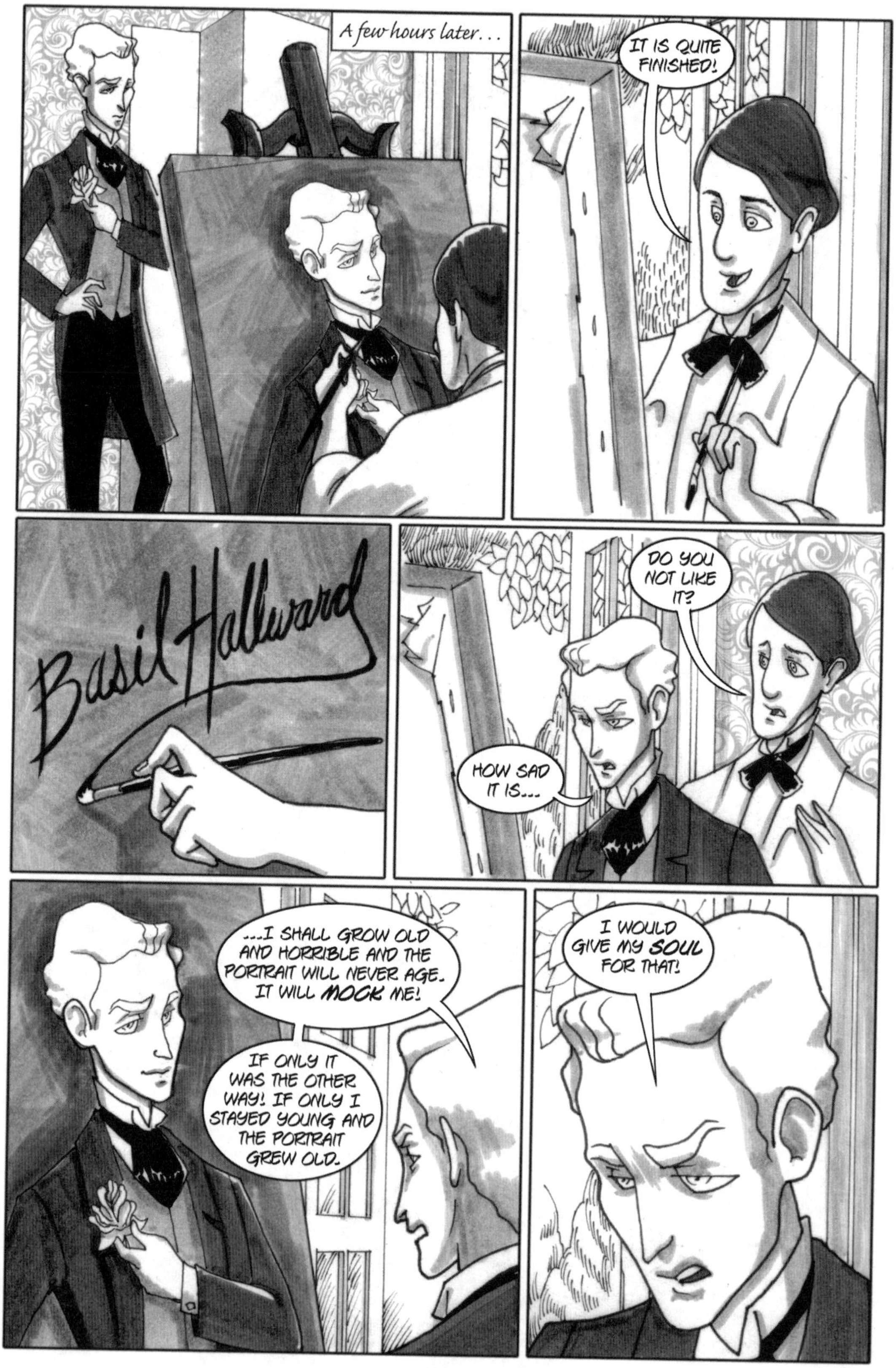
A few hours later...
IT IS QUITE FINISHED!
Basil Hallward
DO YOU NOT LIKE IT?
HOW SAD IT IS...
...I SHALL GROW OLD AND HORRIBLE AND THE PORTRAIT WILL NEVER AGE. IT WILL MOCK ME!
IF ONLY IT WAS THE OTHER WAY! IF ONLY I STAYED YOUNG AND THE PORTRAIT GREW OLD.
I WOULD GIVE MY SOUL FOR THAT!

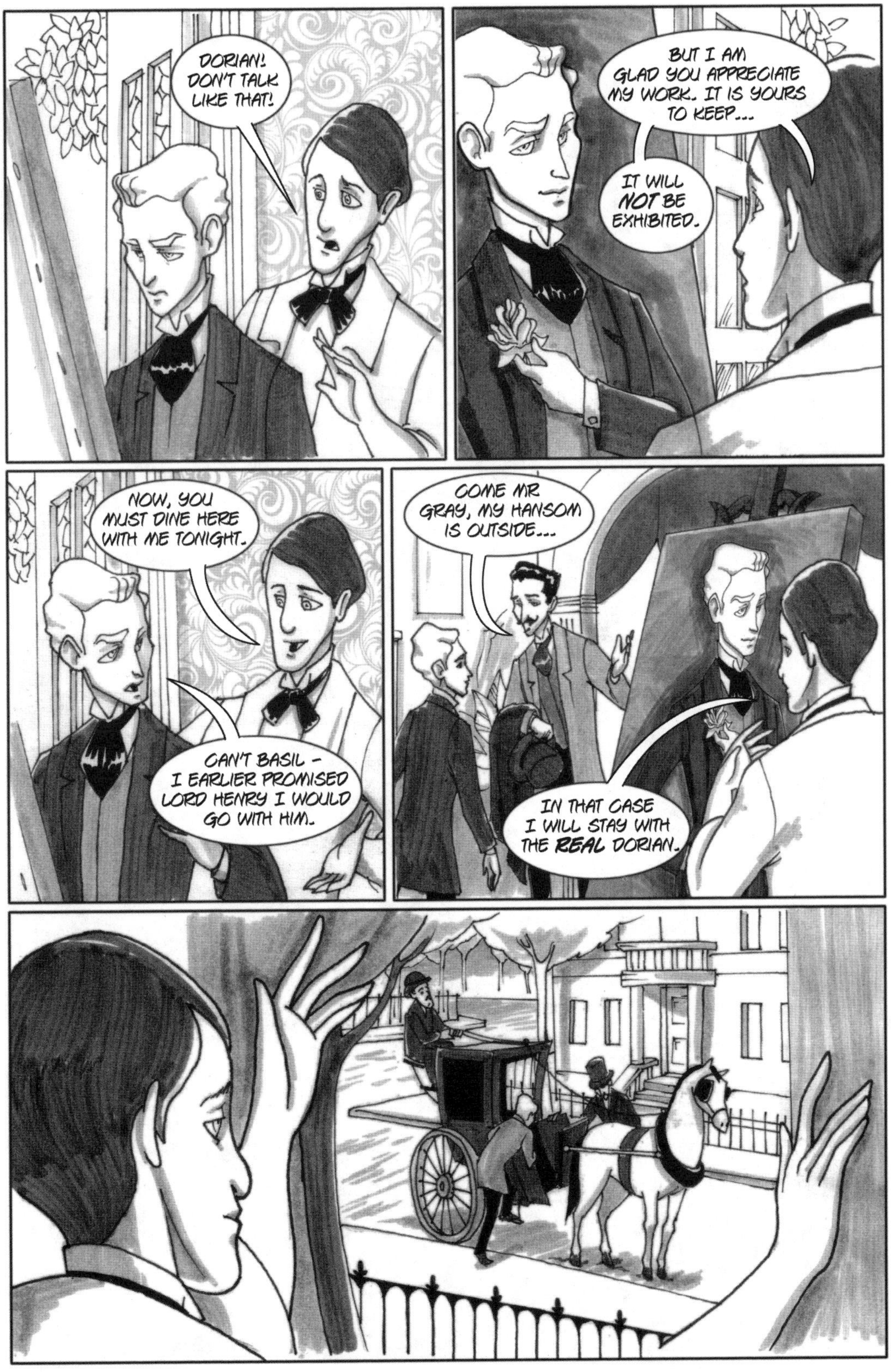
DORIAN! DON'T TALK LIKE THAT!
BUT I AM GLAD YOU APPRECIATE MY WORK. IT IS YOURS TO KEEP...
IT WILL NOT BE EXHIBITED.
NOW, YOU MUST DINE HERE WITH ME TONIGHT.
CAN'T BASIL - I EARLIER PROMISED LORD HENRY I WOULD GO WITH HIM.
COME MR GRAY, MY HANSOM IS OUTSIDE...
IN THAT CASE I WILL STAY WITH THE REAL DORIAN.

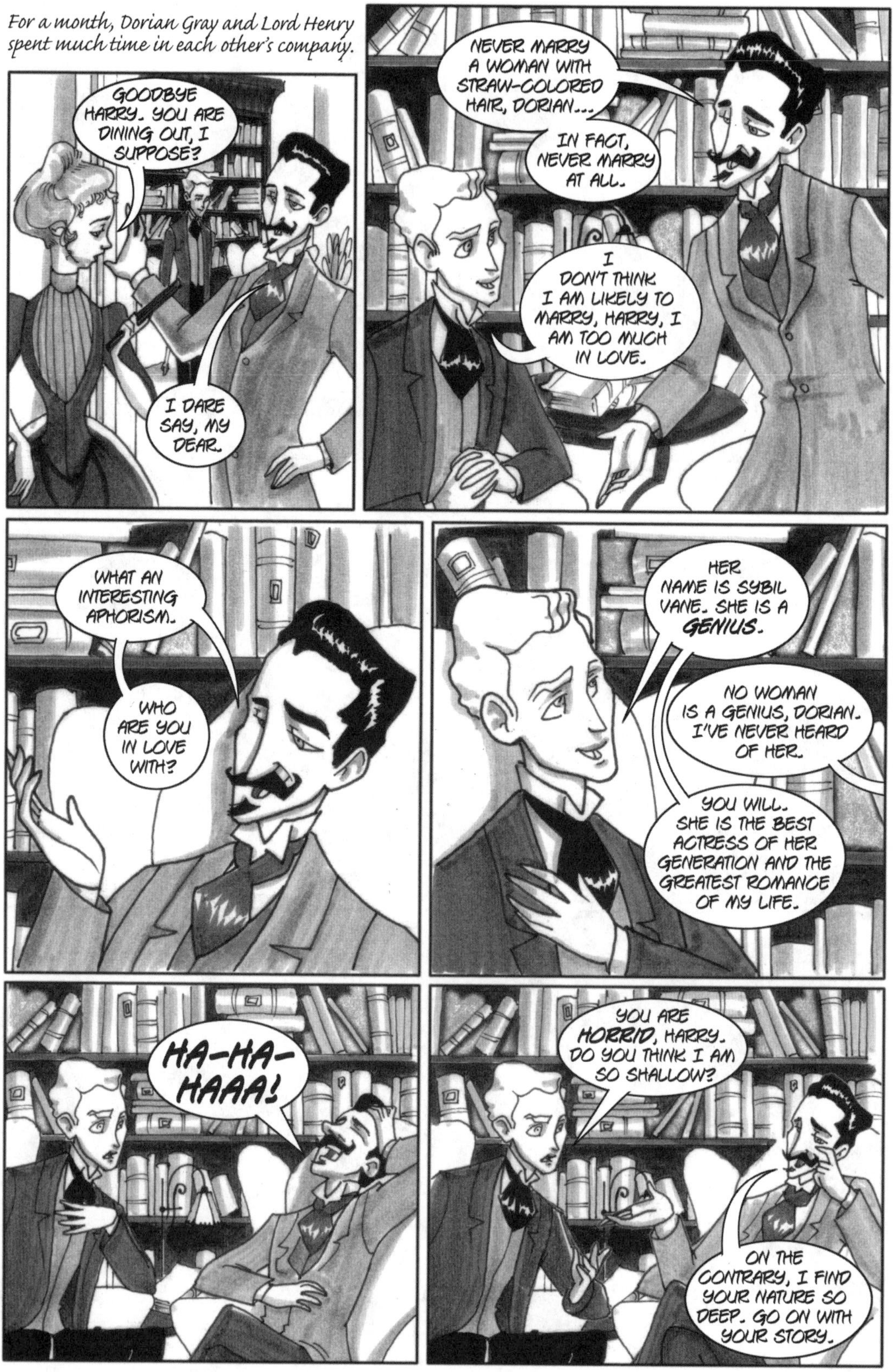
For a month, Dorian Gray and Lord Henry spent much time in each other's company.
GOODBYE HARRY. YOU ARE DINING OUT, I SUPPOSE?
I DARE SAY, MY DEAR.
NEVER MARRY A WOMAN WITH STRAW-COLORED HAIR, DORIAN...
IN FACT, NEVER MARRY AT ALL.
I DON'T THINK I AM LIKELY TO MARRY, HARRY, I AM TOO MUCH IN LOVE.
WHAT AN INTERESTING APHORISM.
WHO ARE YOU IN LOVE WITH?
HER NAME IS SYBIL VANE. SHE IS A GENIUS.
NO WOMAN IS A GENIUS, DORIAN. I'VE NEVER HEARD OF HER.
YOU WILL. SHE IS THE BEST ACTRESS OF HER GENERATION AND THE GREATEST ROMANCE OF MY LIFE.
HA-HA-HAAA!
YOU ARE HORRID, HARRY. DO YOU THINK I AM SO SHALLOW?
ON THE CONTRARY, I FIND YOUR NATURE SO DEEP. GO ON WITH YOUR STORY.

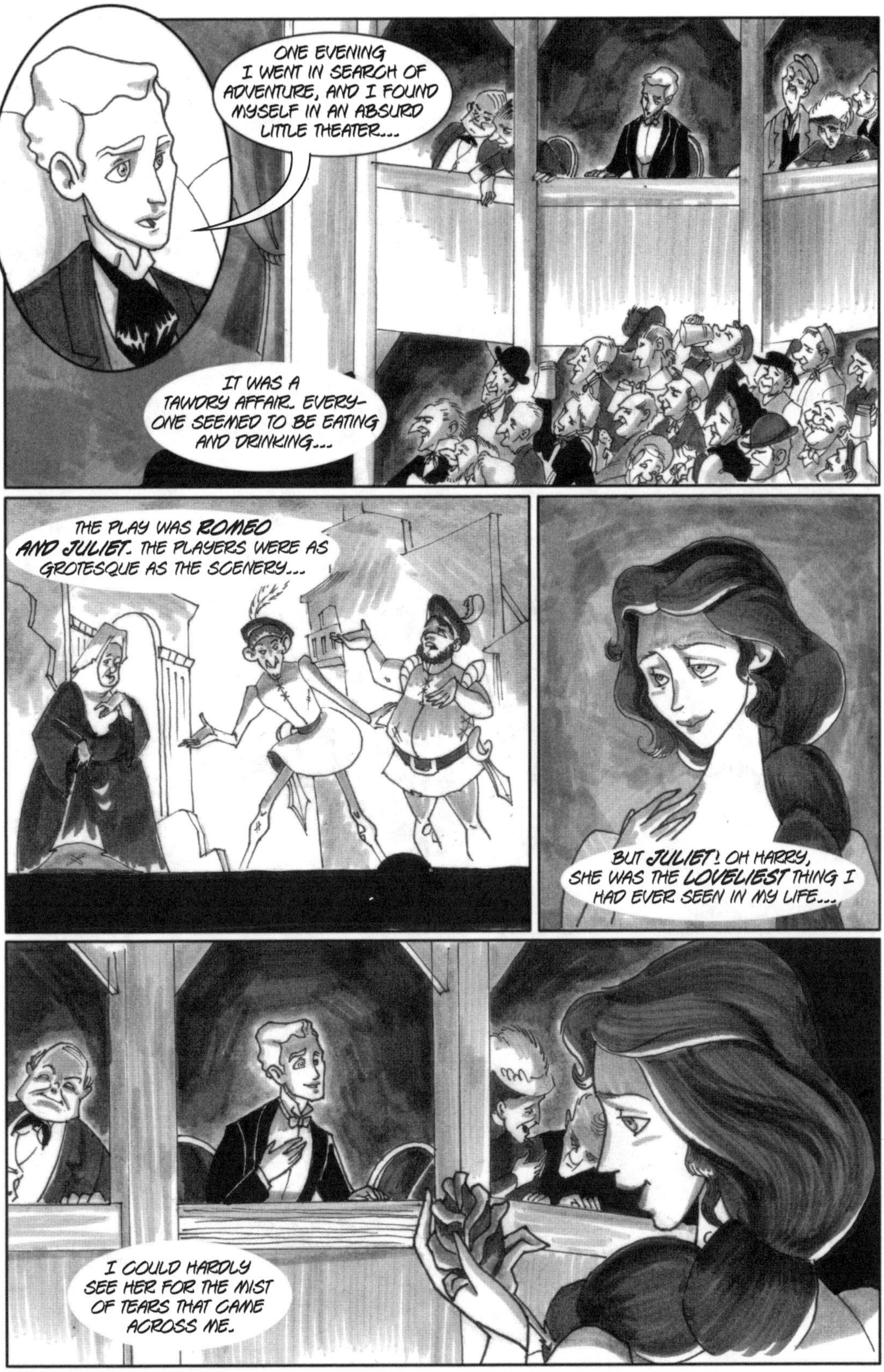
ONE EVENING I WENT IN SEARCH OF ADVENTURE, AND I FOUND MYSELF IN AN ABSURD LITTLE THEATER...
IT WAS A TAWDRY AFFAIR. EVERY-ONE SEEMED TO BE EATING AND DRINKING...
THE PLAY WAS ROMEO AND JULIET. THE PLAYERS WERE AS GROTESQUE AS THE SCENERY...
BUT JULIET! OH HARRY, SHE WAS THE LOVELIEST THING I HAD EVER SEEN IN MY LIFE...
I COULD HARDLY SEE HER FOR THE MIST OF TEARS THAT CAME ACROSS ME.

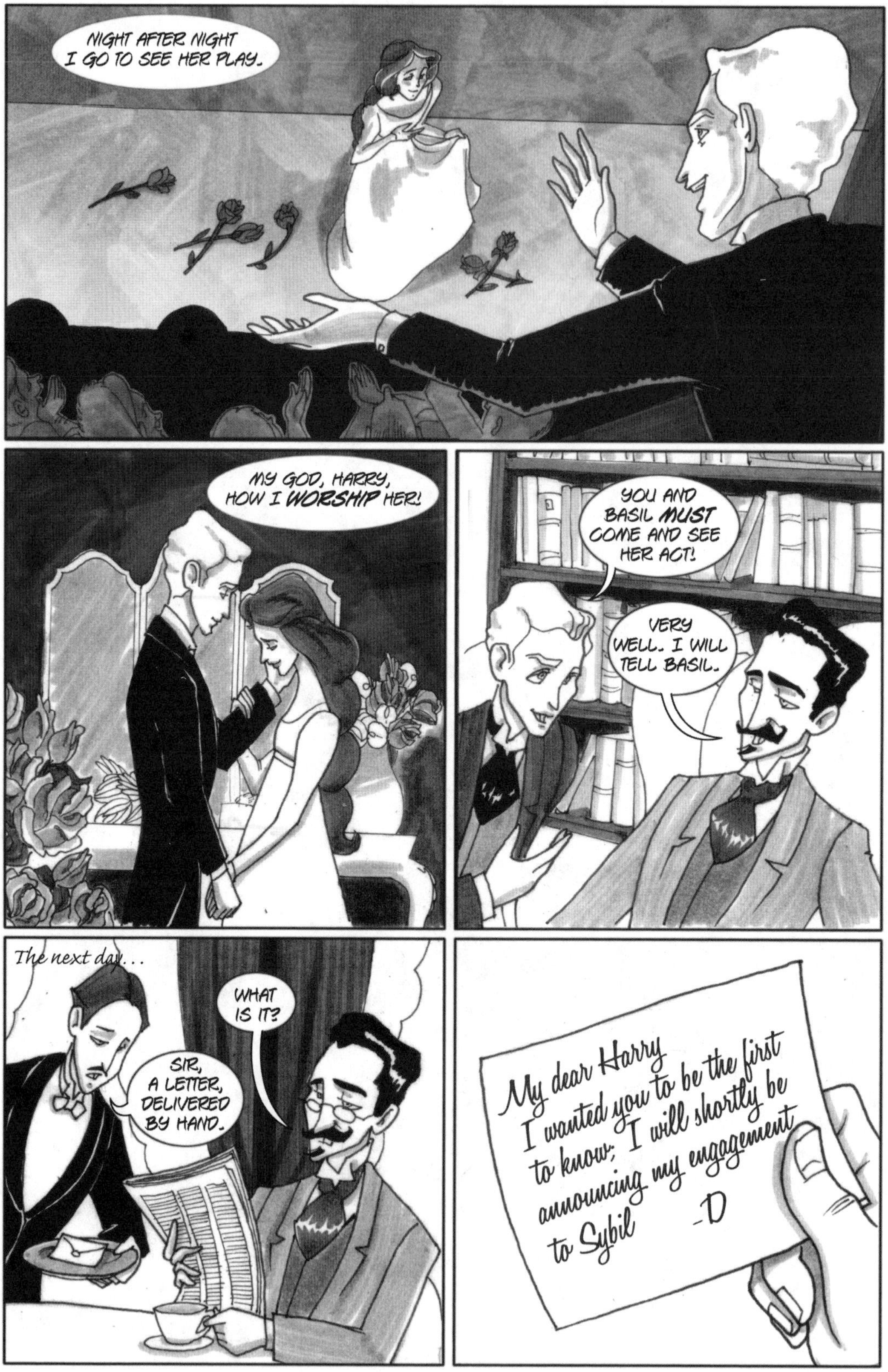
NIGHT AFTER NIGHT I GO TO SEE HER PLAY.
MY GOD, HARRY, HOW I WORSHIP HER!
YOU AND BASIL MUST COME AND SEE HER ACT!
VERY WELL. I WILL TELL BASIL.
The next day...
WHAT IS IT?
SIR, A LETTER, DELIVERED BY HAND.
My dear Harry
I wanted you to be the first
to know; I will shortly be
announcing my engagement
to Sybil -D

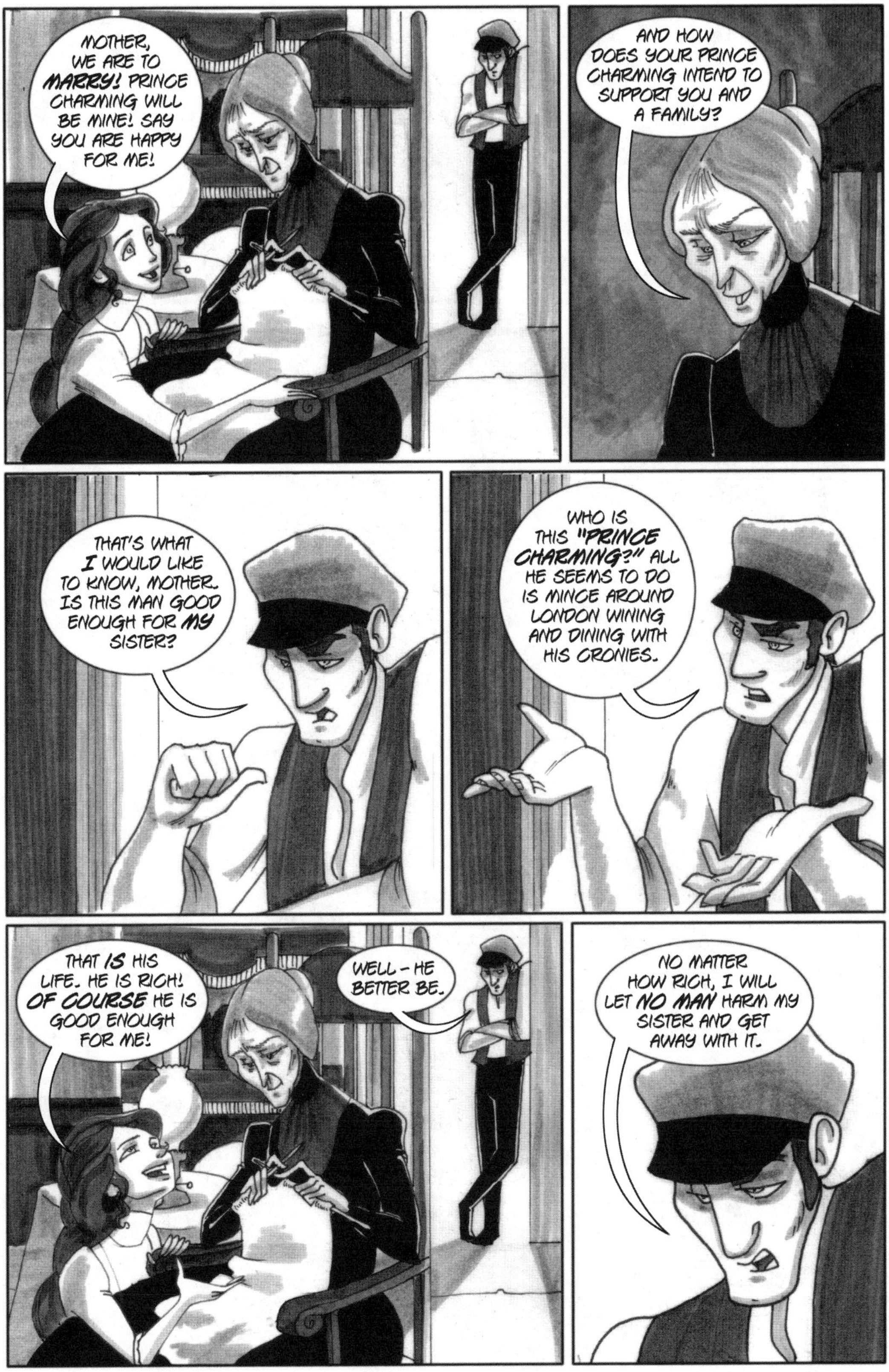
MOTHER, WE ARE TO MARRY! PRINCE CHARMING WILL BE MINE! SAY YOU ARE HAPPY FOR ME!
AND HOW DOES YOUR PRINCE CHARMING INTEND TO SUPPORT YOU AND A FAMILY?
THAT'S WHAT I WOULD LIKE TO KNOW, MOTHER. IS THIS MAN GOOD ENOUGH FOR MY SISTER?
WHO IS THIS "PRINCE CHARMING?" ALL HE SEEMS TO DO IS MINCE AROUND LONDON WINING AND DINING WITH HIS CRONIES.
THAT IS HIS LIFE. HE IS RICH! OF COURSE HE IS GOOD ENOUGH FOR ME!
WELL - HE BETTER BE.
NO MATTER HOW RICH, I WILL LET NO MAN HARM MY SISTER AND GET AWAY WITH IT.

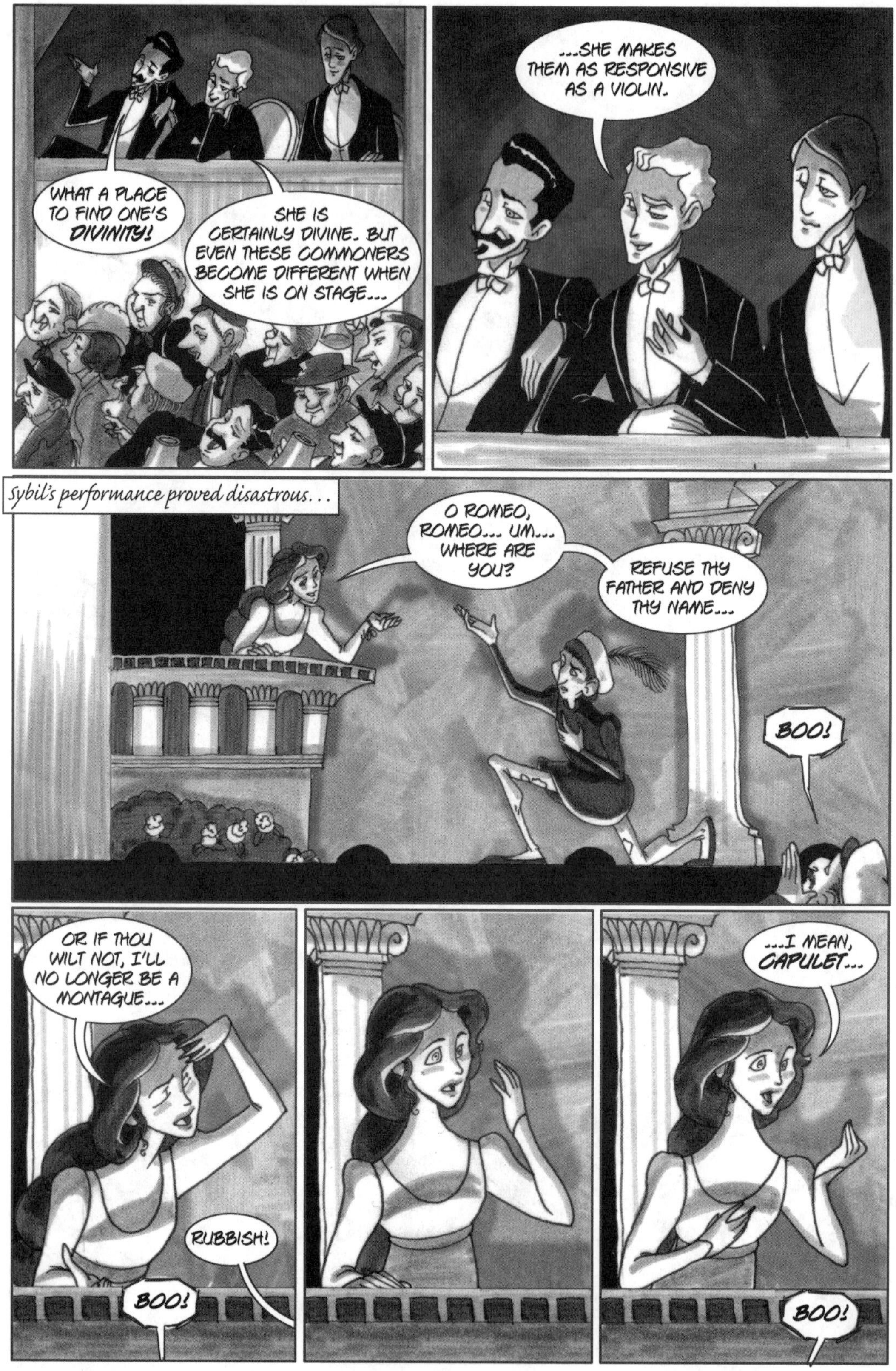
WHAT A PLACE TO FIND ONE'S DIVINITY!
SHE IS CERTAINLY DIVINE. BUT EVEN THESE COMMONERS BECOME DIFFERENT WHEN SHE IS ON STAGE...
...SHE MAKES THEM AS RESPONSIVE AS A VIOLIN.
Sybil's performance proved disastrous...
O ROMEO, ROMEO... UM... WHERE ARE YOU?
REFUSE THY FATHER AND DENY THY NAME...
BOO!
OR IF THOU WILT NOT, I'LL NO LONGER BE A MONTAGUE...
RUBBISH!
BOO!
...I MEAN, CAPULET...
BOO!

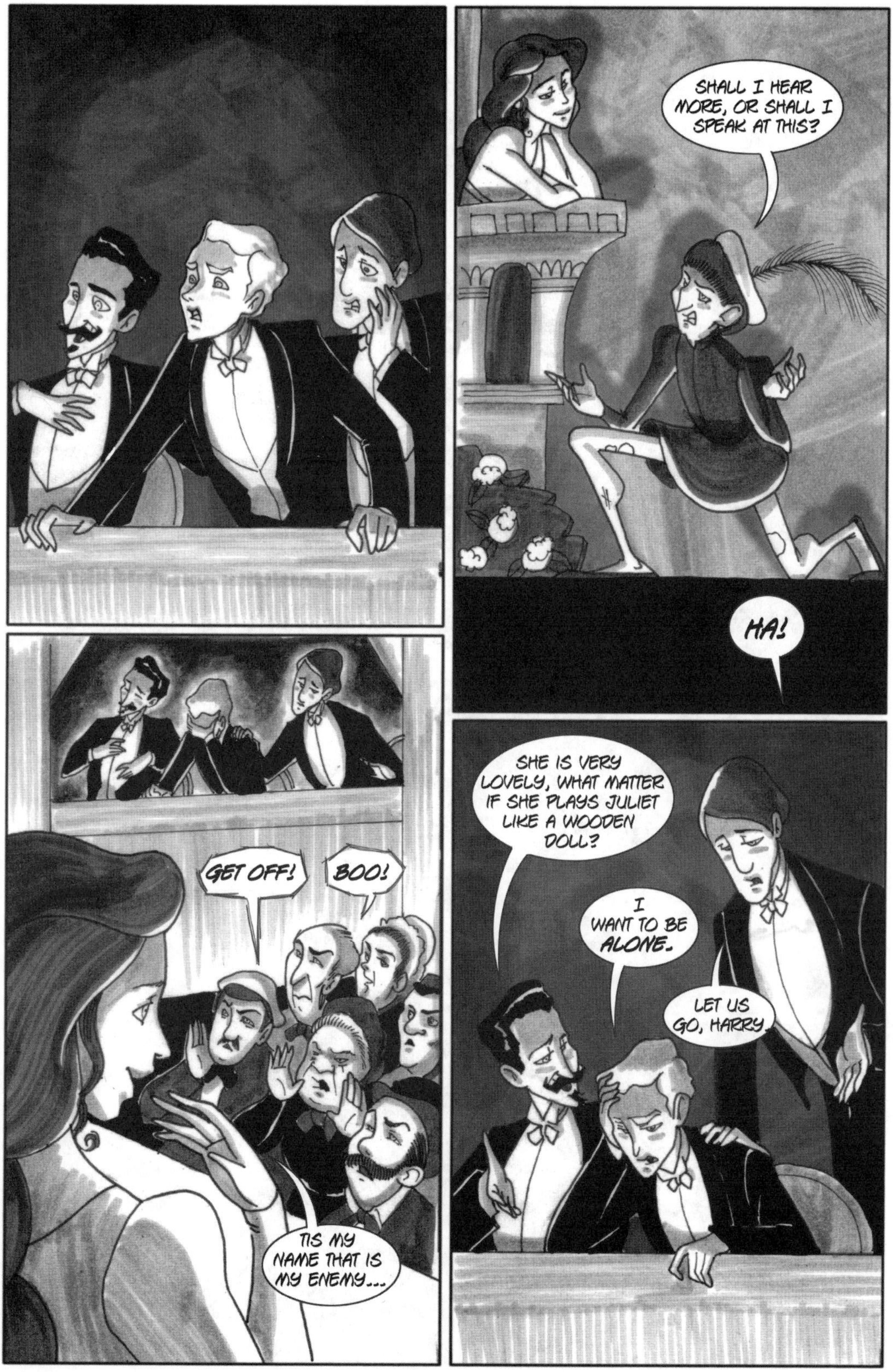
SHALL I HEAR MORE, OR SHALL I SPEAK AT THIS?
HA!
GET OFF!
BOO!
TIS MY NAME THAT IS MY ENEMY...
SHE IS VERY LOVELY, WHAT MATTER IF SHE PLAYS JULIET LIKE A WOODEN DOLL?
I WANT TO BE ALONE.
LET US GO, HARRY.

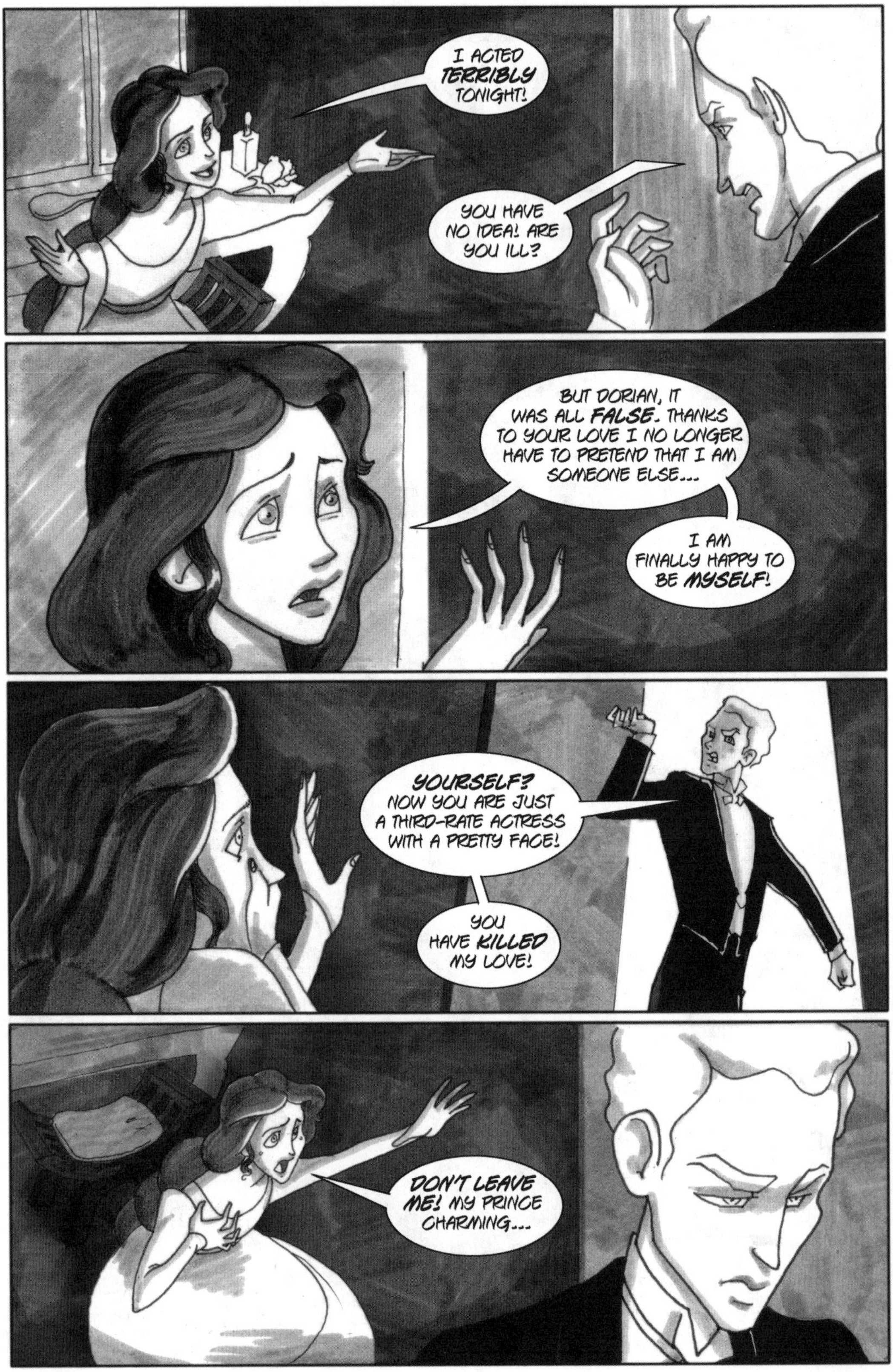
I ACTED TERRIBLY TONIGHT!
YOU HAVE NO IDEA! ARE YOU ILL?
BUT DORIAN, IT WAS ALL FALSE. THANKS TO YOUR LOVE I NO LONGER HAVE TO PRETEND THAT I AM SOMEONE ELSE...
I AM FINALLY HAPPY TO BE MYSELF!
YOURSELF? NOW YOU ARE JUST A THIRD-RATE ACTRESS WITH A PRETTY FACE!
YOU HAVE KILLED MY LOVE!
DON'T LEAVE ME! MY PRINCE CHARMING...

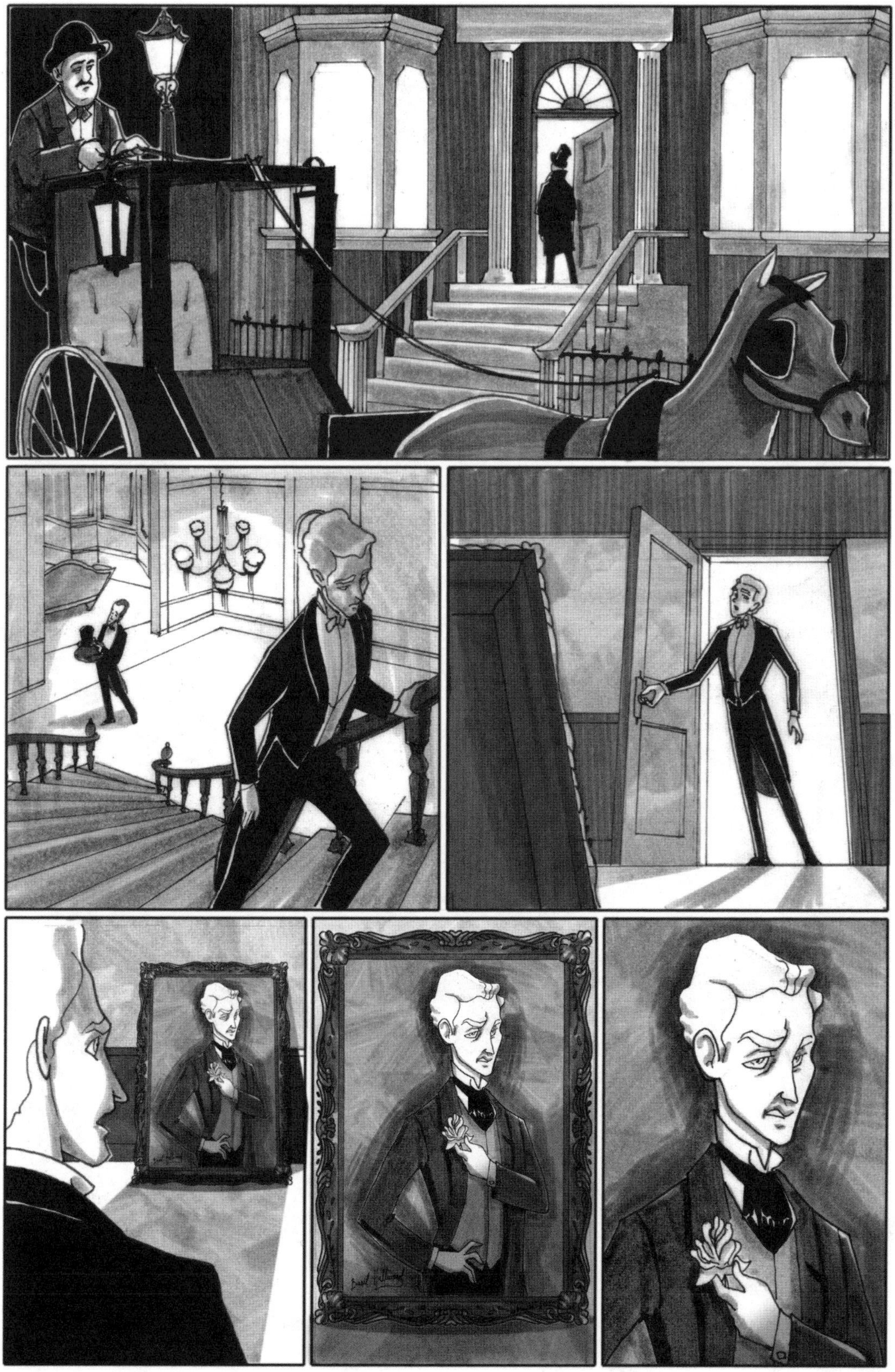

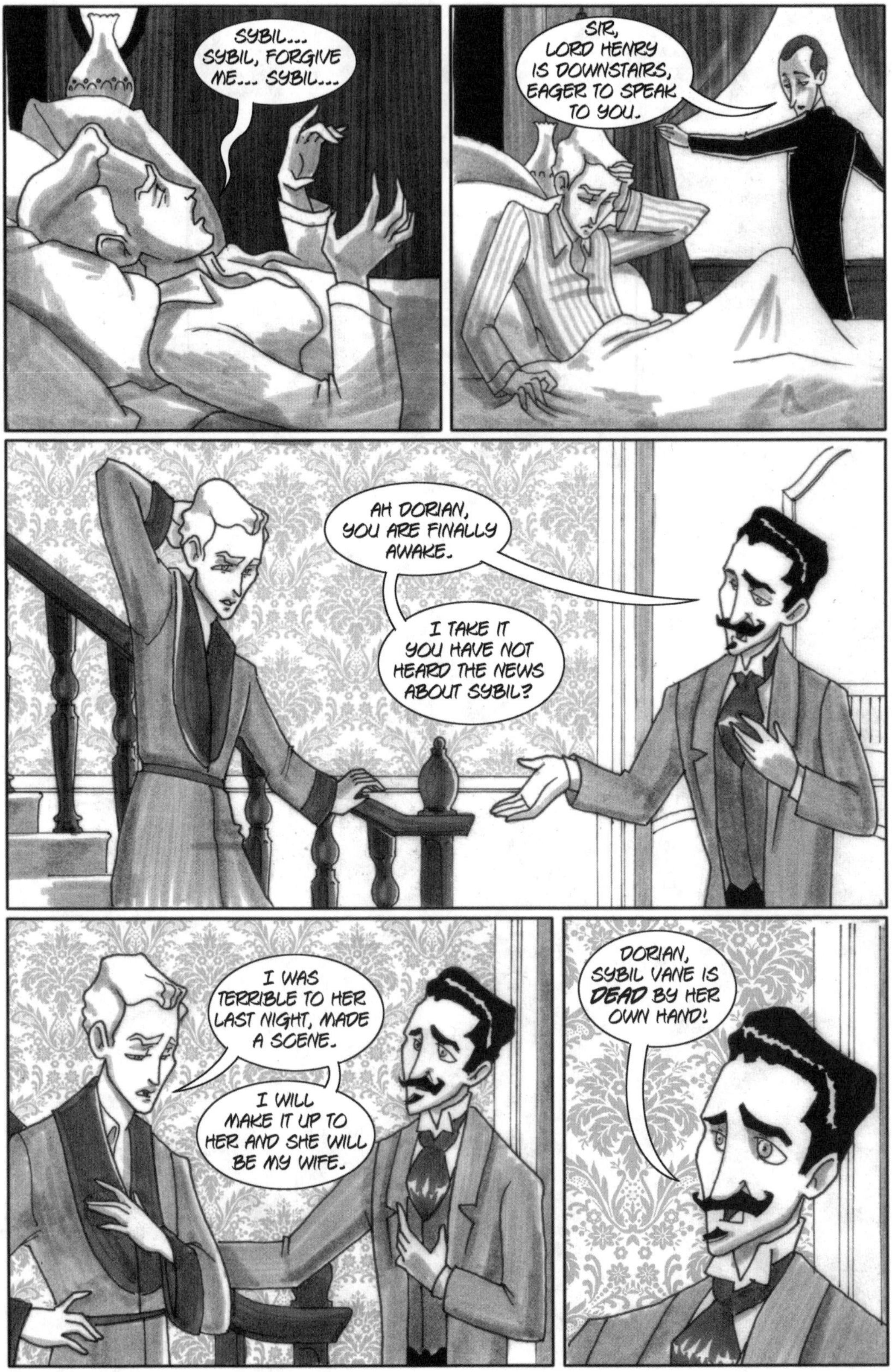
SYBIL... SYBIL, FORGIVE ME... SYBIL...
SIR, LORD HENRY IS DOWNSTAIRS, EAGER TO SPEAK TO YOU.
AH DORIAN, YOU ARE FINALLY AWAKE.
I TAKE IT YOU HAVE NOT HEARD THE NEWS ABOUT SYBIL?
I WAS TERRIBLE TO HER LAST NIGHT, MADE A SCENE.
I WILL MAKE IT UP TO HER AND SHE WILL BE MY WIFE.
DORIAN, SYBIL VANE IS **DEAD** BY HER OWN HAND!

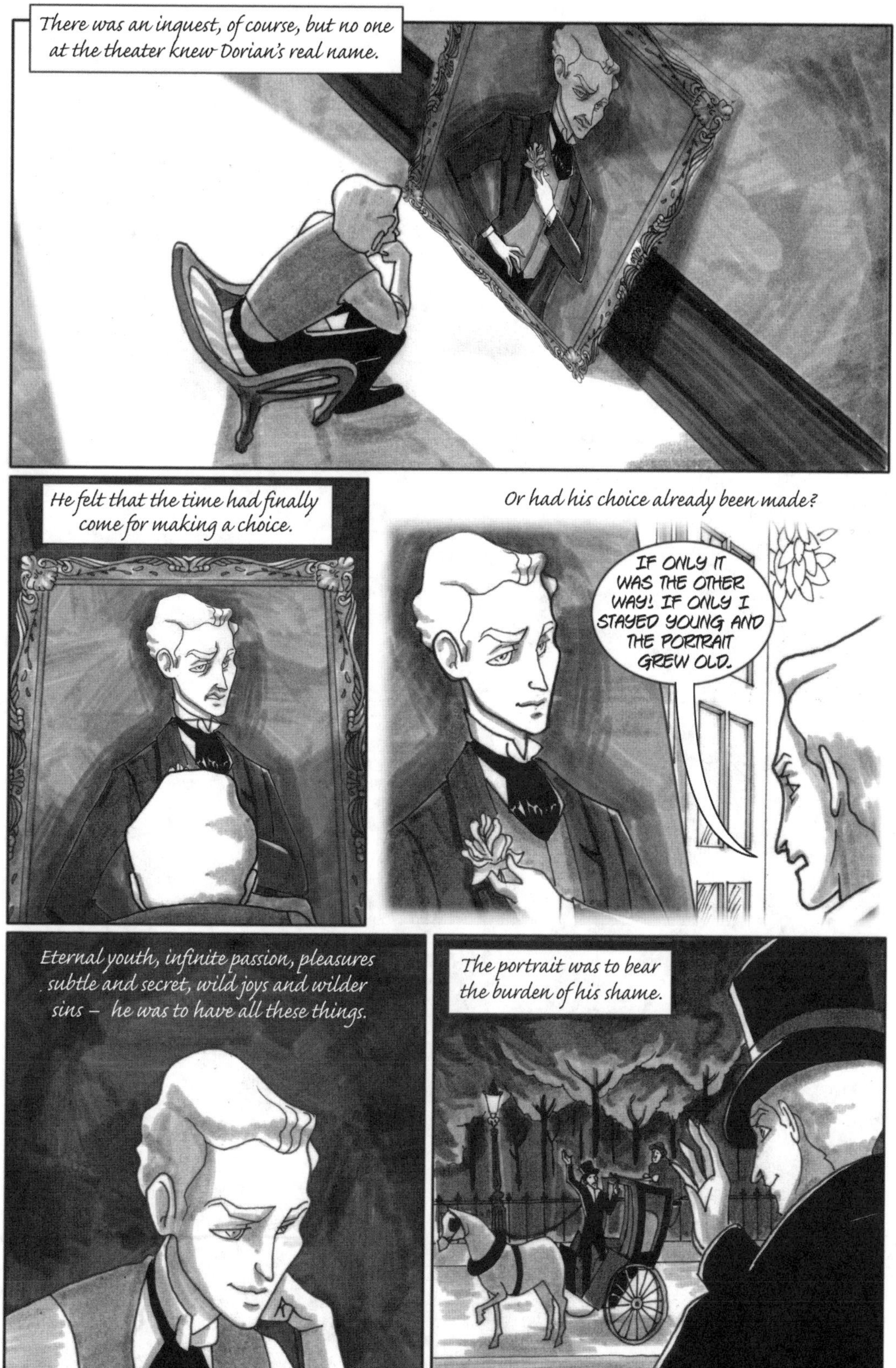
There was an inquest, of course, but no one at the theater knew Dorian's real name.
He felt that the time had finally come for making a choice.
Or had his choice already been made?
IF ONLY IT WAS THE OTHER WAY! IF ONLY I STAYED YOUNG AND THE PORTRAIT GREW OLD.
Eternal youth, infinite passion, pleasures subtle and secret, wild joys and wilder sins – he was to have all these things.
The portrait was to bear the burden of his shame.

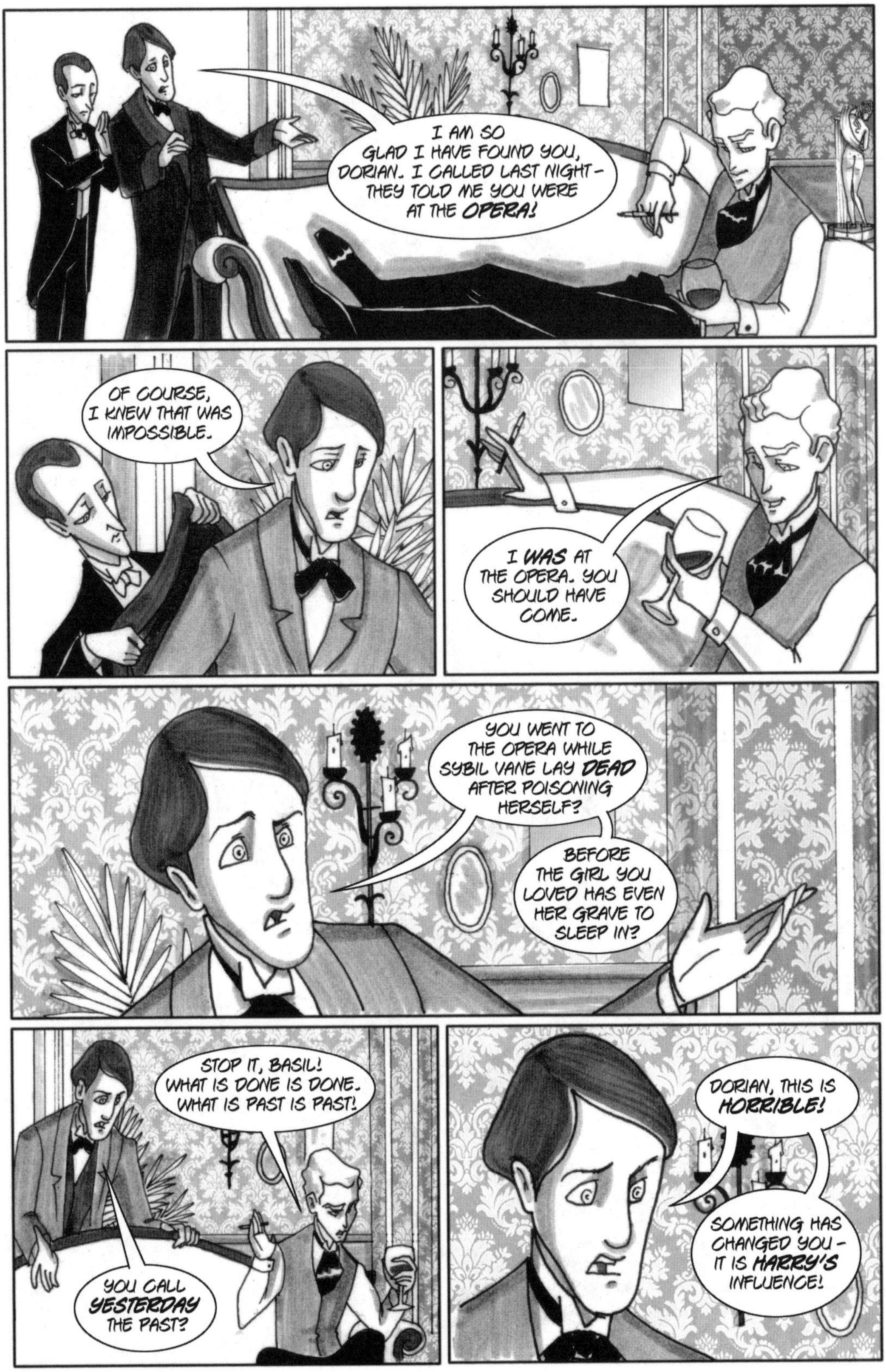
I AM SO GLAD I HAVE FOUND YOU, DORIAN. I CALLED LAST NIGHT - THEY TOLD ME YOU WERE AT THE OPERA!
OF COURSE, I KNEW THAT WAS IMPOSSIBLE.
I WAS AT THE OPERA. YOU SHOULD HAVE COME.
YOU WENT TO THE OPERA WHILE SYBIL VANE LAY DEAD AFTER POISONING HERSELF?
BEFORE THE GIRL YOU LOVED HAS EVEN HER GRAVE TO SLEEP IN?
STOP IT, BASIL! WHAT IS DONE IS DONE. WHAT IS PAST IS PAST!
YOU CALL YESTERDAY THE PAST?
DORIAN, THIS IS HORRIBLE!
SOMETHING HAS CHANGED YOU - IT IS HARRY'S INFLUENCE!

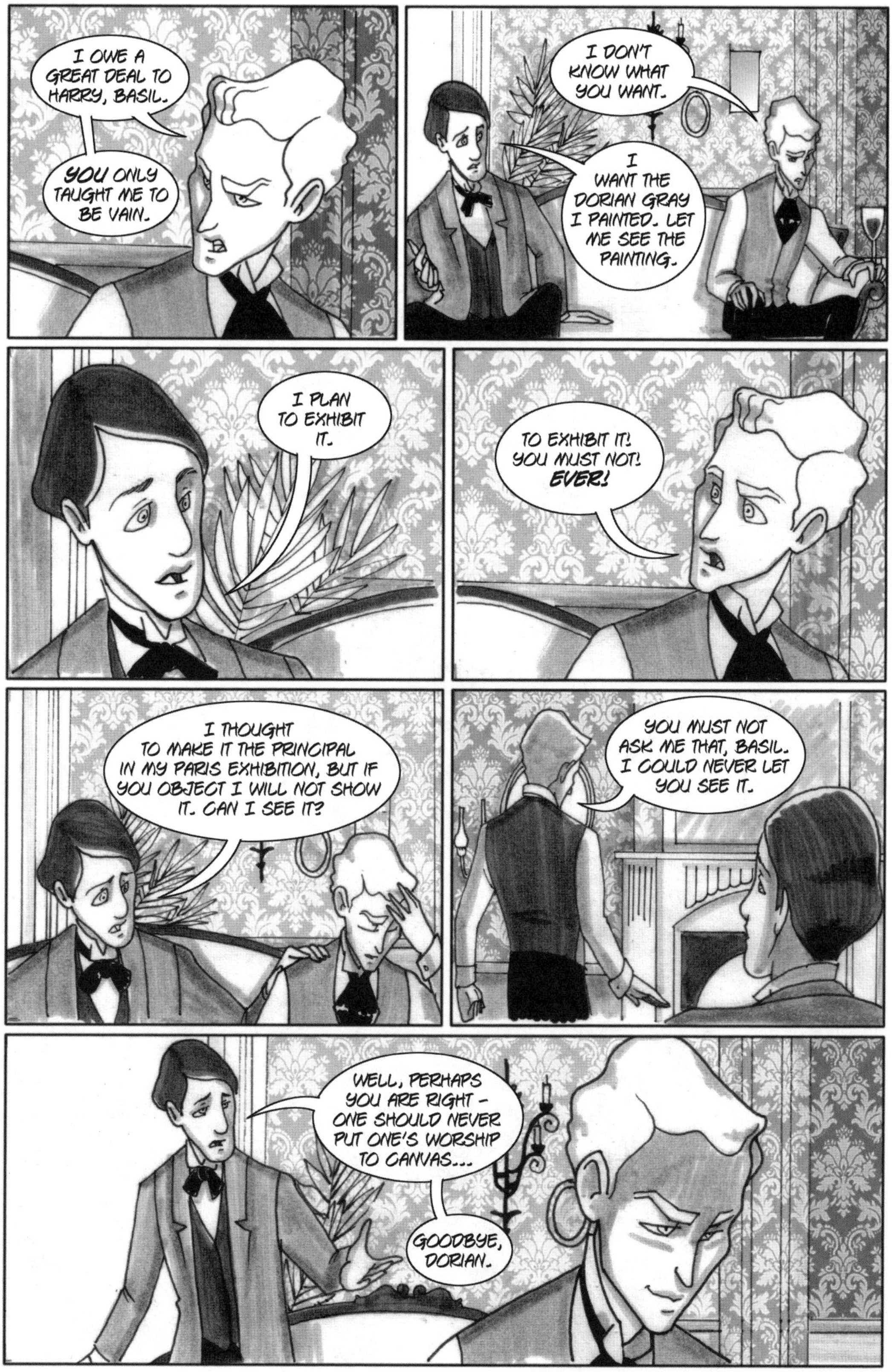
I OWE A GREAT DEAL TO HARRY, BASIL.
YOU ONLY TAUGHT ME TO BE VAIN.
I DON'T KNOW WHAT YOU WANT.
I WANT THE DORIAN GRAY I PAINTED. LET ME SEE THE PAINTING.
I PLAN TO EXHIBIT IT.
TO EXHIBIT IT! YOU MUST NOT! EVER!
I THOUGHT TO MAKE IT THE PRINCIPAL IN MY PARIS EXHIBITION, BUT IF YOU OBJECT I WILL NOT SHOW IT. CAN I SEE IT?
YOU MUST NOT ASK ME THAT, BASIL. I COULD NEVER LET YOU SEE IT.
WELL, PERHAPS YOU ARE RIGHT - ONE SHOULD NEVER PUT ONE'S WORSHIP TO CANVAS...
GOODBYE, DORIAN.

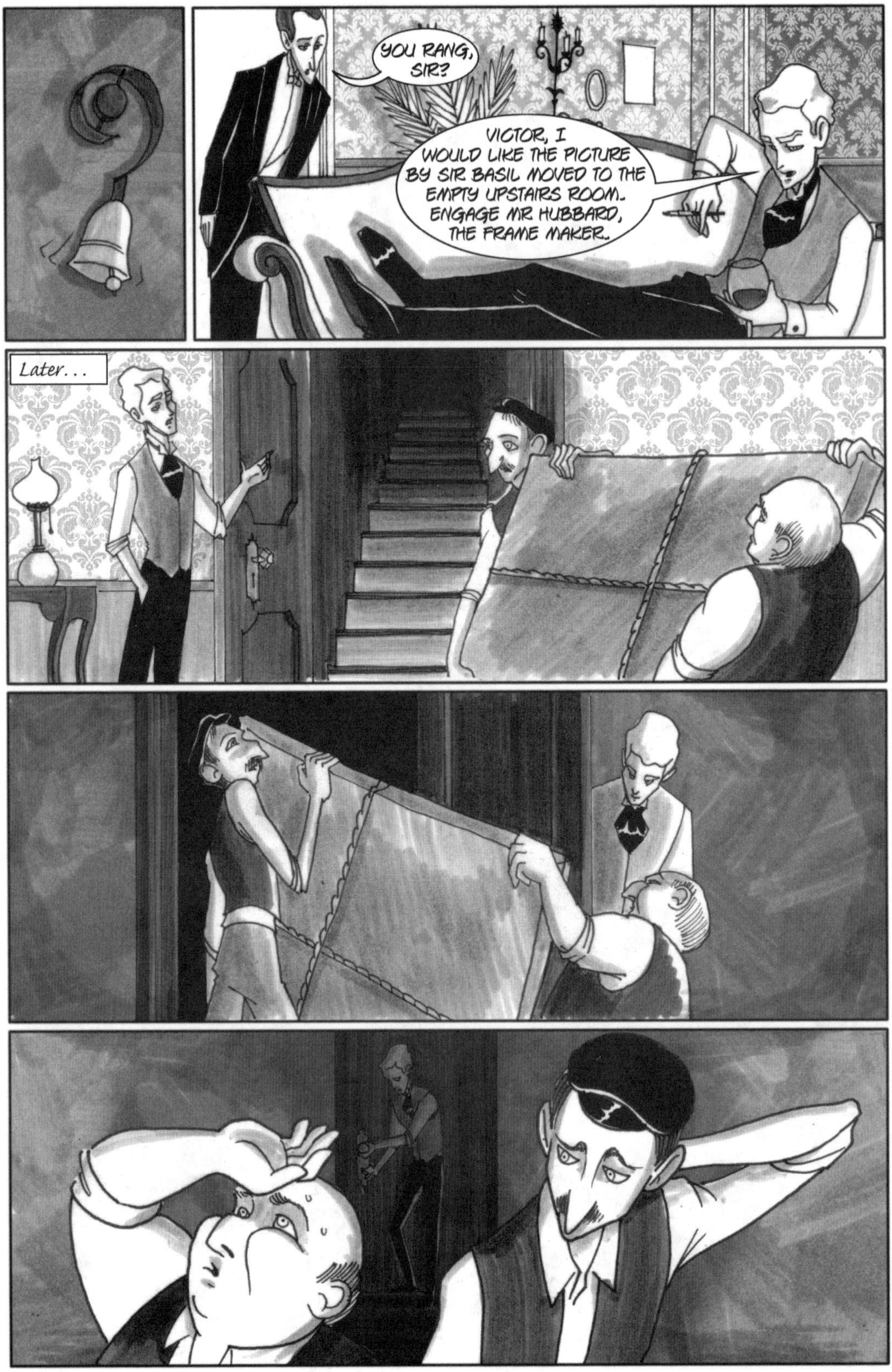
YOU RANG, SIR?
VICTOR, I WOULD LIKE THE PICTURE BY SIR BASIL MOVED TO THE EMPTY UPSTAIRS ROOM. ENGAGE MR HUBBARD, THE FRAME MAKER.
Later...

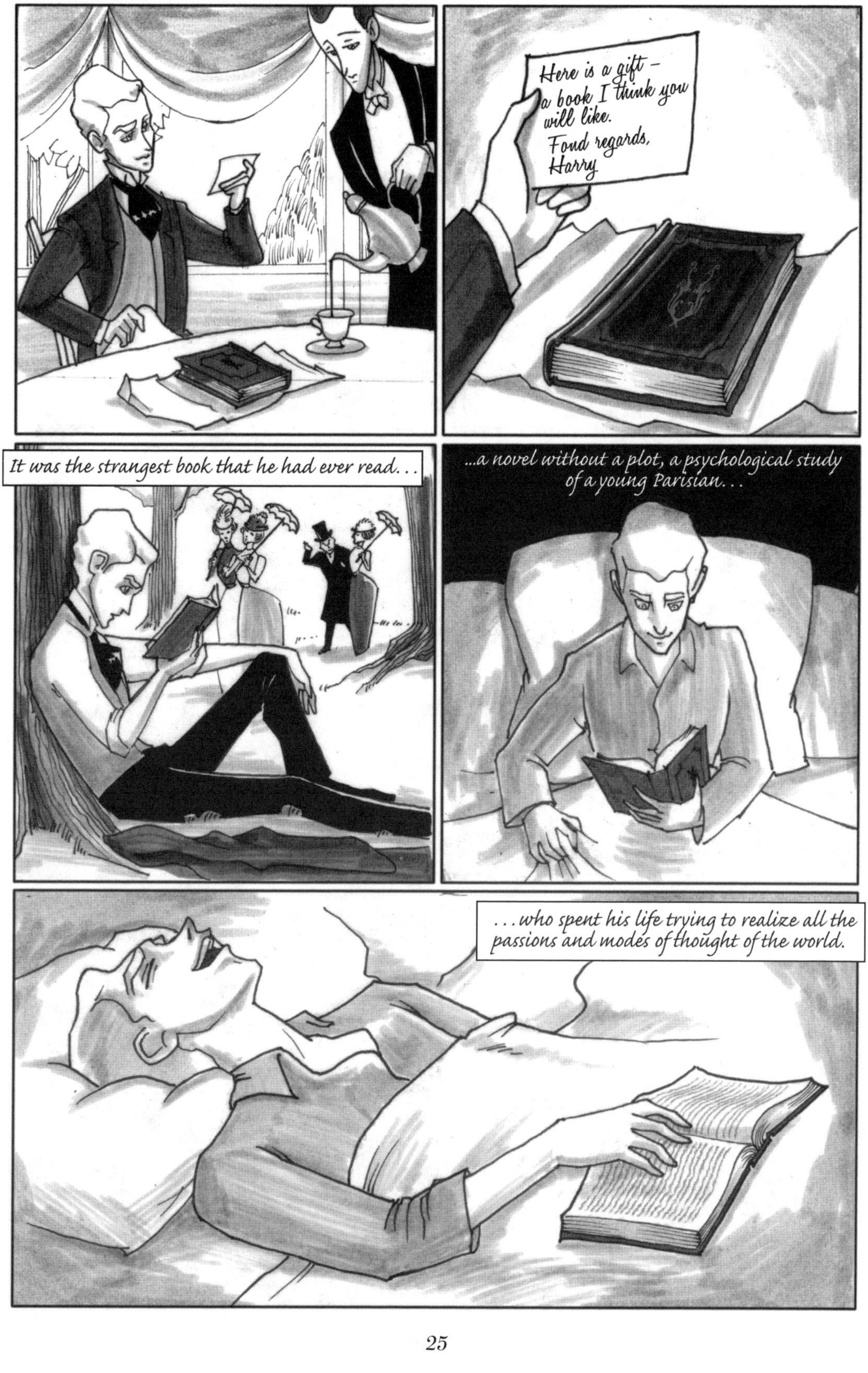
Here is a gift –
a book I think you
will like.
Fond regards,
Harry
It was the strangest book that he had ever read...
...a novel without a plot, a psychological study of a young Parisian...
...who spent his life trying to realize all the passions and modes of thought of the world.

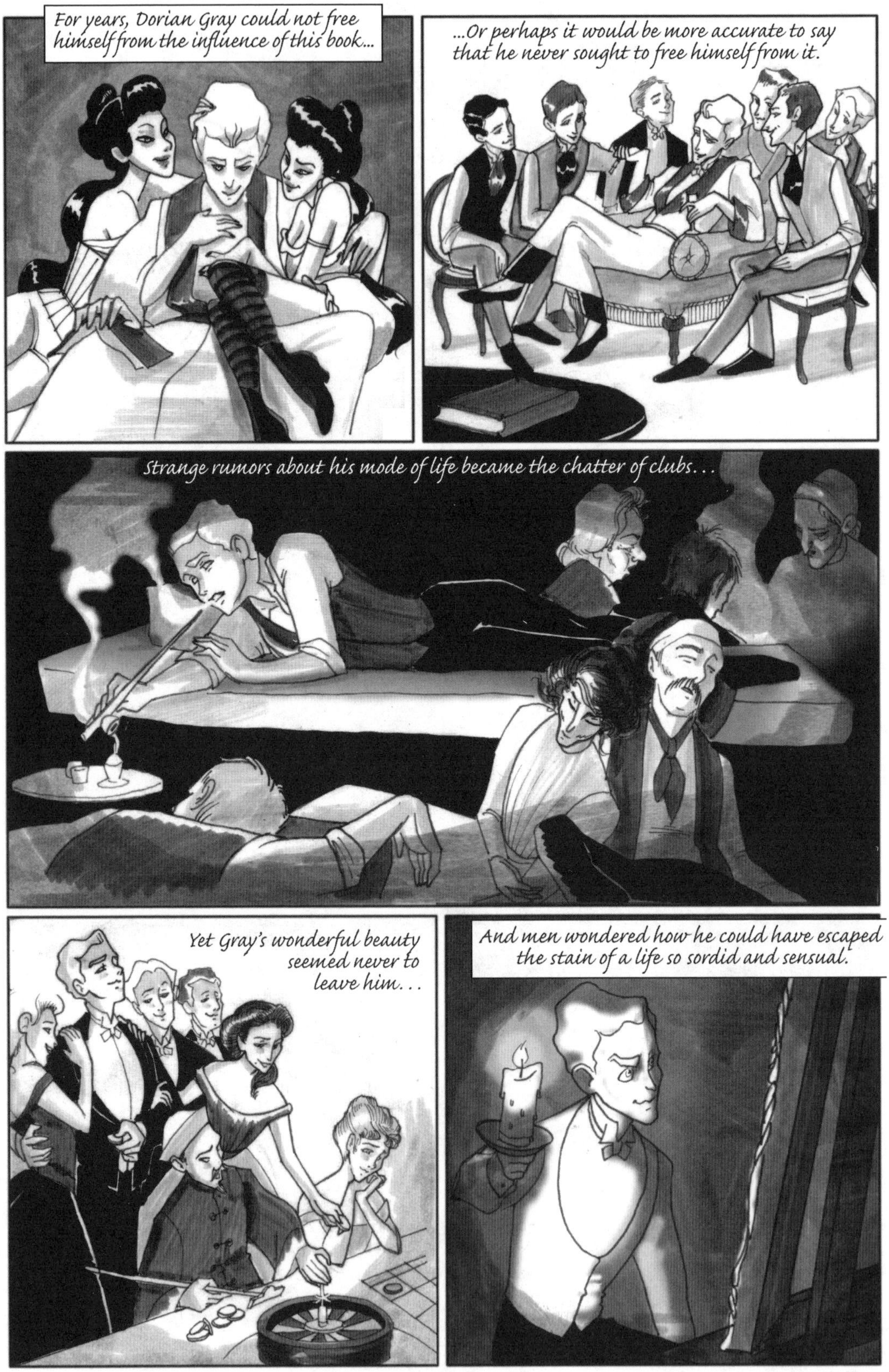
For years, Dorian Gray could not free himself from the influence of this book...
...Or perhaps it would be more accurate to say that he never sought to free himself from it.
Strange rumors about his mode of life became the chatter of clubs. . .
Yet Gray's wonderful beauty seemed never to leave him. . .
And men wondered how he could have escaped the stain of a life so sordid and sensual.

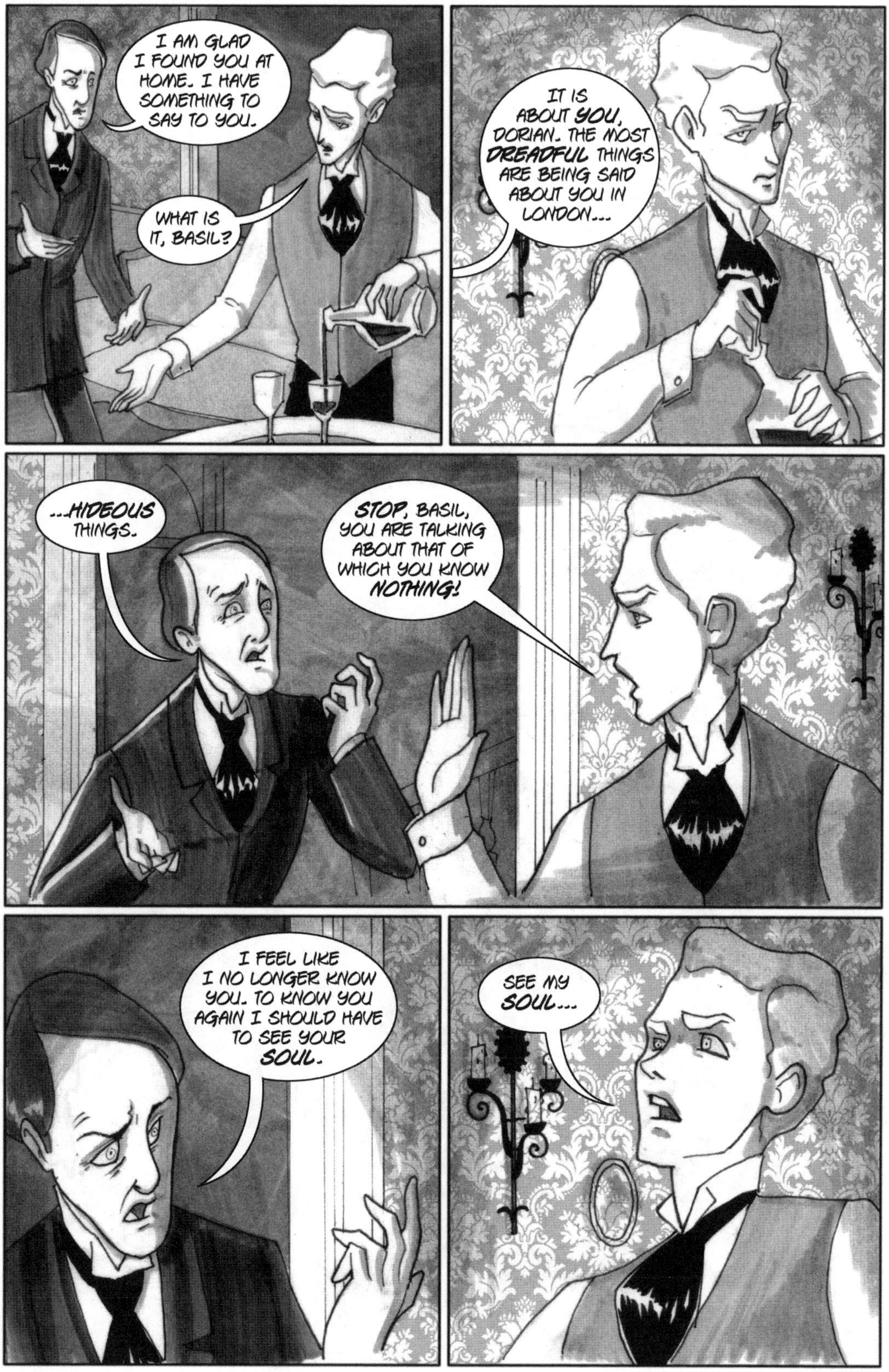
I AM GLAD I FOUND YOU AT HOME. I HAVE SOMETHING TO SAY TO YOU.
WHAT IS IT, BASIL?
IT IS ABOUT YOU, DORIAN. THE MOST DREADFUL THINGS ARE BEING SAID ABOUT YOU IN LONDON...
...HIDEOUS THINGS.
STOP, BASIL, YOU ARE TALKING ABOUT THAT OF WHICH YOU KNOW NOTHING!
I FEEL LIKE I NO LONGER KNOW YOU. TO KNOW YOU AGAIN I SHOULD HAVE TO SEE YOUR SOUL.
SEE MY SOUL...

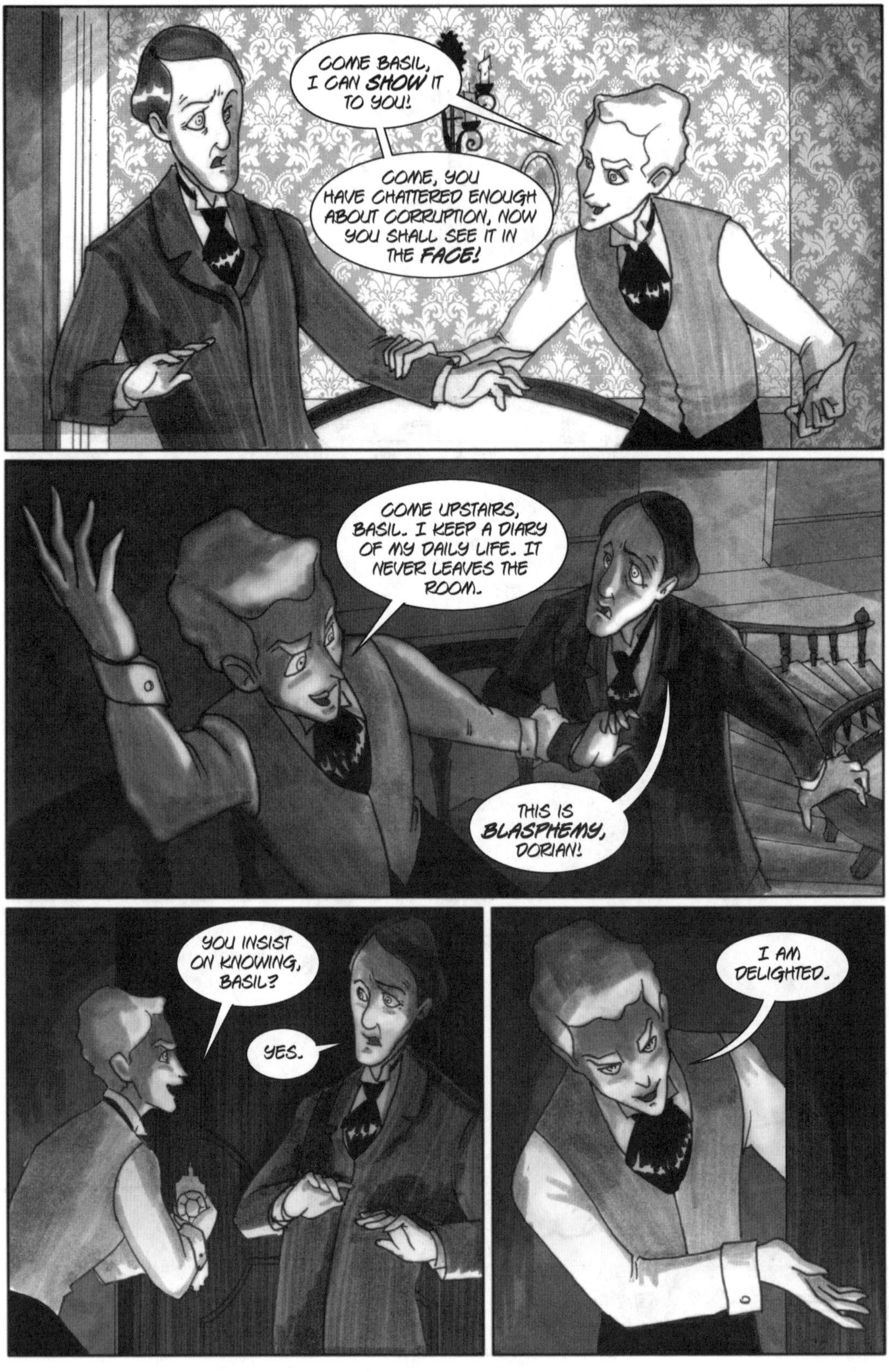
COME BASIL, I CAN SHOW IT TO YOU!
COME, YOU HAVE CHATTERED ENOUGH ABOUT CORRUPTION, NOW YOU SHALL SEE IT IN THE FACE!
COME UPSTAIRS, BASIL. I KEEP A DIARY OF MY DAILY LIFE. IT NEVER LEAVES THE ROOM.
THIS IS BLASPHEMY, DORIAN!
YOU INSIST ON KNOWING, BASIL?
YES.
I AM DELIGHTED.

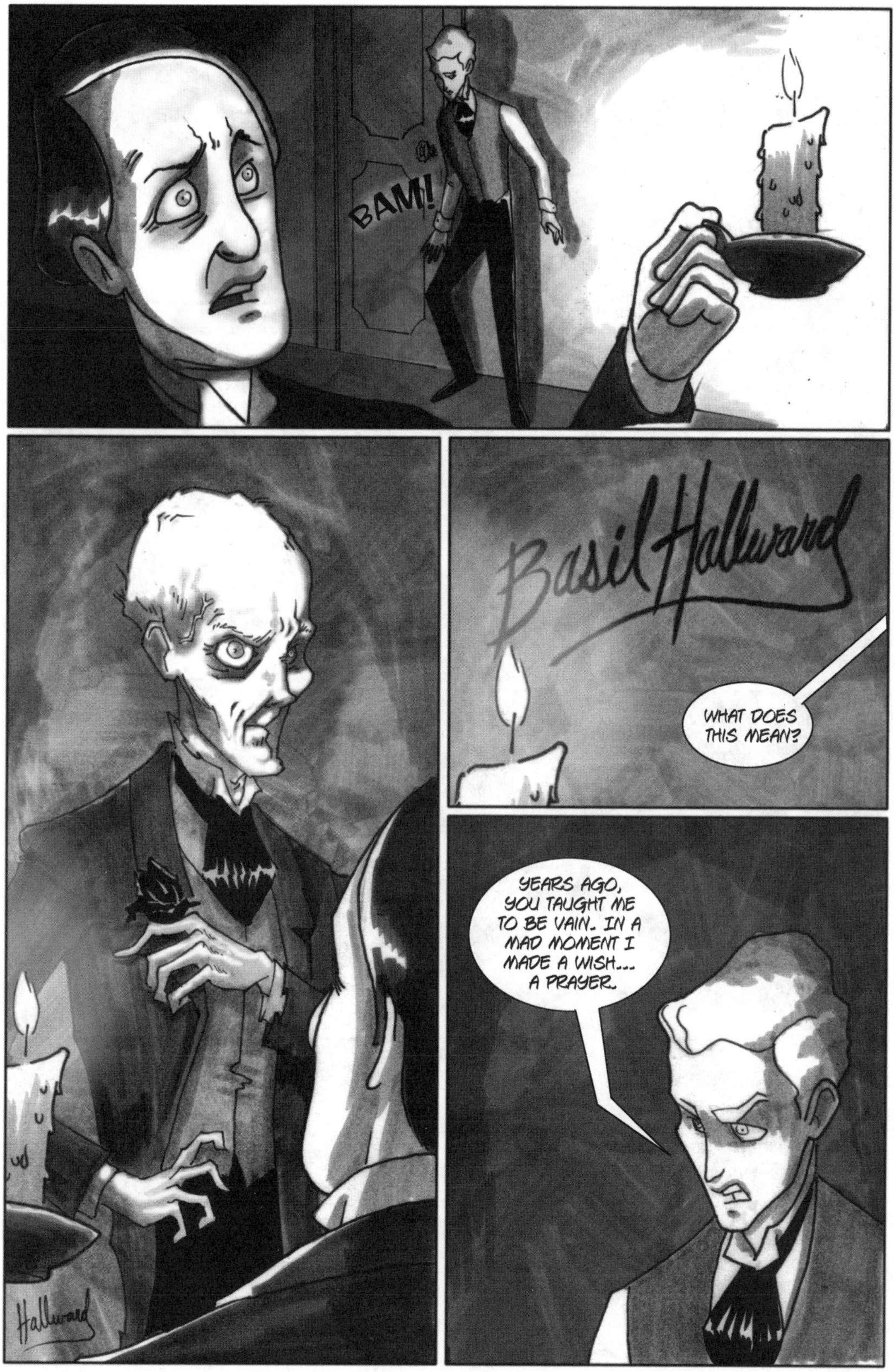
BAM!
Basil Hallward
WHAT DOES THIS MEAN?
YEARS AGO, YOU TAUGHT ME TO BE VAIN. IN A MAD MOMENT I MADE A WISH... A PRAYER.
Hallward

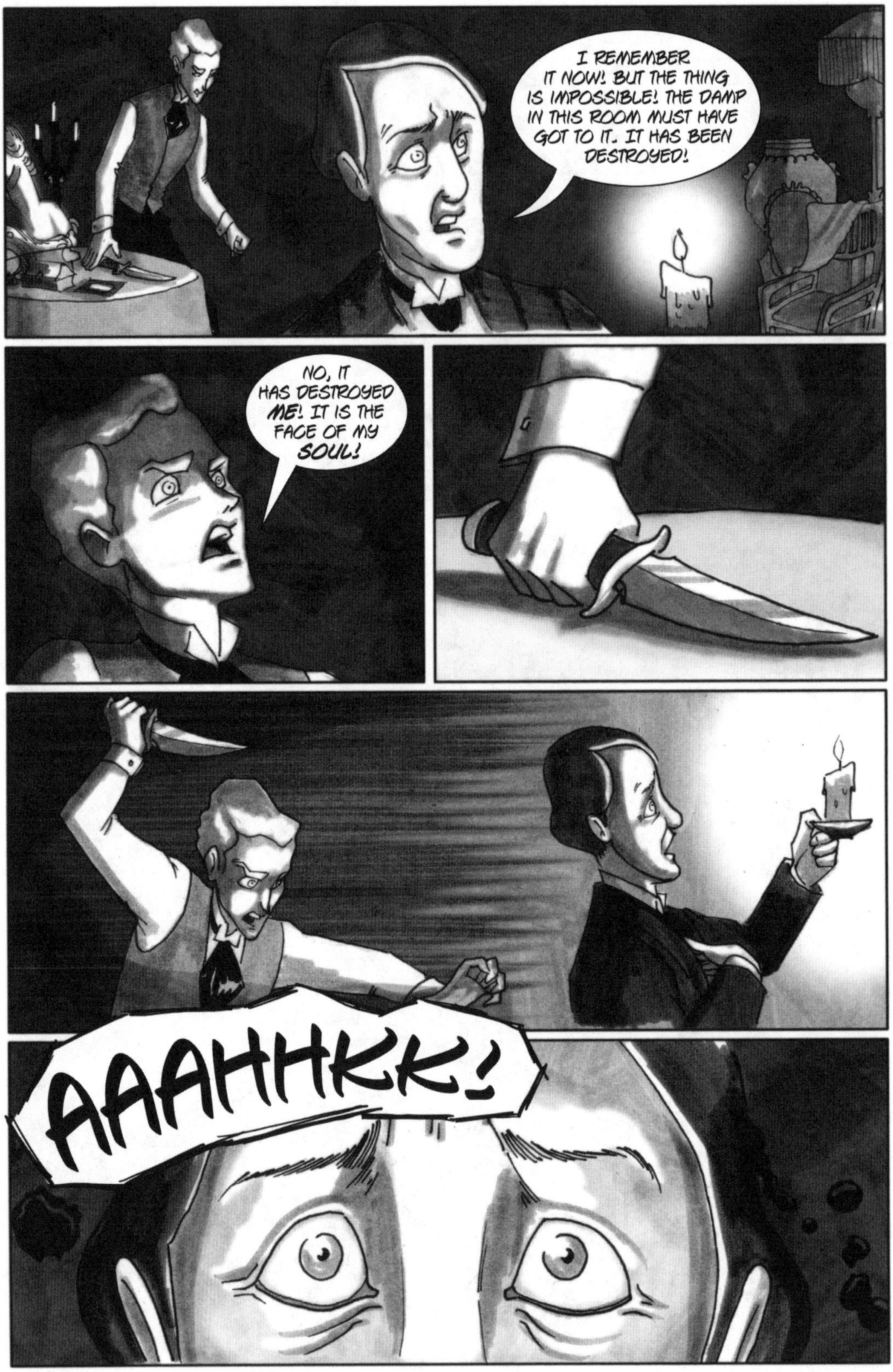
I REMEMBER IT NOW! BUT THE THING IS IMPOSSIBLE! THE DAMP IN THIS ROOM MUST HAVE GOT TO IT. IT HAS BEEN DESTROYED!
NO, IT HAS DESTROYED ME! IT IS THE FACE OF MY SOUL!
AAAHHKK!

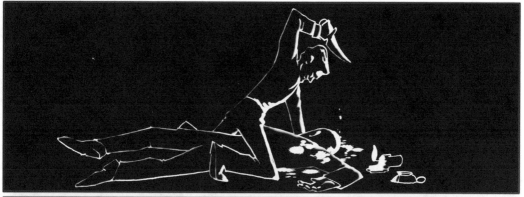

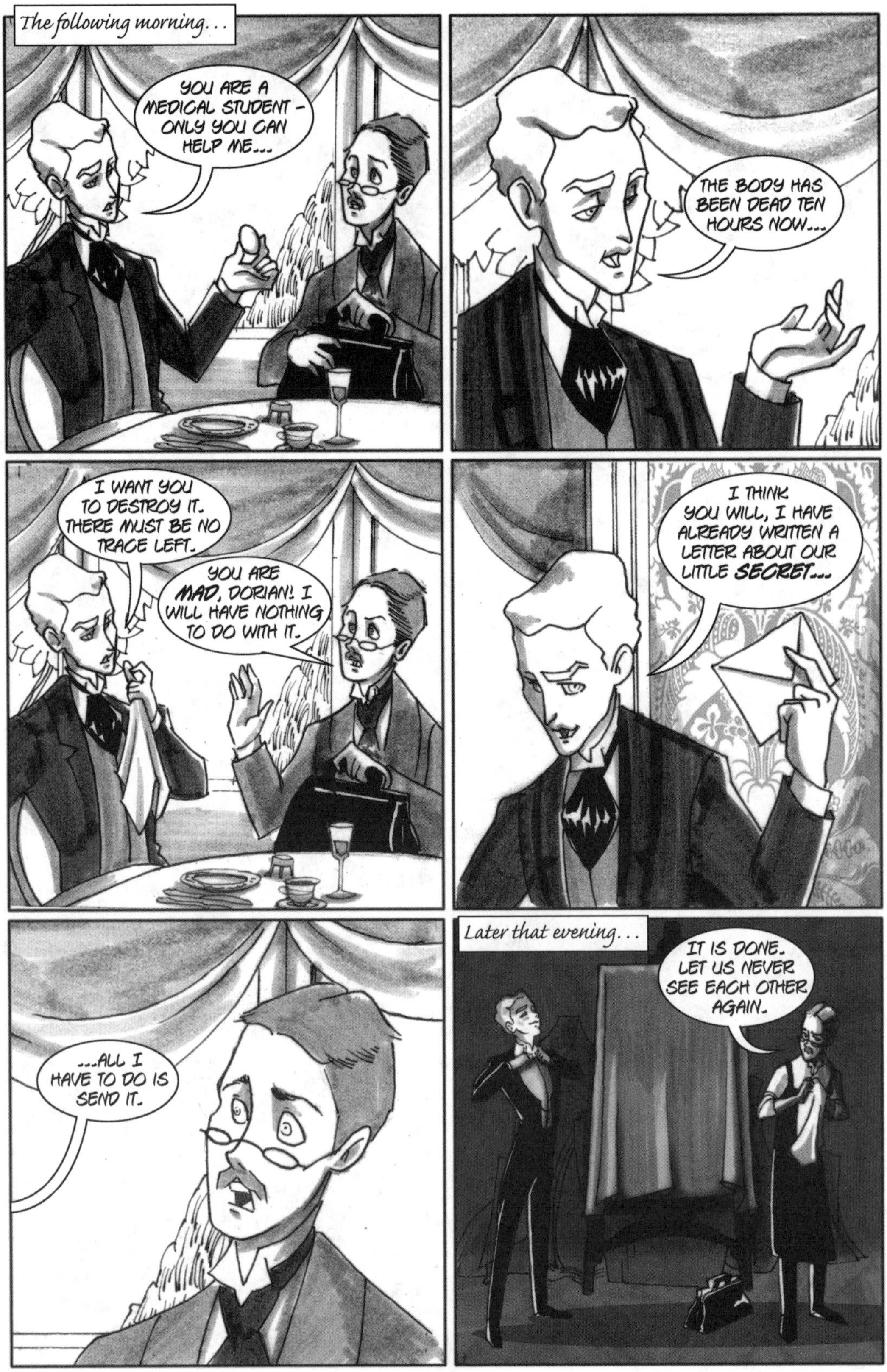
The following morning. . .
YOU ARE A MEDICAL STUDENT - ONLY YOU CAN HELP ME...
THE BODY HAS BEEN DEAD TEN HOURS NOW...
I WANT YOU TO DESTROY IT. THERE MUST BE NO TRACE LEFT.
YOU ARE MAD, DORIAN! I WILL HAVE NOTHING TO DO WITH IT.
I THINK YOU WILL, I HAVE ALREADY WRITTEN A LETTER ABOUT OUR LITTLE SECRET...
...ALL I HAVE TO DO IS SEND IT.
Later that evening. . .
IT IS DONE. LET US NEVER SEE EACH OTHER AGAIN.

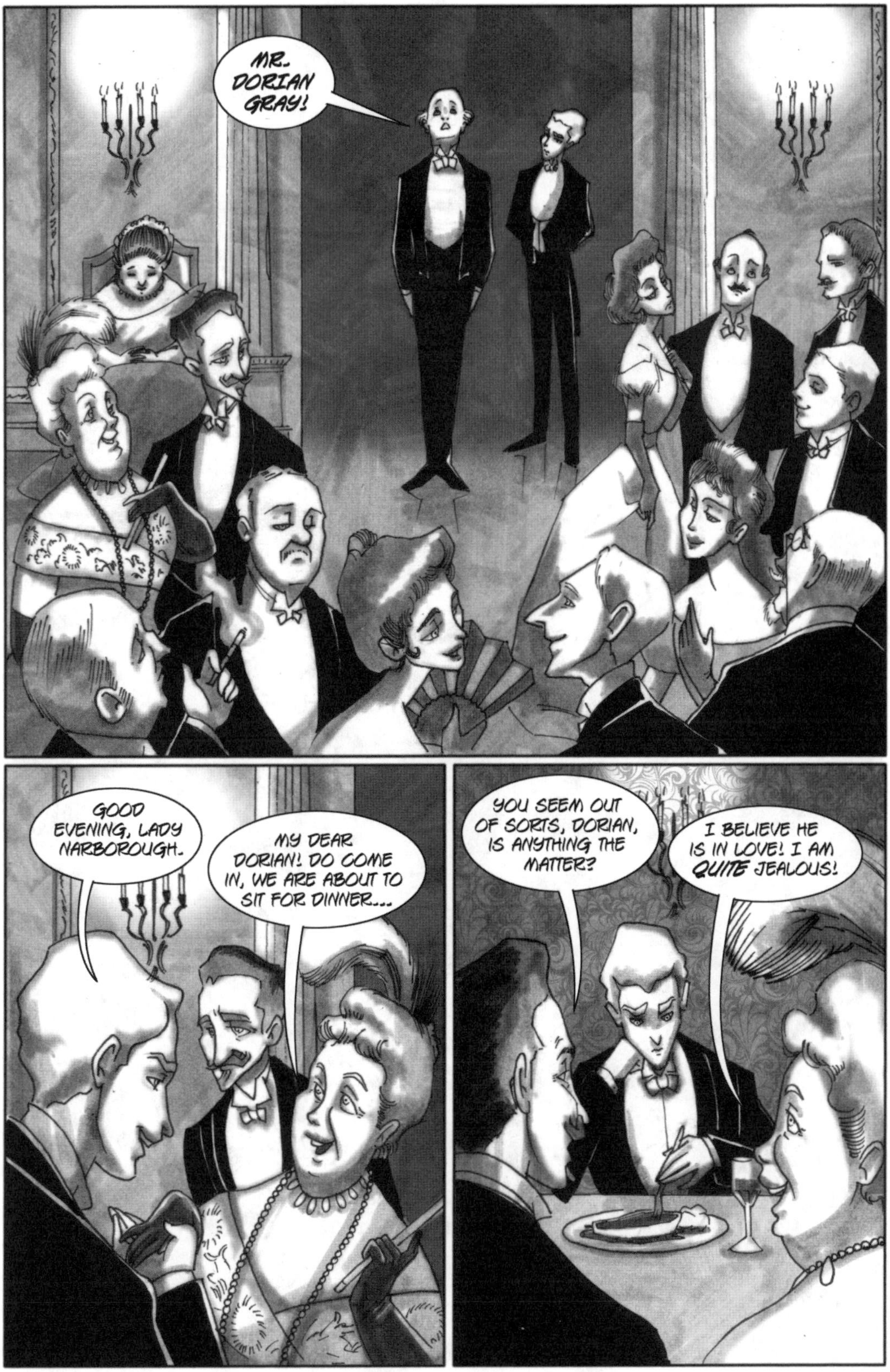
MR. DORIAN GRAY!
GOOD EVENING, LADY NARBOROUGH.
MY DEAR DORIAN! DO COME IN, WE ARE ABOUT TO SIT FOR DINNER...
YOU SEEM OUT OF SORTS, DORIAN, IS ANYTHING THE MATTER?
I BELIEVE HE IS IN LOVE! I AM *QUITE* JEALOUS!

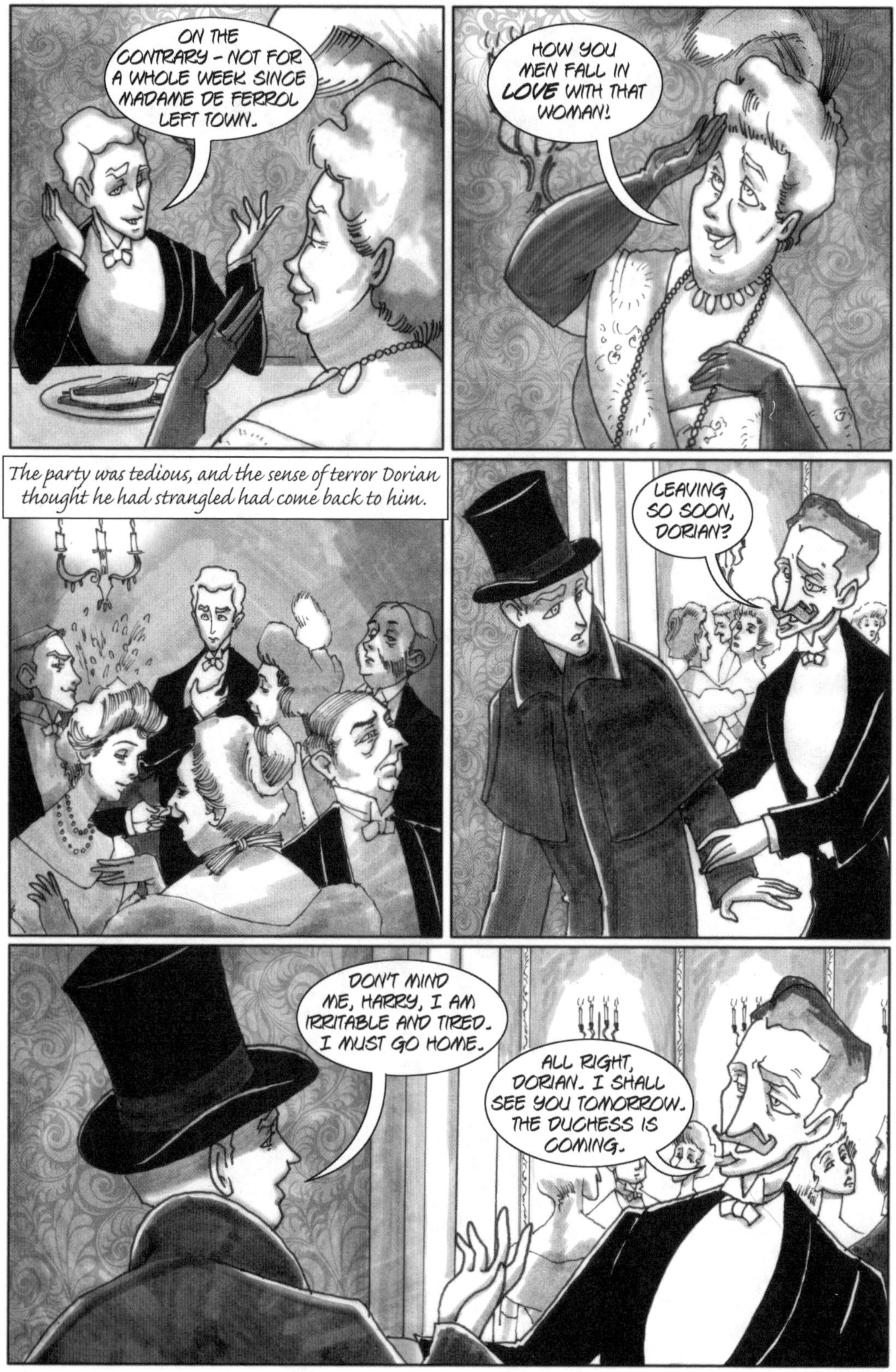
ON THE CONTRARY - NOT FOR A WHOLE WEEK SINCE MADAME DE FERROL LEFT TOWN.
HOW YOU MEN FALL IN LOVE WITH THAT WOMAN!
The party was tedious, and the sense of terror Dorian thought he had strangled had come back to him.
LEAVING SO SOON, DORIAN?
DON'T MIND ME, HARRY, I AM IRRITABLE AND TIRED. I MUST GO HOME.
ALL RIGHT, DORIAN. I SHALL SEE YOU TOMORROW. THE DUCHESS IS COMING.

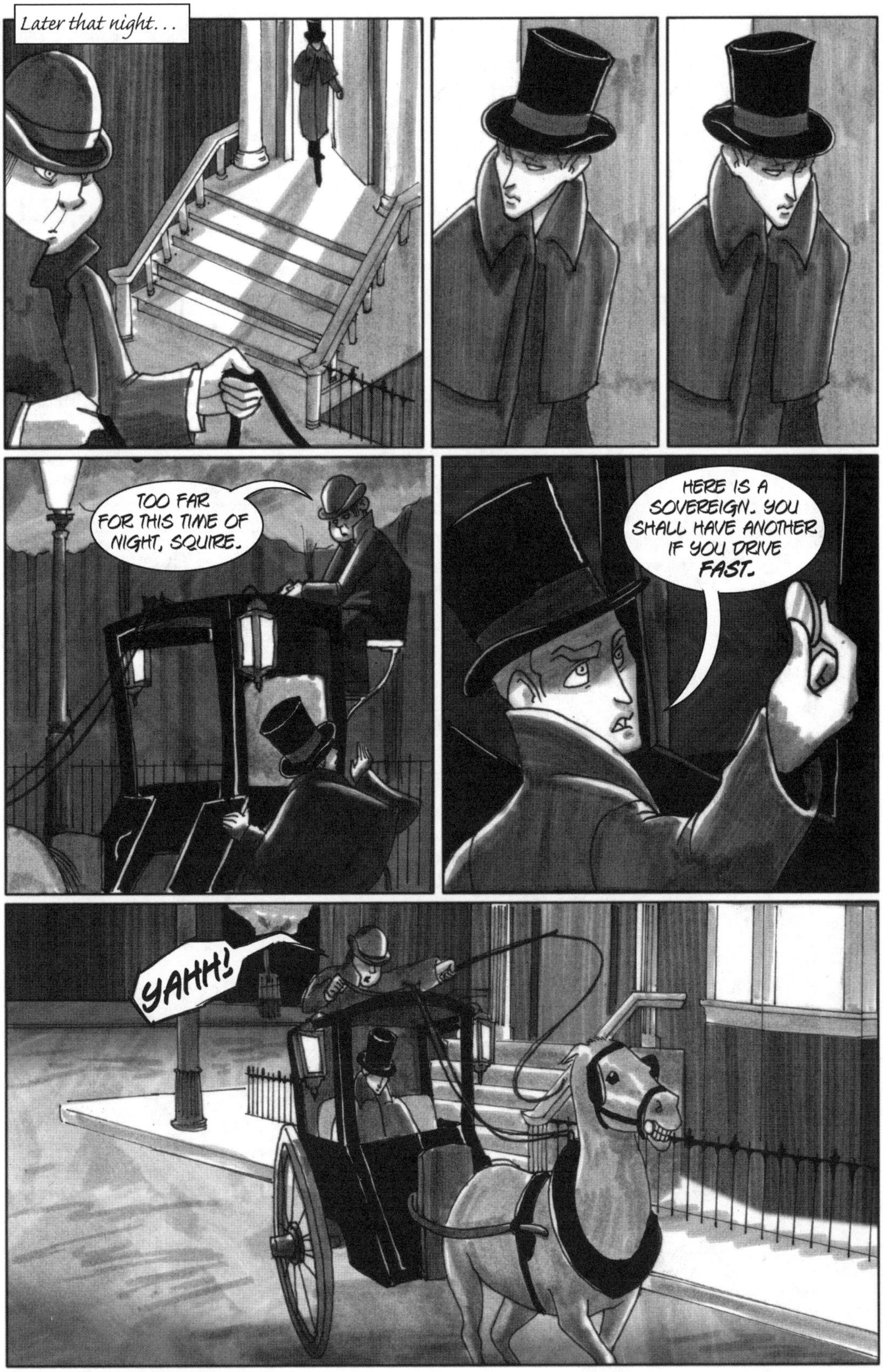
Later that night...
TOO FAR FOR THIS TIME OF NIGHT, SQUIRE.
HERE IS A SOVEREIGN. YOU SHALL HAVE ANOTHER IF YOU DRIVE FAST.
YAHH!

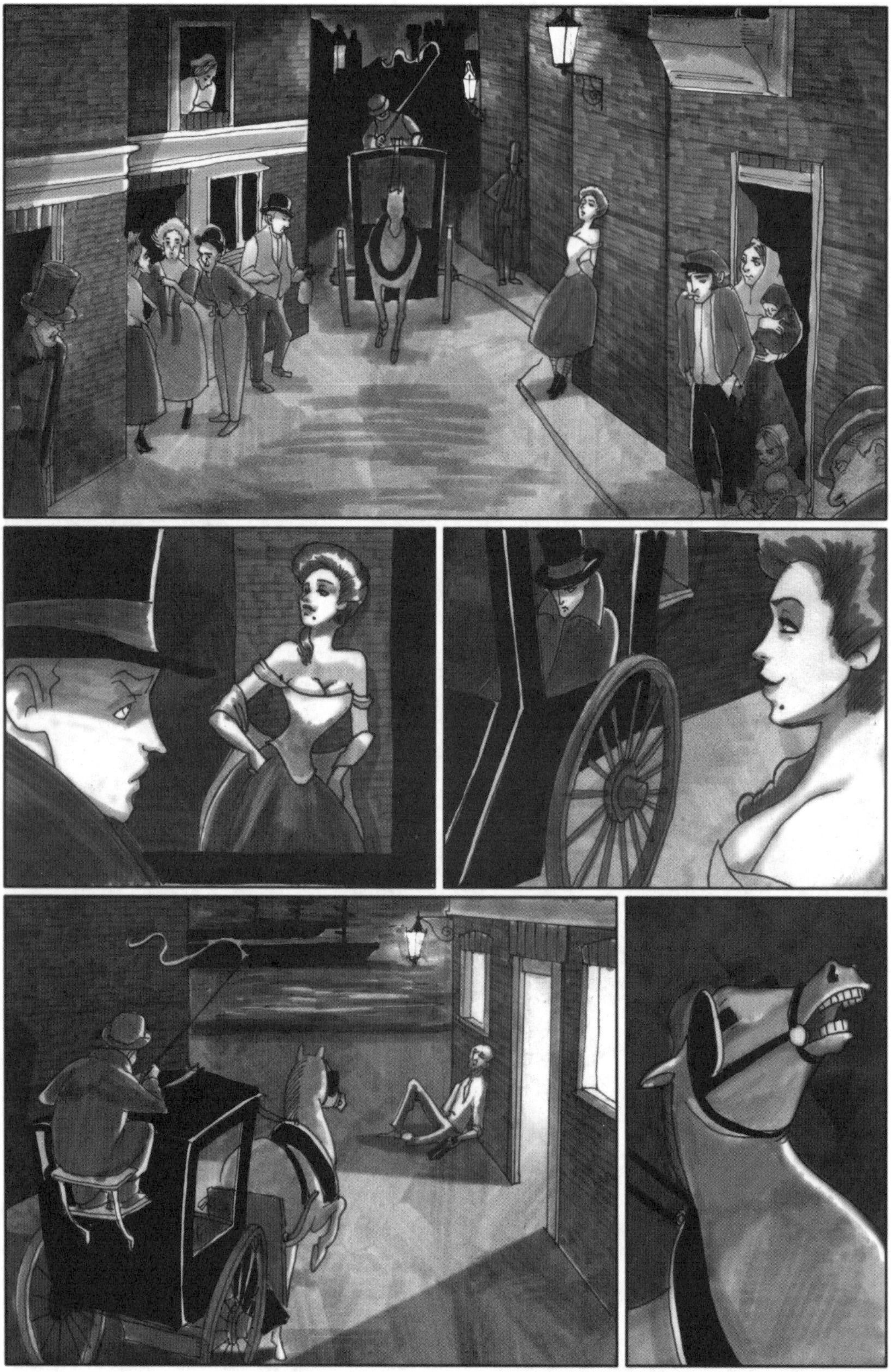

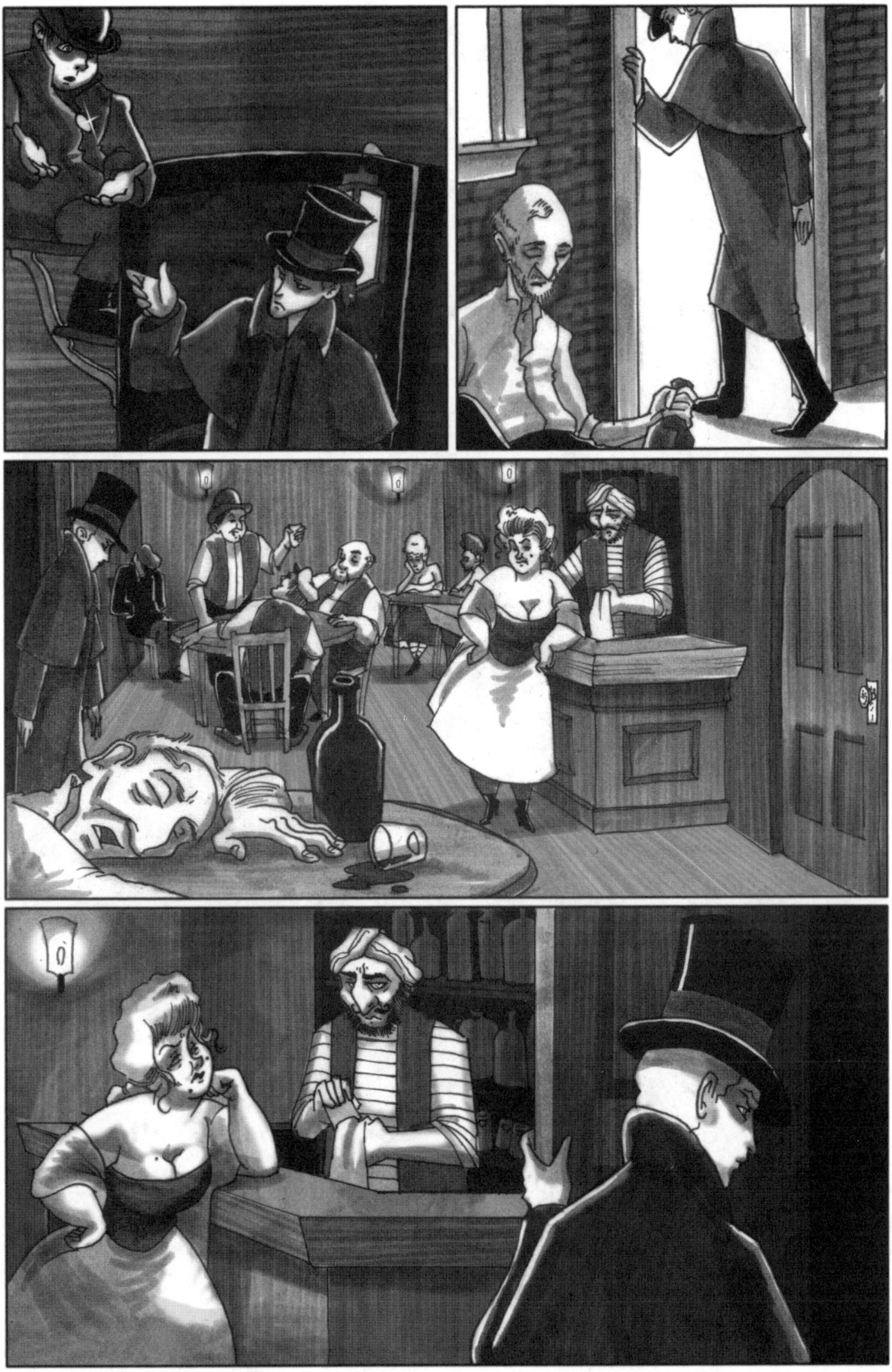

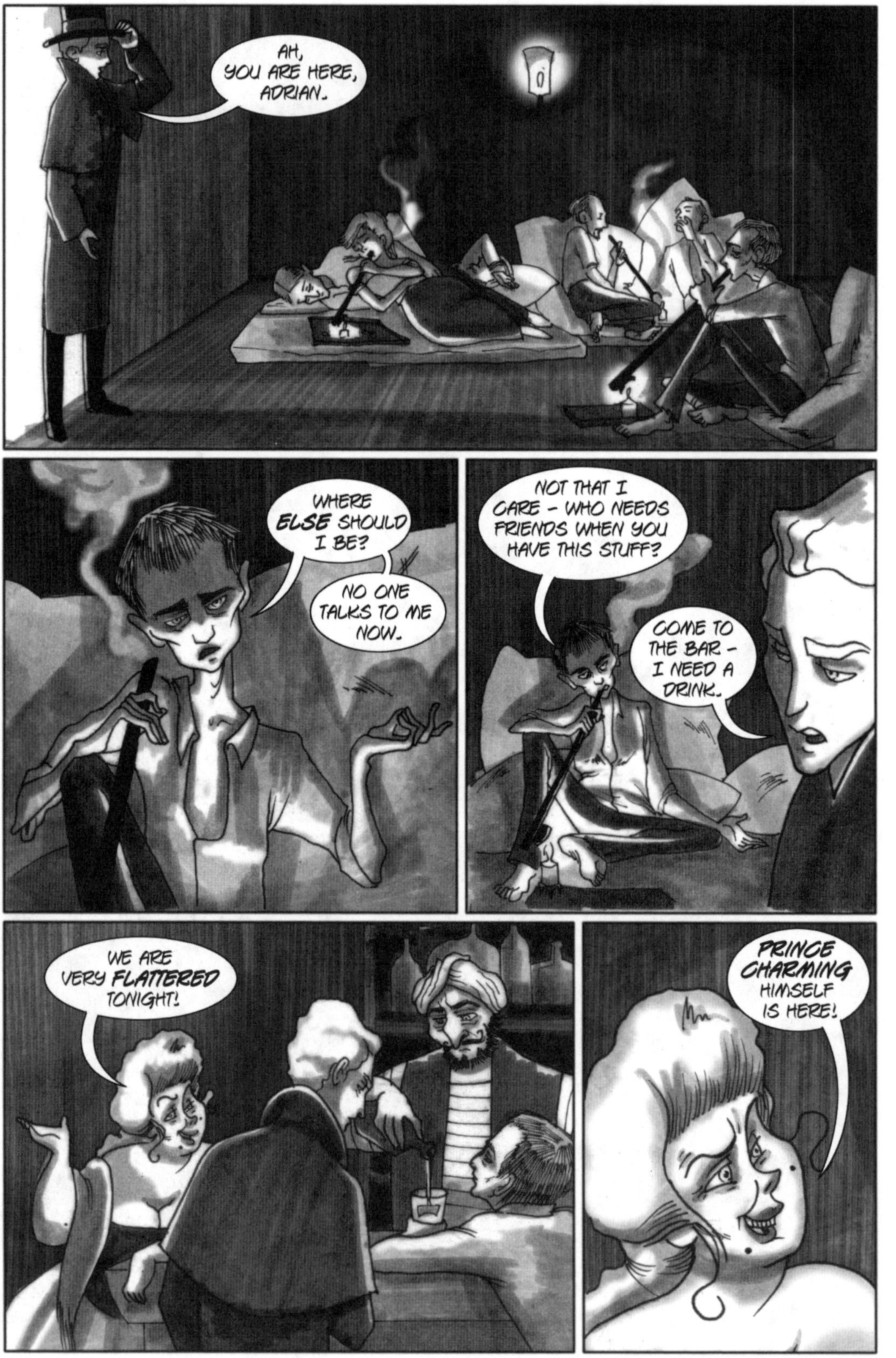
AH, YOU ARE HERE, ADRIAN.
WHERE ELSE SHOULD I BE?
NO ONE TALKS TO ME NOW.
NOT THAT I CARE - WHO NEEDS FRIENDS WHEN YOU HAVE THIS STUFF?
COME TO THE BAR - I NEED A DRINK.
WE ARE VERY FLATTERED TONIGHT!
PRINCE CHARMING HIMSELF IS HERE!

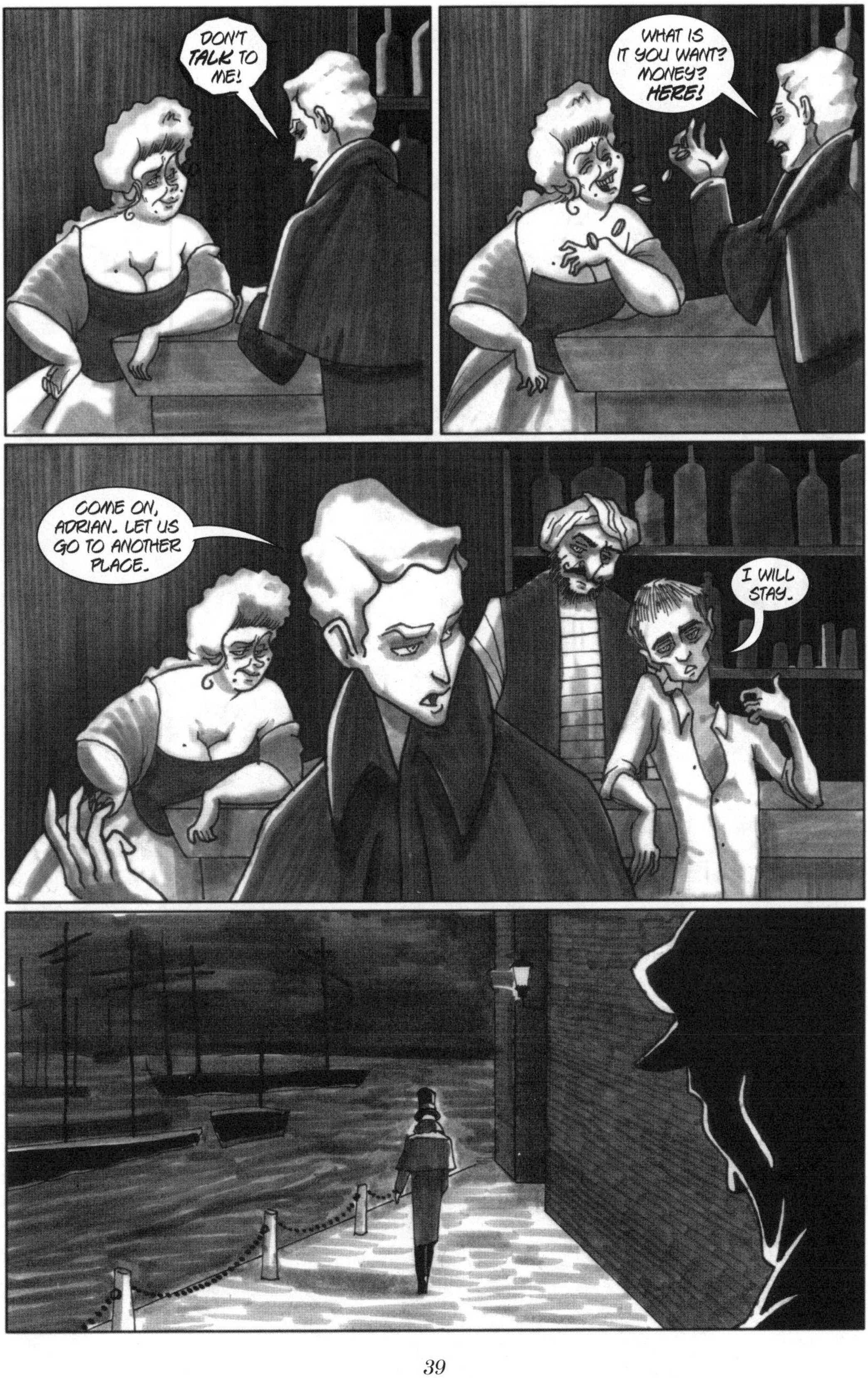
DON'T *TALK* TO ME!
WHAT IS IT YOU WANT? MONEY? *HERE!*
COME ON, ADRIAN. LET US GO TO ANOTHER PLACE.
I WILL STAY.

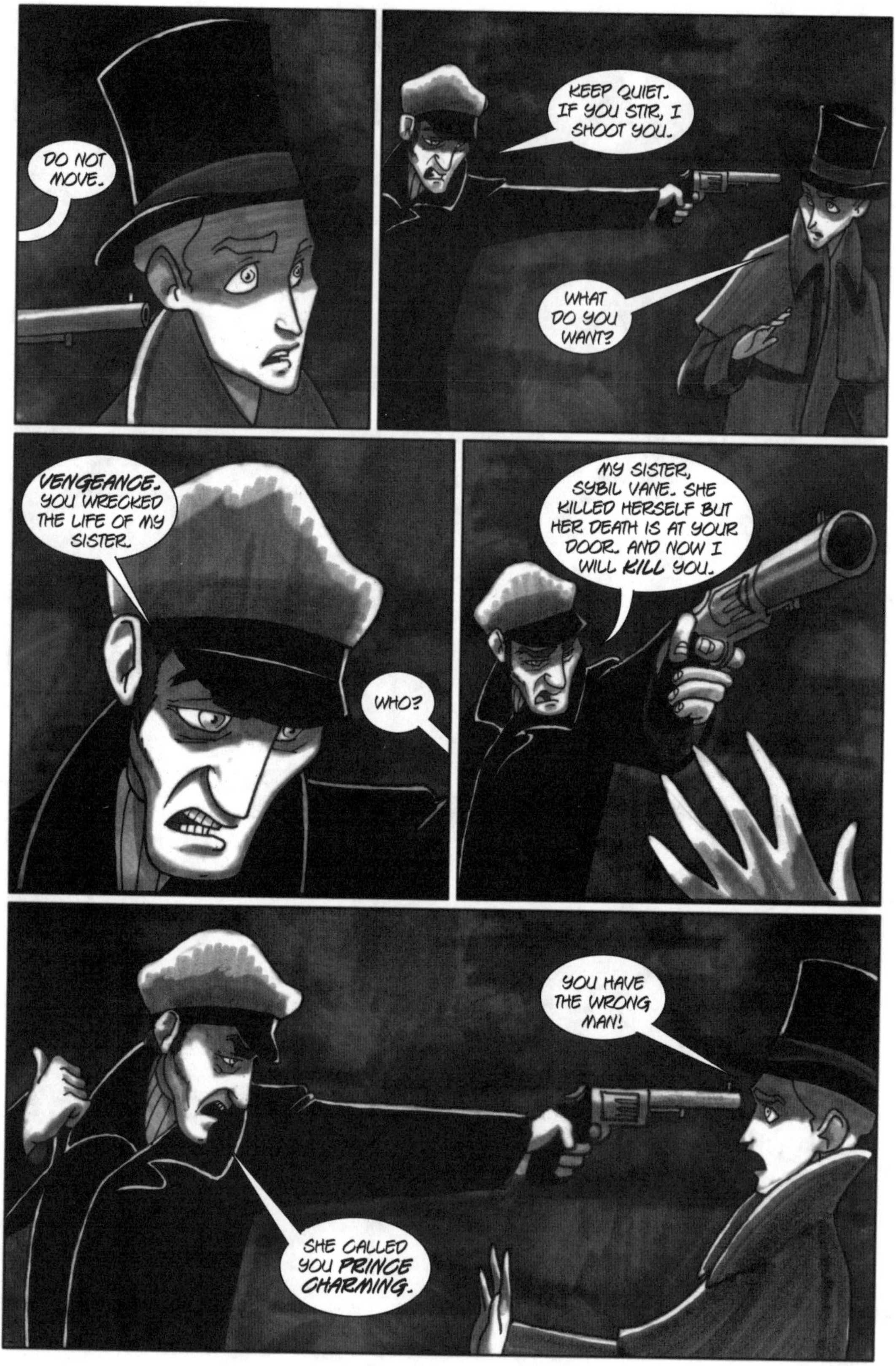
DO NOT MOVE.
KEEP QUIET. IF YOU STIR, I SHOOT YOU.
WHAT DO YOU WANT?
VENGEANCE. YOU WRECKED THE LIFE OF MY SISTER.
WHO?
MY SISTER, SYBIL VANE. SHE KILLED HERSELF BUT HER DEATH IS AT YOUR DOOR. AND NOW I WILL KILL YOU.
YOU HAVE THE WRONG MAN!
SHE CALLED YOU PRINCE CHARMING.

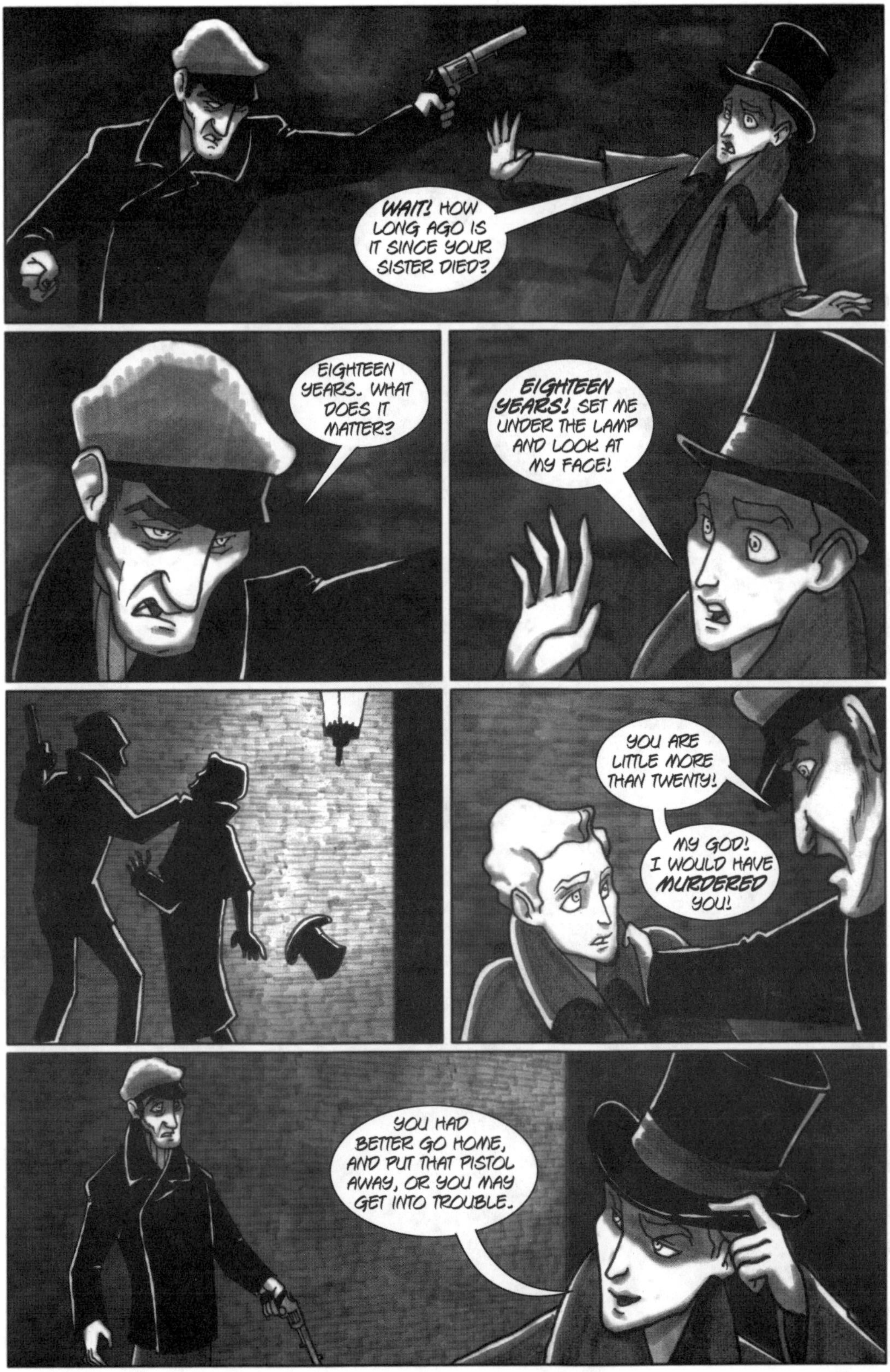
WAIT! HOW LONG AGO IS IT SINCE YOUR SISTER DIED?
EIGHTEEN YEARS. WHAT DOES IT MATTER?
EIGHTEEN YEARS! SET ME UNDER THE LAMP AND LOOK AT MY FACE!
YOU ARE LITTLE MORE THAN TWENTY!
MY GOD! I WOULD HAVE MURDERED YOU!
YOU HAD BETTER GO HOME, AND PUT THAT PISTOL AWAY, OR YOU MAY GET INTO TROUBLE.

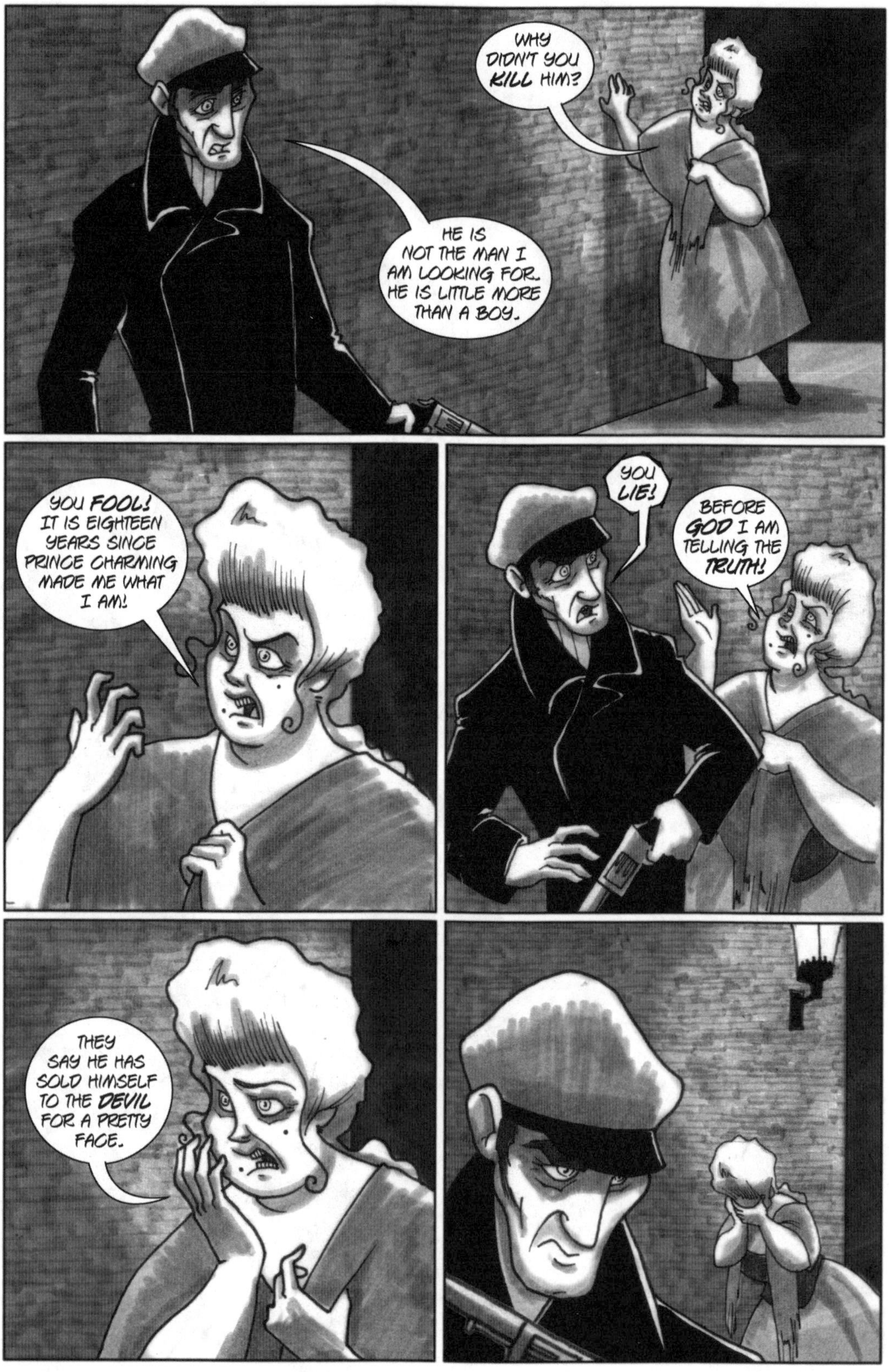
WHY DIDN'T YOU KILL HIM?
HE IS NOT THE MAN I AM LOOKING FOR. HE IS LITTLE MORE THAN A BOY.
YOU FOOL! IT IS EIGHTEEN YEARS SINCE PRINCE CHARMING MADE ME WHAT I AM!
YOU LIE!
BEFORE GOD I AM TELLING THE TRUTH!
THEY SAY HE HAS SOLD HIMSELF TO THE DEVIL FOR A PRETTY FACE.

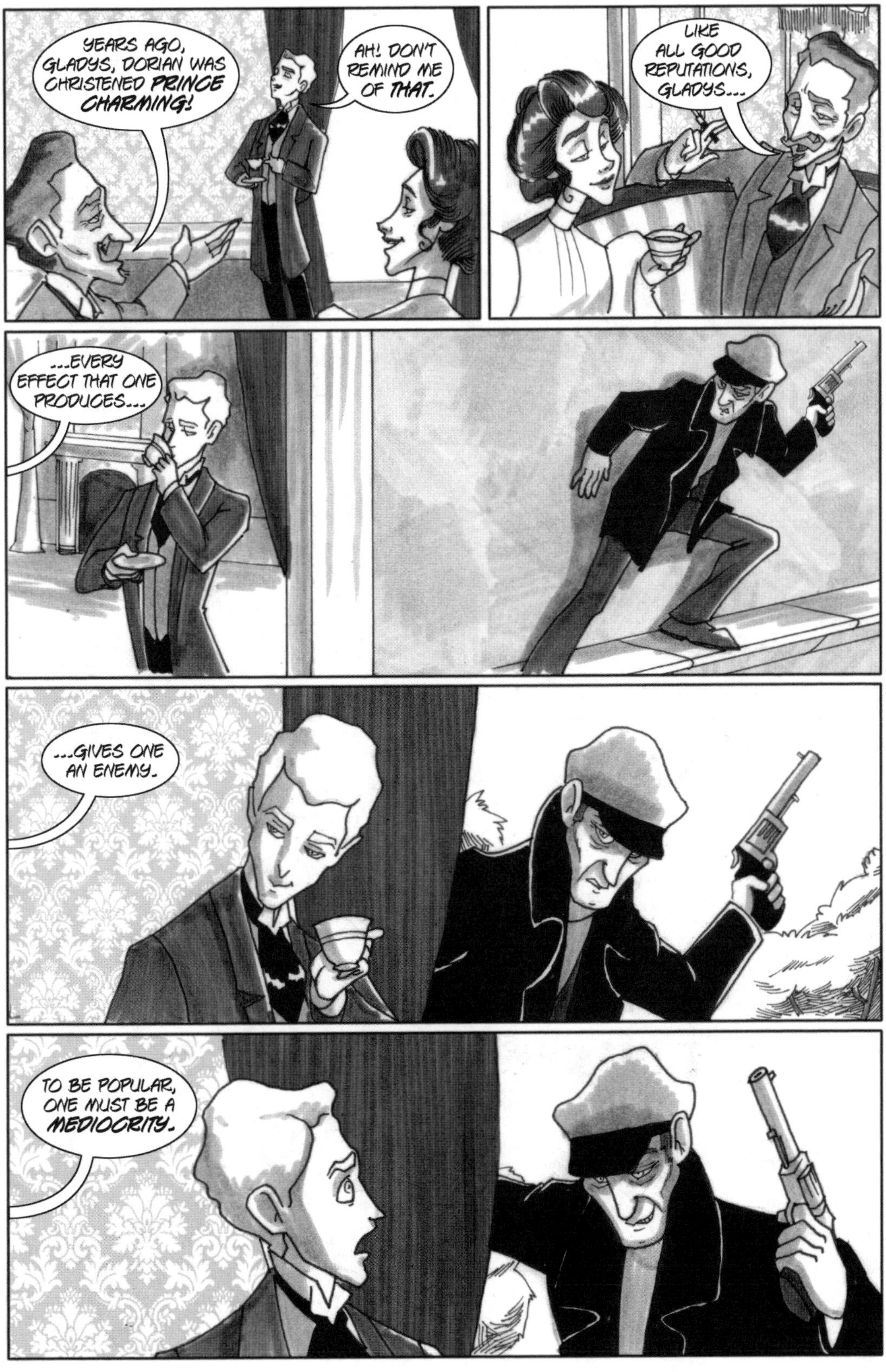
YEARS AGO, GLADYS, DORIAN WAS CHRISTENED **PRINCE CHARMING**!
AH! DON'T REMIND ME OF **THAT**.
LIKE ALL GOOD REPUTATIONS, GLADYS...
...EVERY EFFECT THAT ONE PRODUCES...
...GIVES ONE AN ENEMY.
TO BE POPULAR, ONE MUST BE A **MEDIOCRITY**.

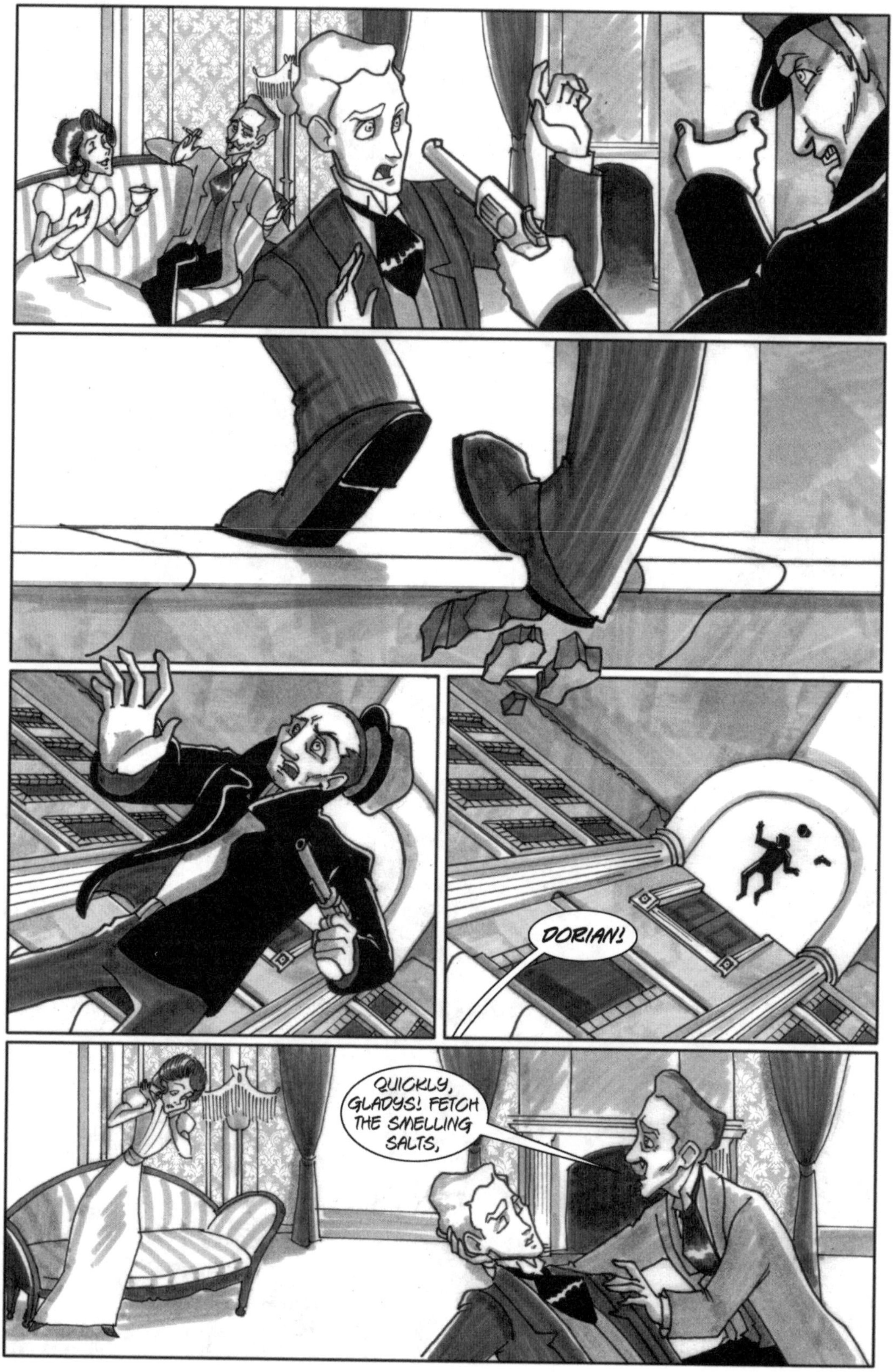
DORIAN!
QUICKLY, GLADYS! FETCH THE SMELLING SALTS,

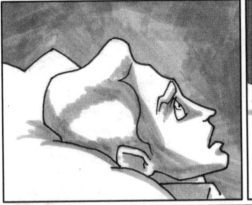

WHAT HAS HAPPENED? AM I SAFE?

YOU MERELY FAINTED. LADY NARBOROUGH INSISTED THAT WE PUT YOU TO BED HERE.

THE GROUNDSMAN AT THE HOUSE FOUND A POACHER, DEAD.

POOR DEVIL. PERHAPS THAT IS WHAT GAVE YOU A START.

YES, YES, THAT WAS IT.

I WILL LEAVE SO YOU CAN REST.

I WANT TO ESCAPE... TO FORGET...

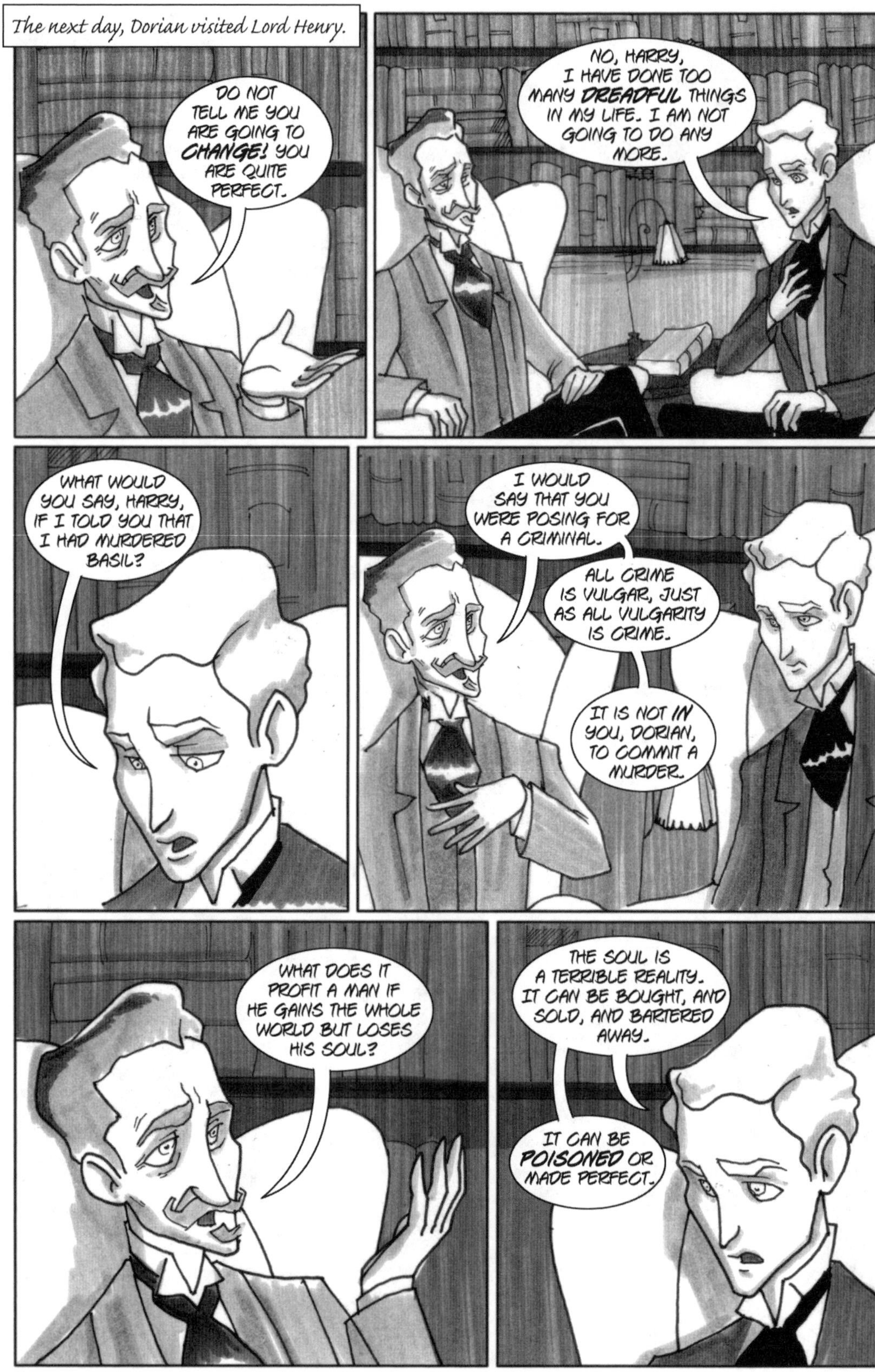
The next day, Dorian visited Lord Henry.
DO NOT TELL ME YOU ARE GOING TO CHANGE! YOU ARE QUITE PERFECT.
NO, HARRY, I HAVE DONE TOO MANY DREADFUL THINGS IN MY LIFE. I AM NOT GOING TO DO ANY MORE.
WHAT WOULD YOU SAY, HARRY, IF I TOLD YOU THAT I HAD MURDERED BASIL?
I WOULD SAY THAT YOU WERE POSING FOR A CRIMINAL.
ALL CRIME IS VULGAR, JUST AS ALL VULGARITY IS CRIME.
IT IS NOT IN YOU, DORIAN, TO COMMIT A MURDER.
WHAT DOES IT PROFIT A MAN IF HE GAINS THE WHOLE WORLD BUT LOSES HIS SOUL?
THE SOUL IS A TERRIBLE REALITY. IT CAN BE BOUGHT, AND SOLD, AND BARTERED AWAY.
IT CAN BE POISONED OR MADE PERFECT.

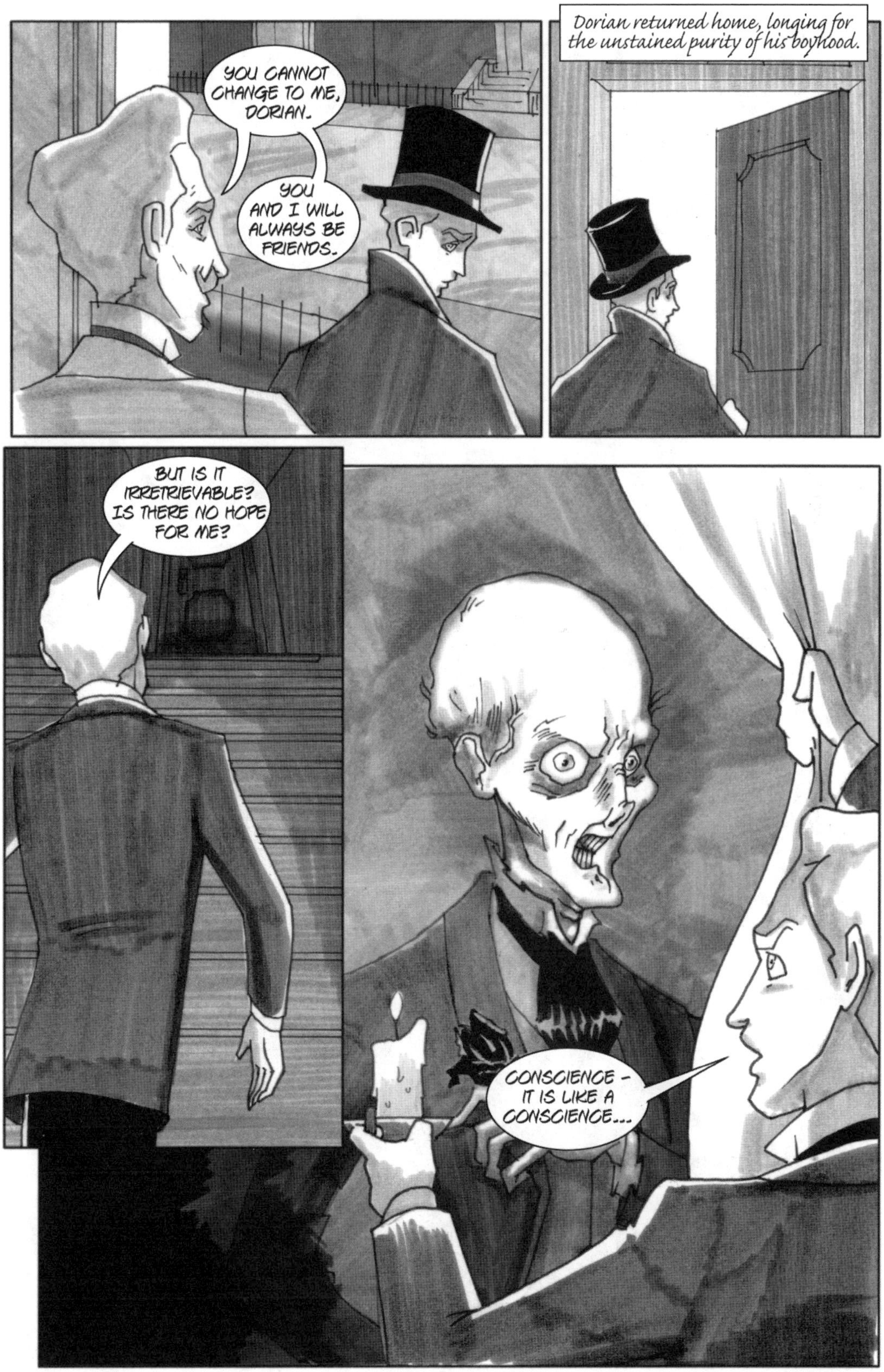
YOU CANNOT CHANGE TO ME, DORIAN.
YOU AND I WILL ALWAYS BE FRIENDS.
Dorian returned home, longing for the unstained purity of his boyhood.
BUT IS IT IRRETRIEVABLE? IS THERE NO HOPE FOR ME?
CONSCIENCE - IT IS LIKE A CONSCIENCE...

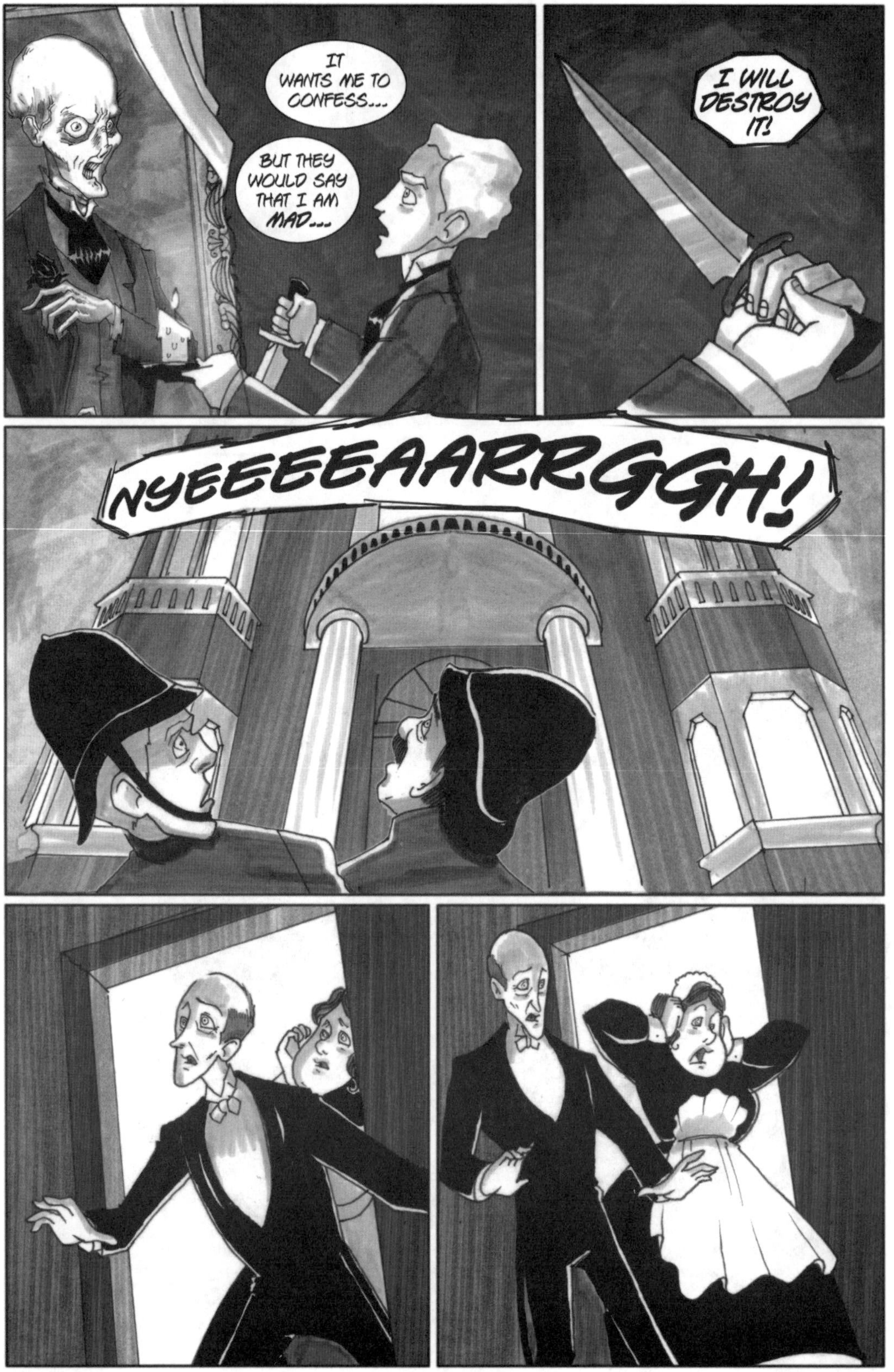
IT WANTS ME TO CONFESS...
BUT THEY WOULD SAY THAT I AM MAD...
I WILL DESTROY IT!
NYEEEEAARRGGH!

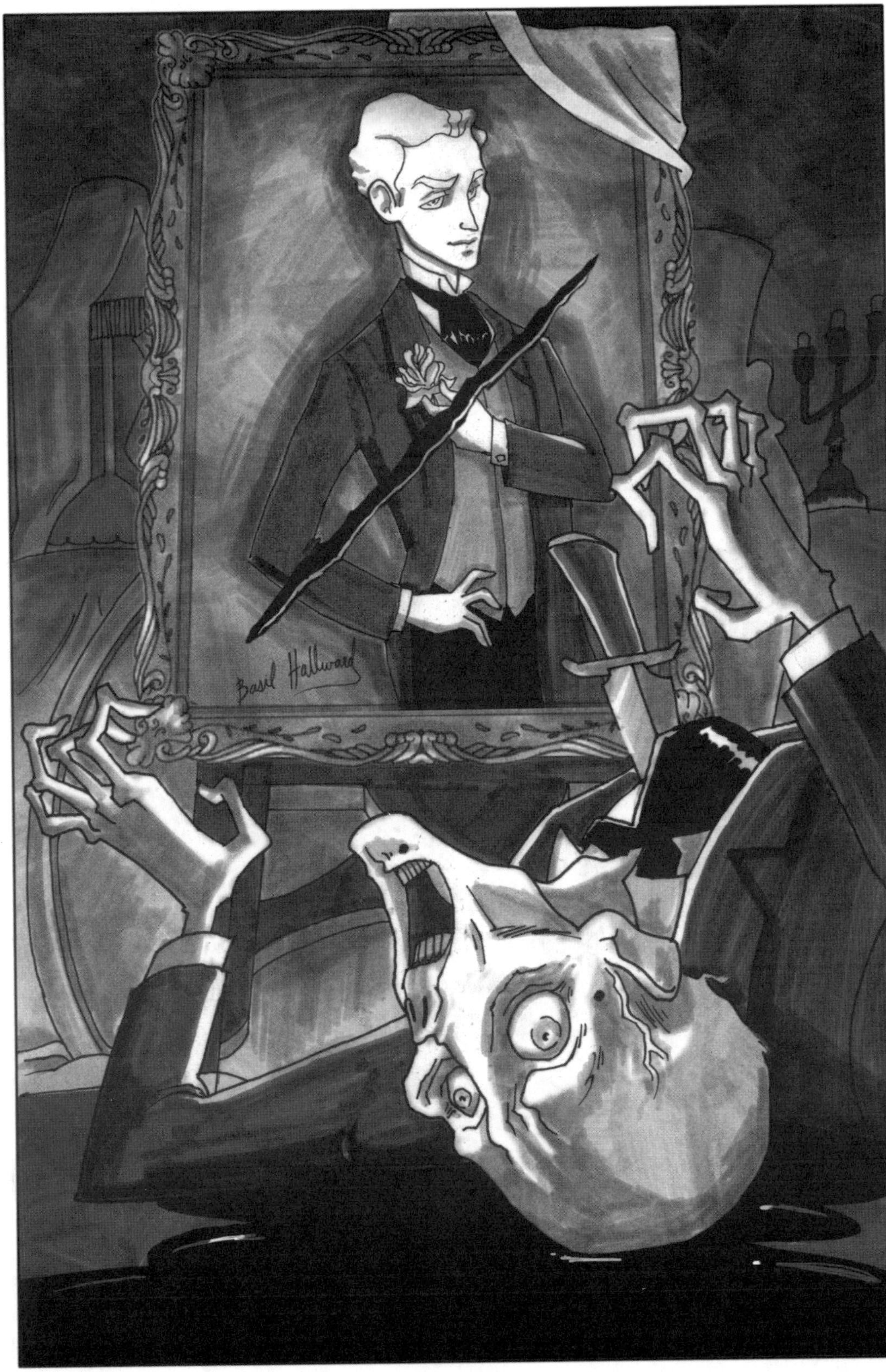
Basil Hallward

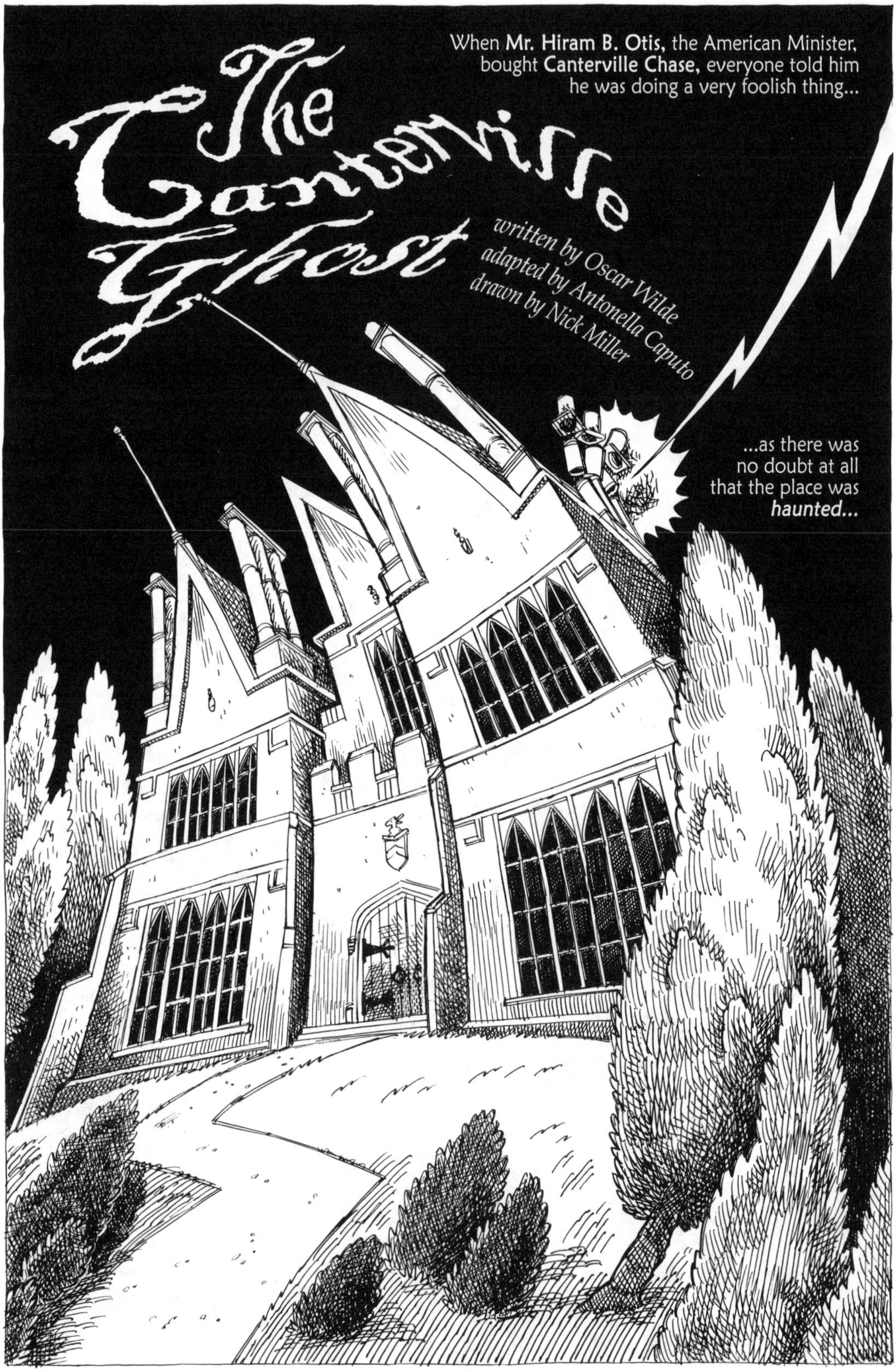
When Mr. Hiram B. Otis, the American Minister, bought Canterville Chase, everyone told him he was doing a very foolish thing...
The Canterville Ghost
written by Oscar Wilde
adapted by Antonella Caputo
drawn by Nick Miller
...as there was no doubt at all that the place was haunted...

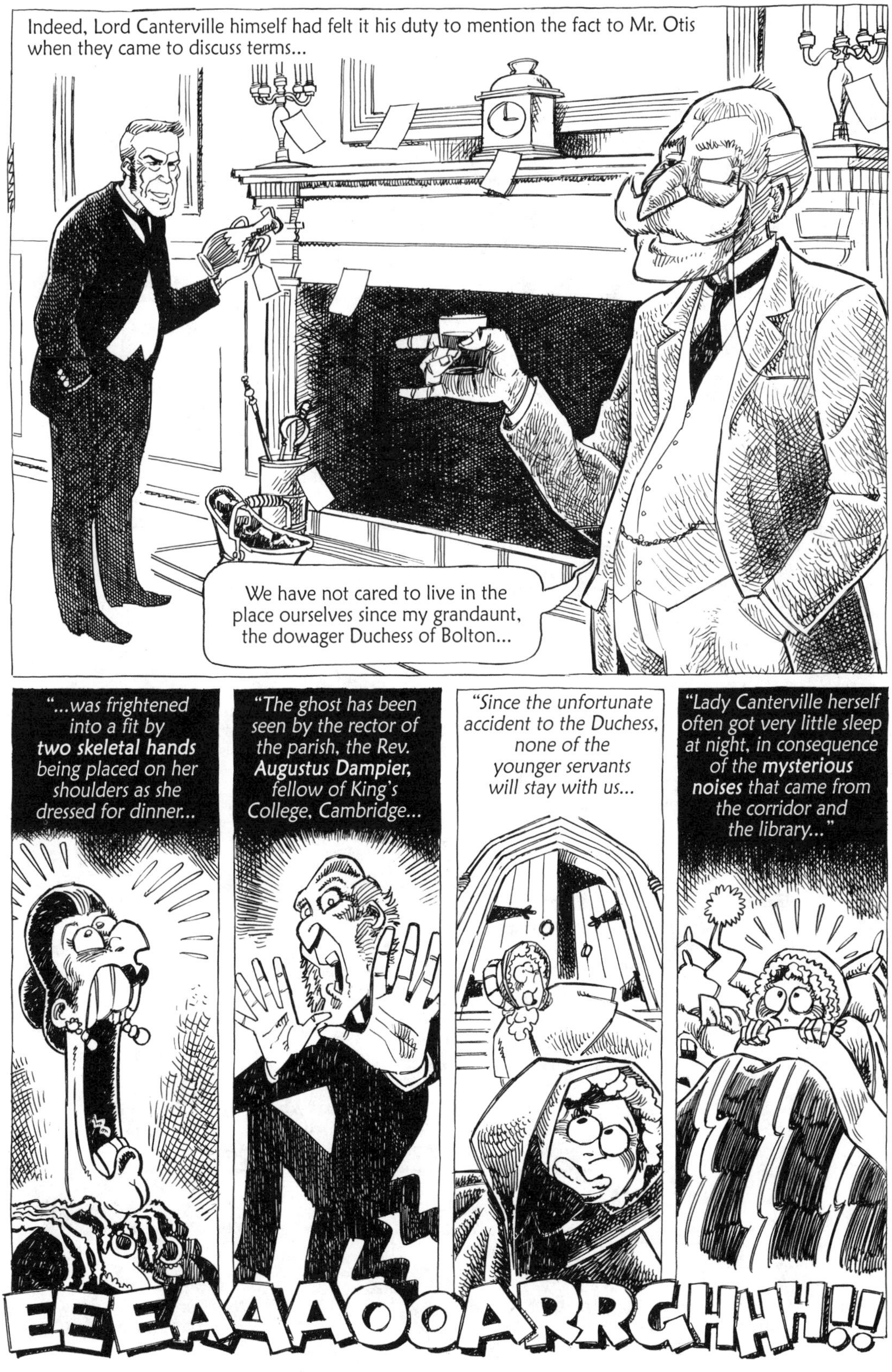
Indeed, Lord Canterville himself had felt it his duty to mention the fact to Mr. Otis when they came to discuss terms...
We have not cared to live in the place ourselves since my grandaunt, the dowager Duchess of Bolton...
"...was frightened into a fit by two skeletal hands being placed on her shoulders as she dressed for dinner...
"The ghost has been seen by the rector of the parish, the Rev. Augustus Dampier, fellow of King's College, Cambridge...
"Since the unfortunate accident to the Duchess, none of the younger servants will stay with us...
"Lady Canterville herself often got very little sleep at night, in consequence of the mysterious noises that came from the corridor and the library..."
EEEAAAOOARRGHHH!!

My Lord, I will take the furniture *and* the ghost at a valuation! I come from a **modern country,** where we can have everything that money can buy...

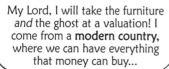

"*...and with our spry young fellows painting the Old World red...*

"*...and carrying off your best actresses...*

STAGE DOOR

"*...I reckon if there were such a thing as a ghost in Europe, we'd have it at home in very short time in one of our **public museums,** or on the **road** as a **show..!**"*

Laydeez an' genn'lmen! **Step this way** t'see the **REAL ENGLISH GHOST!** Thrill t'the *awful noise* of his *rattling chains...!!*

The English Ghost!

SHILL   RUBE   SUCKER   MARK   PUNTER

I fear the ghost *exists!* It has been in the house since **1584,** and always makes its appearance before the death of **any member** of our family!

So does the family doctor! There's **no such thing as a ghost,** and I guess the **laws of nature** are not to be **suspended** for the British aristocracy!

You are certainly very *natural* in America, and if you don't mind a **ghost** in the house, it is all right. Only you **must** remember I *warned* you!

A few weeks after this the purchase was **completed,** and the Minister and his family went down to **Canterville Chase.**

52

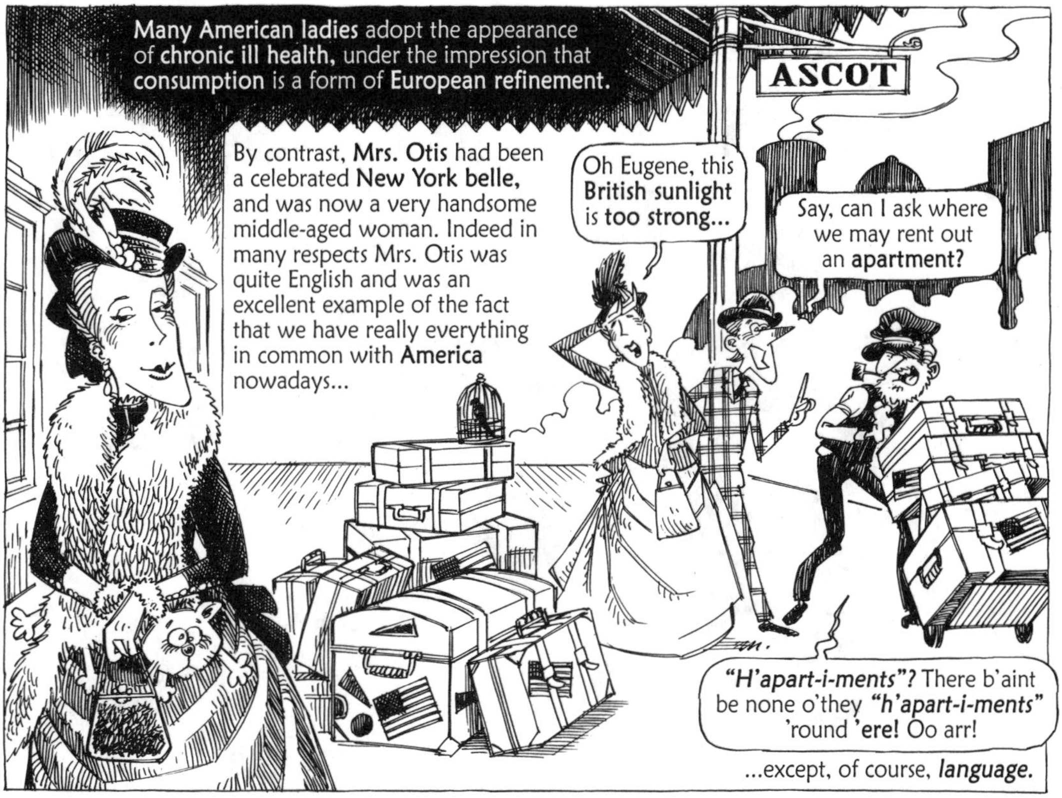
Many American ladies adopt the appearance of chronic ill health, under the impression that consumption is a form of European refinement.
ASCOT
By contrast, Mrs. Otis had been a celebrated New York belle, and was now a very handsome middle-aged woman. Indeed in many respects Mrs. Otis was quite English and was an excellent example of the fact that we have really everything in common with America nowadays...
Oh Eugene, this British sunlight is too strong...
Say, can I ask where we may rent out an apartment?
"H'apart-i-ments"? There b'aint be none o'they "h'apart-i-ments" 'round 'ere! Oo arr!
...except, of course, language.

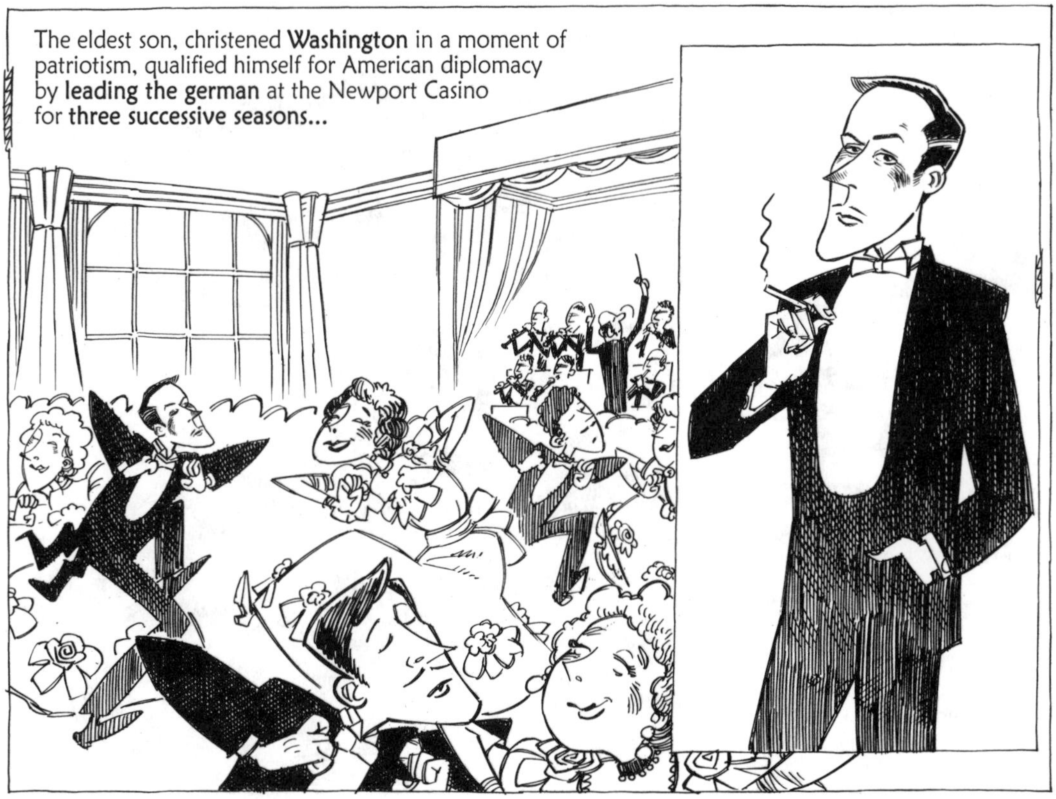
The eldest son, christened Washington in a moment of patriotism, qualified himself for American diplomacy by leading the german at the Newport Casino for three successive seasons...

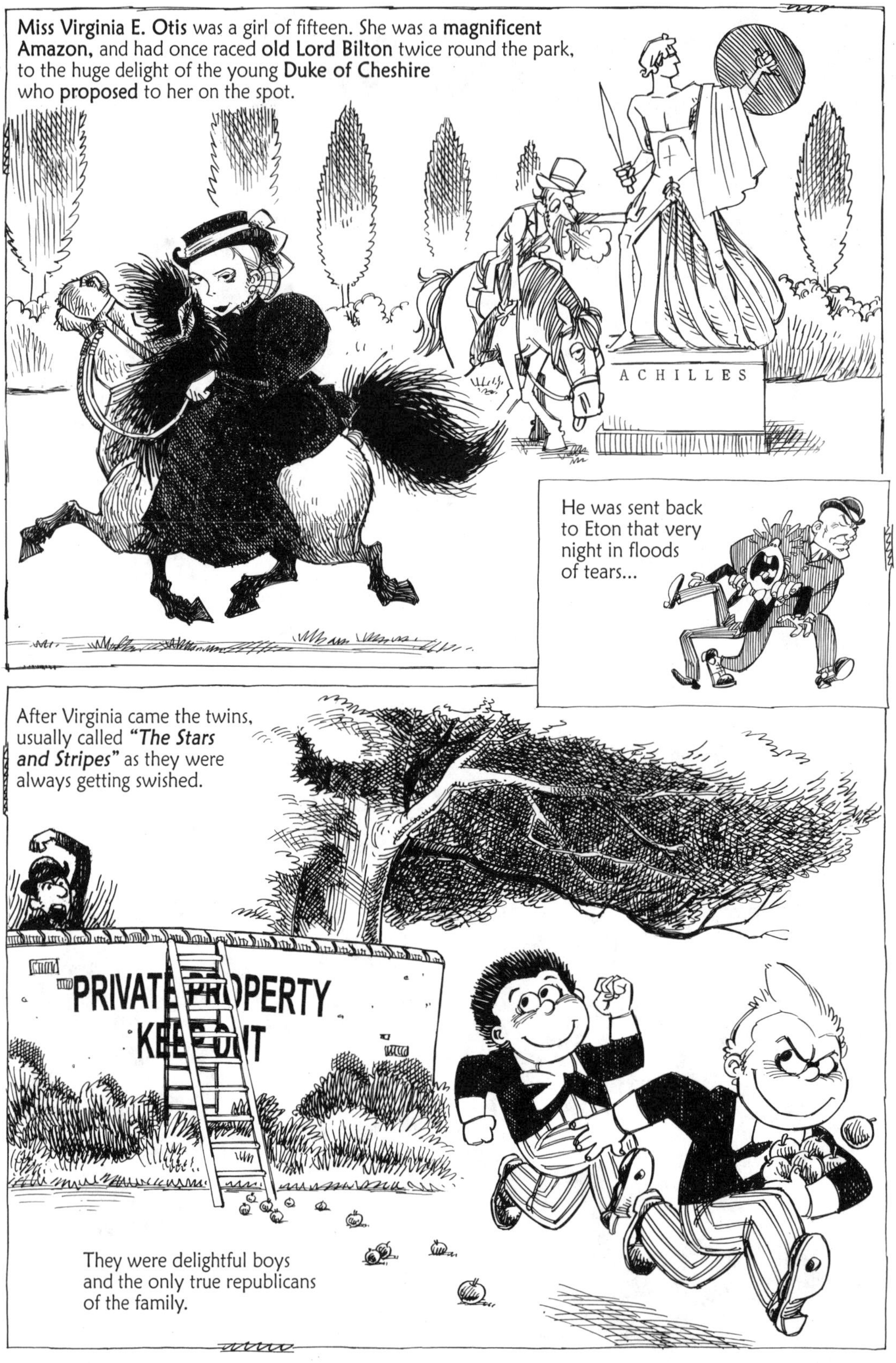
Miss Virginia E. Otis was a girl of fifteen. She was a **magnificent Amazon,** and had once raced **old Lord Bilton** twice round the park, to the huge delight of the young **Duke of Cheshire** who **proposed** to her on the spot.
ACHILLES
He was sent back to Eton that very night in floods of tears...
After Virginia came the twins, usually called ***"The Stars and Stripes"*** as they were always getting swished.
PRIVATE PROPERTY
KEEP OUT
They were delightful boys and the only true republicans of the family.

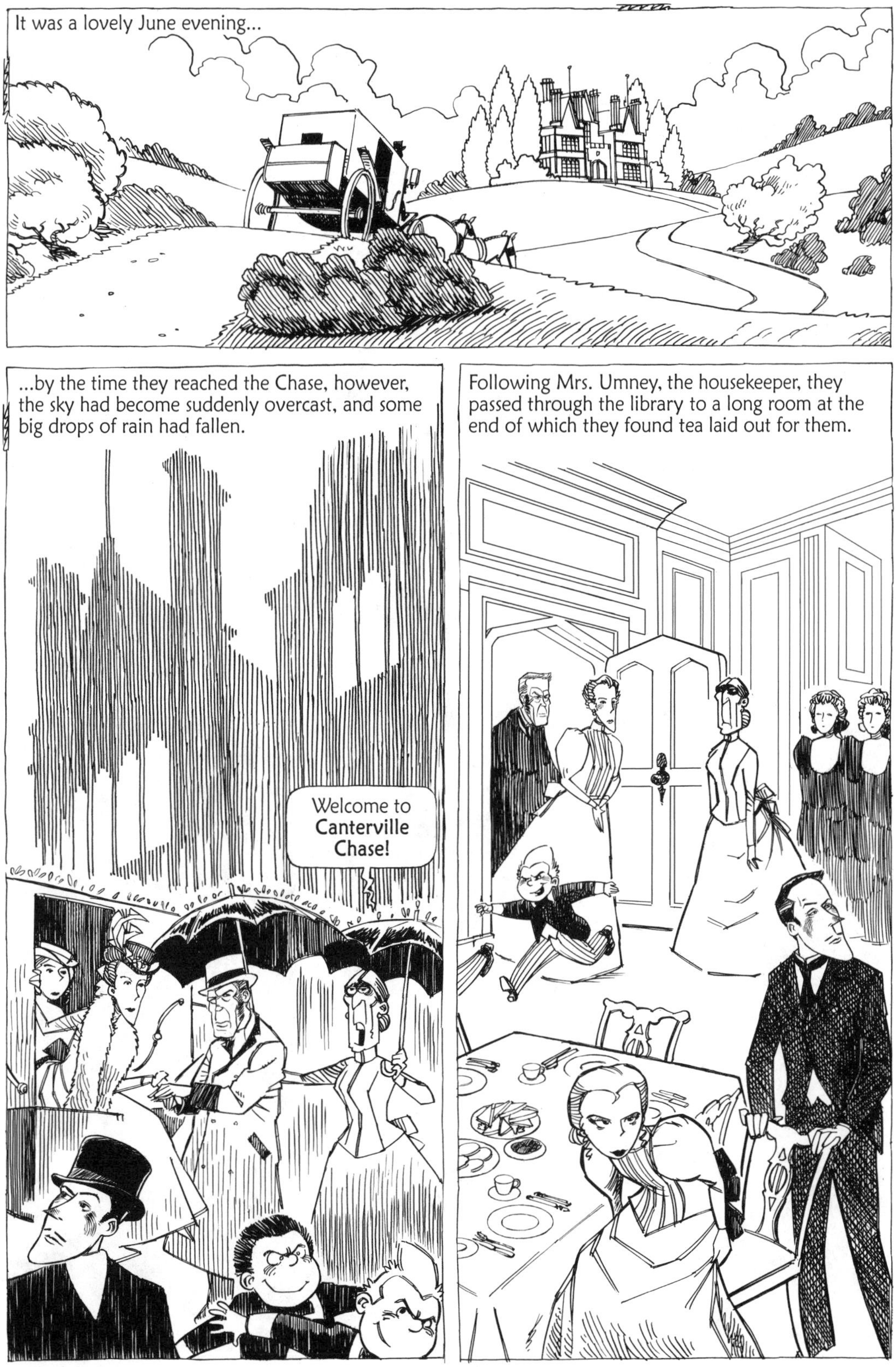
It was a lovely June evening...
...by the time they reached the Chase, however, the sky had become suddenly overcast, and some big drops of rain had fallen.
Welcome to Canterville Chase!
Following Mrs. Umney, the housekeeper, they passed through the library to a long room at the end of which they found tea laid out for them.

I'm afraid something has been spilt there!

Yes madam, BLOOD has been spilt on that spot. It is the blood of Lady Eleanore de Canterville...

"...who was murdered on that spot by her own husband Sir Simon in 1575...

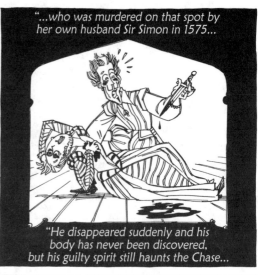

"He disappeared suddenly and his body has never been discovered, but his guilty spirit still haunts the Chase...

"The blood stain has been much admired by tourists ever since and cannot be removed!"

That is all nonsense...!

PINKERTON'S CHAMPION STAIN REMOVER AND PARAGON DETERGENT will clean it up in no time..!!

And before the terrified housekeeper he had fallen upon his knees and scoured the floor with the small black bottle.

There! I knew PINKERTON'S would do the trick!

BAROOMM!!

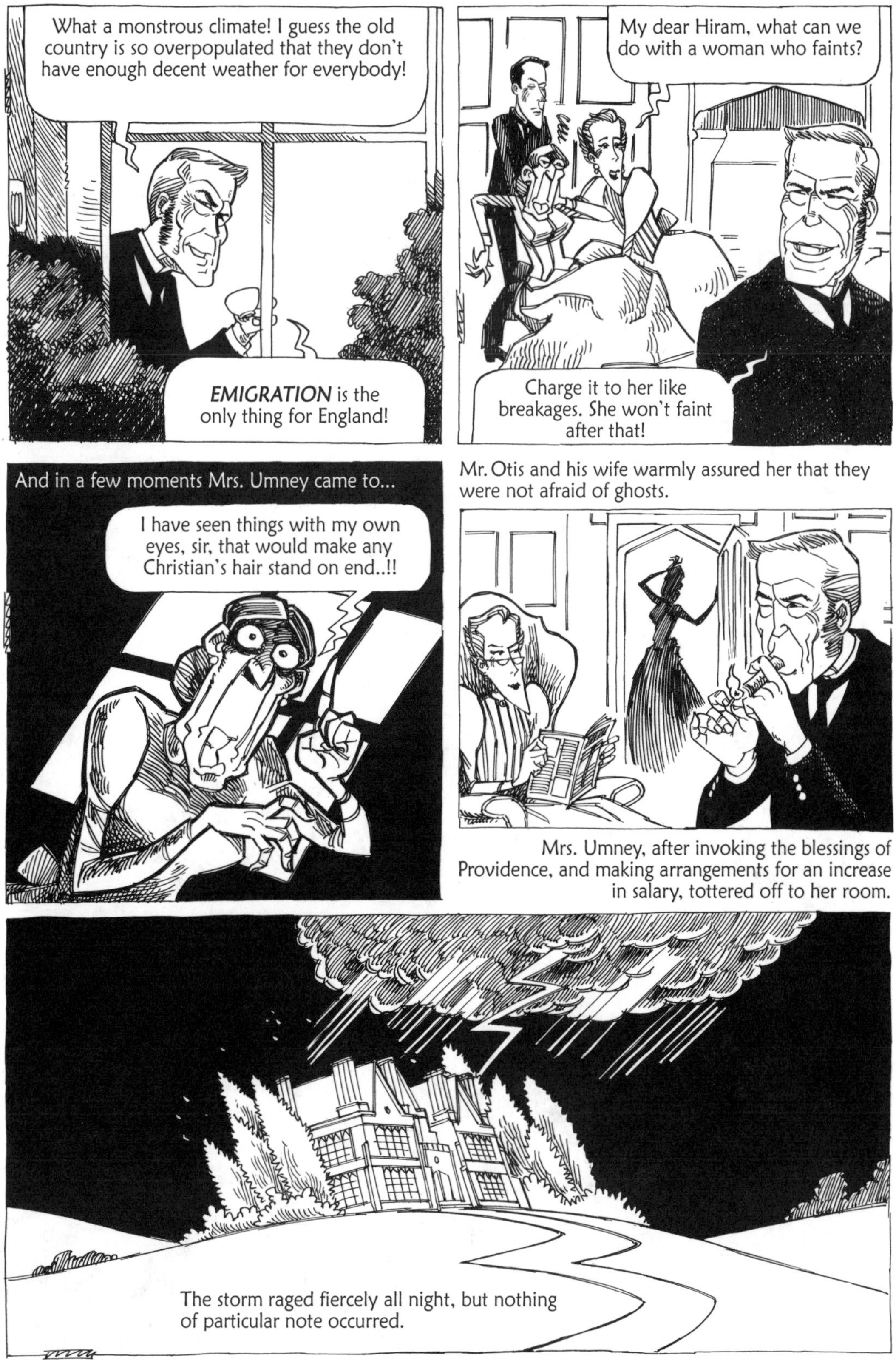
What a monstrous climate! I guess the old country is so overpopulated that they don't have enough decent weather for everybody!
EMIGRATION is the only thing for England!
My dear Hiram, what can we do with a woman who faints?
Charge it to her like breakages. She won't faint after that!
And in a few moments Mrs. Umney came to...
I have seen things with my own eyes, sir, that would make any Christian's hair stand on end..!!
Mr. Otis and his wife warmly assured her that they were not afraid of ghosts.
Mrs. Umney, after invoking the blessings of Providence, and making arrangements for an increase in salary, tottered off to her room.
The storm raged fiercely all night, but nothing of particular note occurred.

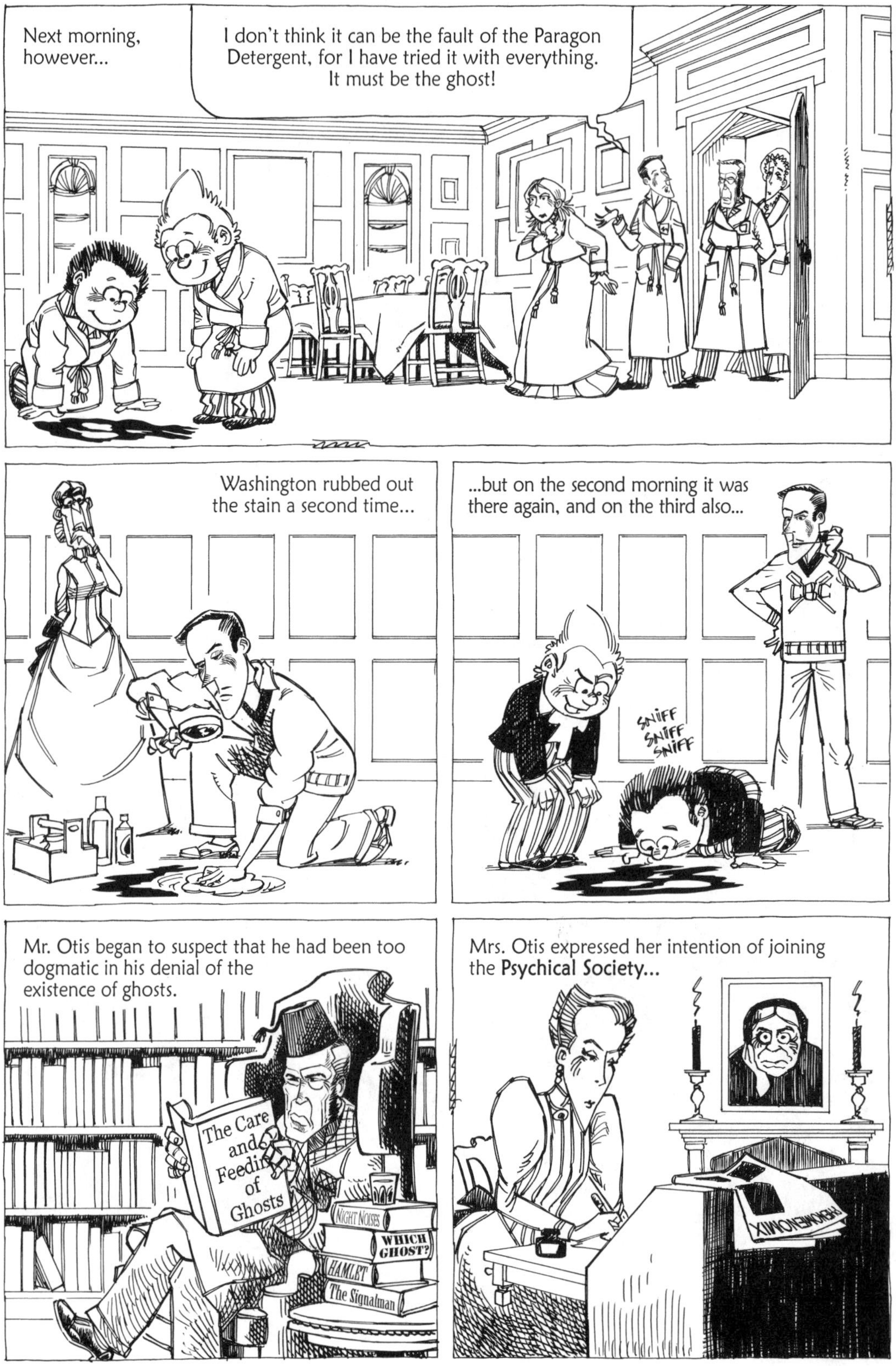
Next morning, however...
I don't think it can be the fault of the Paragon Detergent, for I have tried it with everything. It must be the ghost!
Washington rubbed out the stain a second time...
...but on the second morning it was there again, and on the third also...
SNIFF
SNIFF
SNIFF
Mr. Otis began to suspect that he had been too dogmatic in his denial of the existence of ghosts.
The Care and Feedin of Ghosts
NIGHT NOISES
WHICH GHOST?
HAMLET
The Signalman
Mrs. Otis expressed her intention of joining the **Psychical Society...**

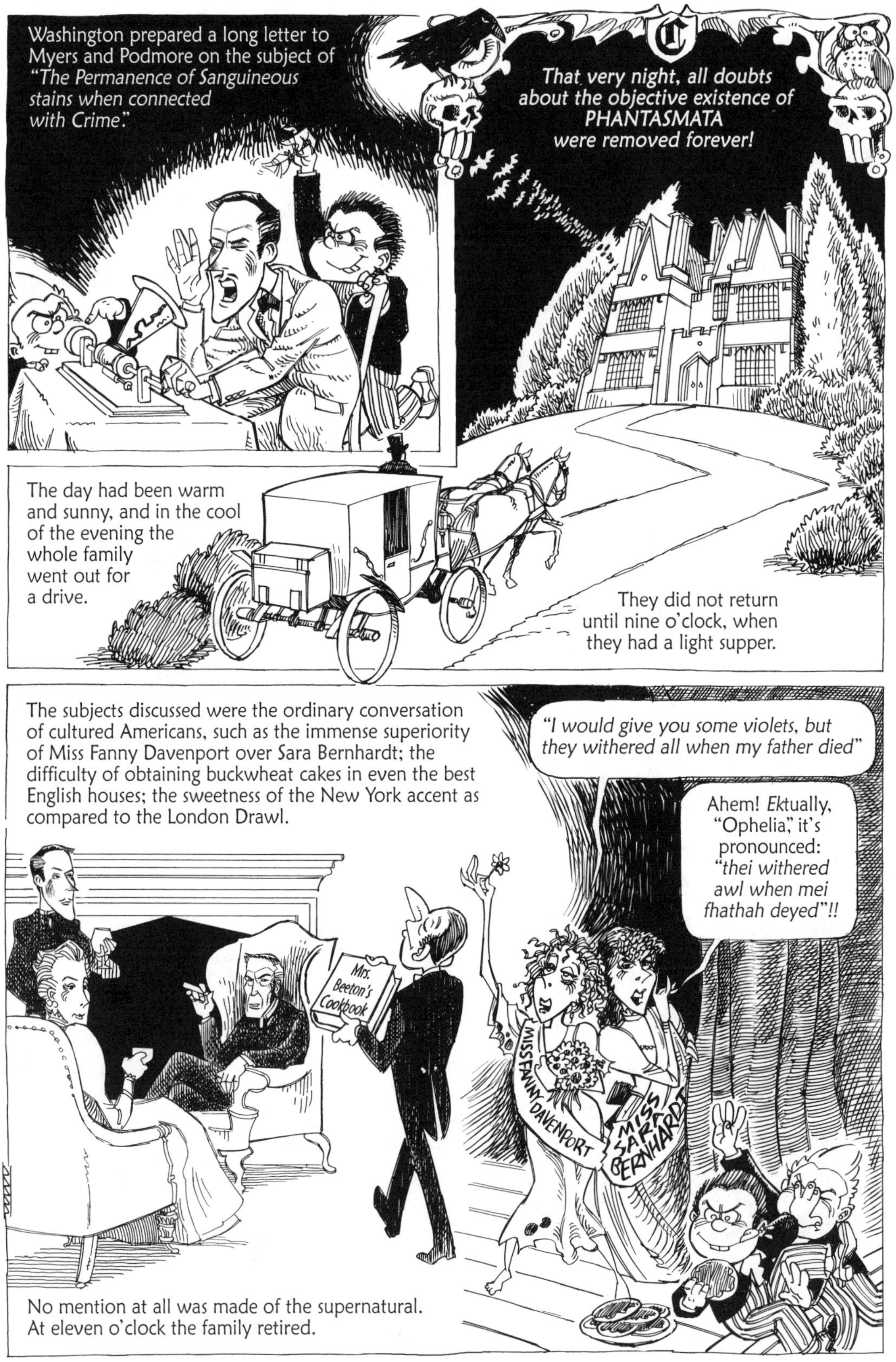
Washington prepared a long letter to Myers and Podmore on the subject of *"The Permanence of Sanguineous stains when connected with Crime."*
That very night, all doubts about the objective existence of PHANTASMATA were removed forever!
The day had been warm and sunny, and in the cool of the evening the whole family went out for a drive.
They did not return until nine o'clock, when they had a light supper.
The subjects discussed were the ordinary conversation of cultured Americans, such as the immense superiority of Miss Fanny Davenport over Sara Bernhardt; the difficulty of obtaining buckwheat cakes in even the best English houses; the sweetness of the New York accent as compared to the London Drawl.
"I would give you some violets, but they withered all when my father died"
Ahem! *Ek*tually, "Ophelia," it's pronounced: *"thei withered awl when mei fhathah deyed"!!*
Mrs. Beeton's Cookbook
MISS FANNY DAVENPORT
MISS SARA BERNHARDT
No mention at all was made of the supernatural. At eleven o'clock the family retired.

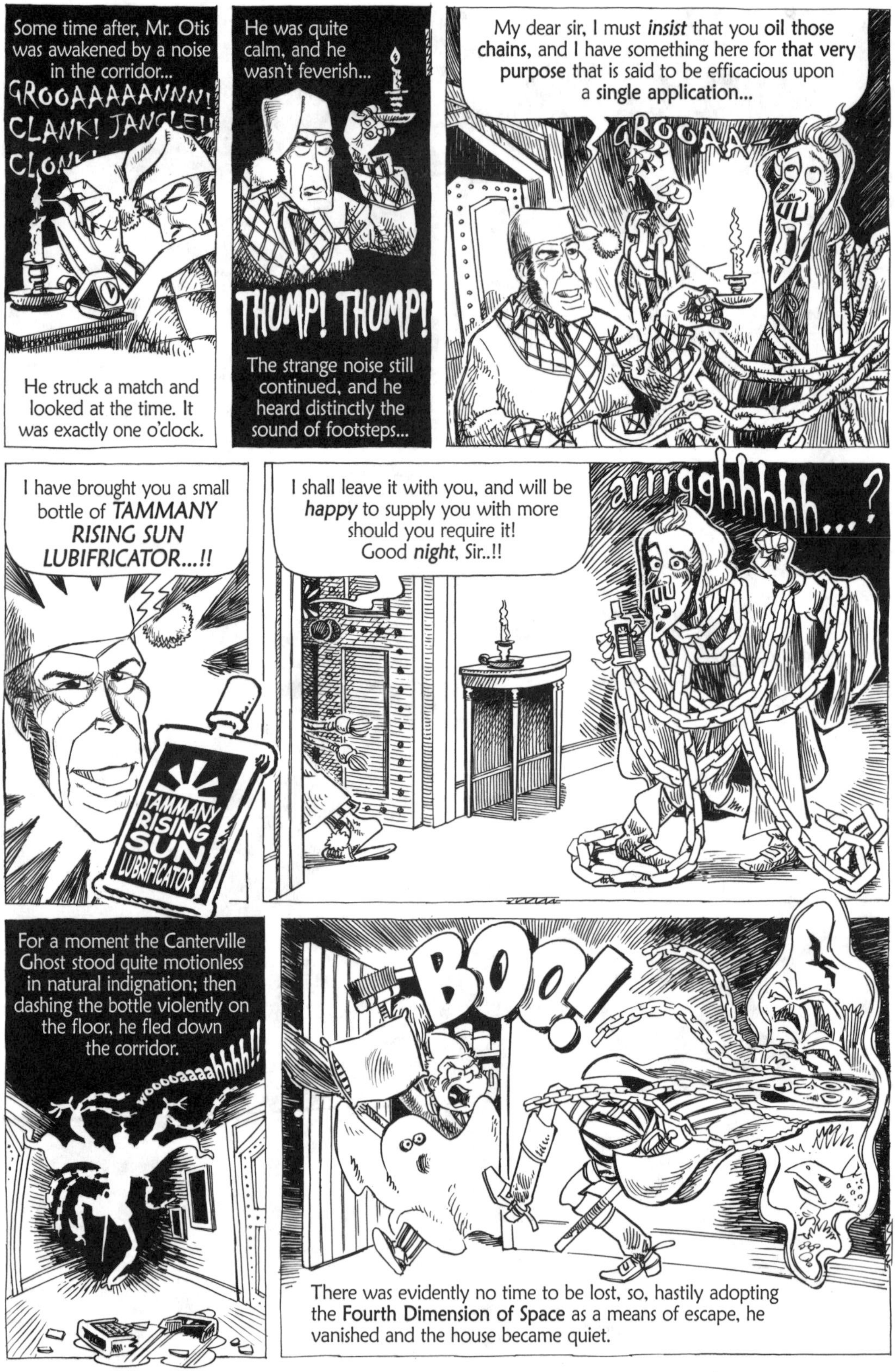

Some time after, Mr. Otis was awakened by a noise in the corridor...
GROOAAAAANNN!
CLANK! JANGLE!!
He struck a match and looked at the time. It was exactly one o'clock.
He was quite calm, and he wasn't feverish...
THUMP! THUMP!
The strange noise still continued, and he heard distinctly the sound of footsteps...
My dear sir, I must ***insist*** that you **oil those chains**, and I have something here for **that very purpose** that is said to be efficacious upon a **single application...**
GROOAA—
I have brought you a small bottle of ***TAMMANY RISING SUN LUBIFRICATOR...!!***
TAMMANY RISING SUN LUBRIFICATOR
I shall leave it with you, and will be ***happy*** to supply you with more should you require it! Good ***night***, Sir..!!
arrrgghhhhh...?
For a moment the Canterville Ghost stood quite motionless in natural indignation; then dashing the bottle violently on the floor, he fled down the corridor.
woooaaaahhhh!!
BOO!
There was evidently no time to be lost, so, hastily adopting the **Fourth Dimension of Space** as a means of escape, he vanished and the house became quiet.

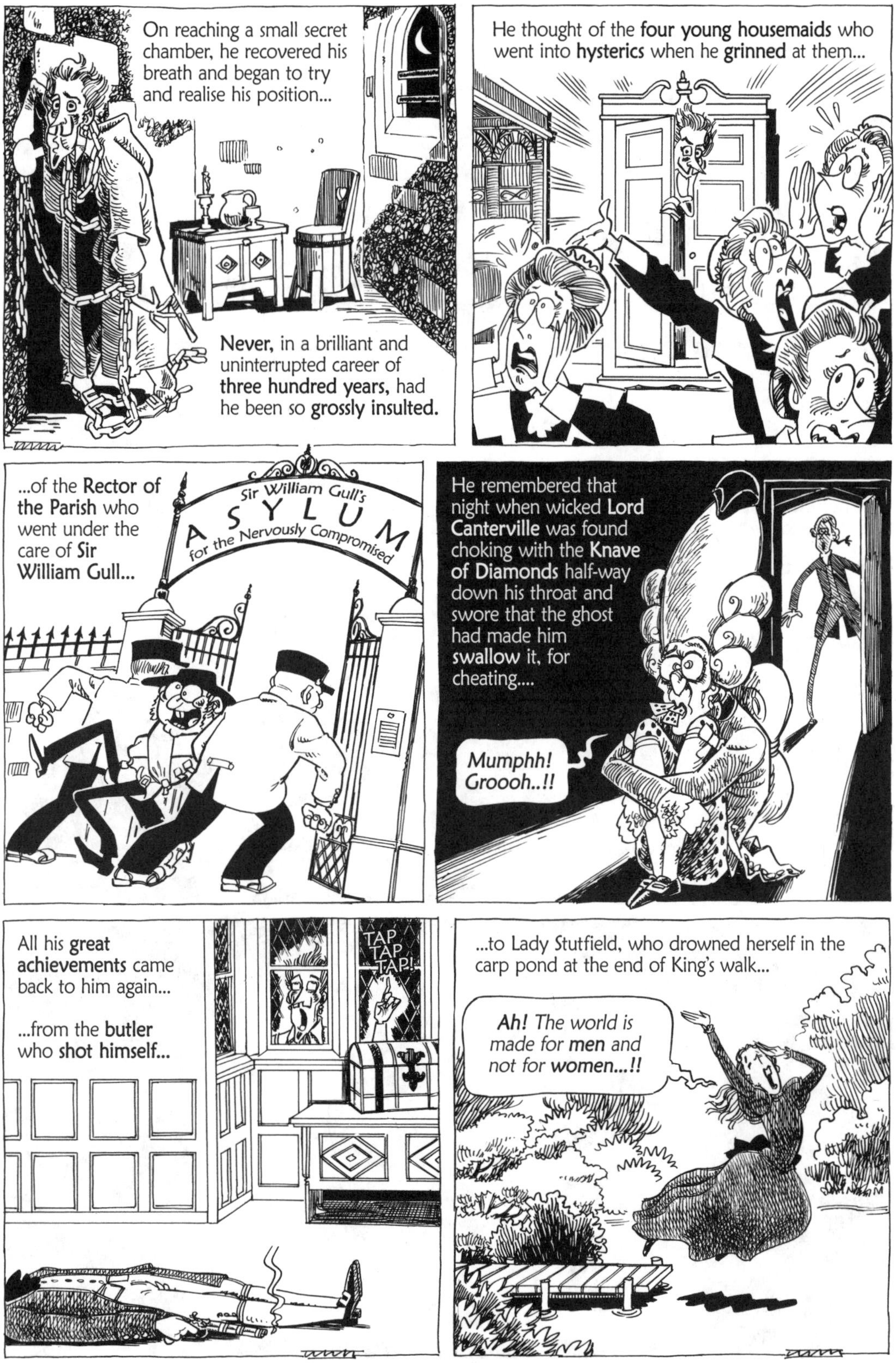
On reaching a small secret chamber, he recovered his breath and began to try and realise his position...
Never, in a brilliant and uninterrupted career of **three hundred years,** had he been so **grossly insulted.**
He thought of the **four young housemaids** who went into **hysterics** when he **grinned** at them...
...of the **Rector of the Parish** who went under the care of **Sir William Gull...**
Sir William Gull's
ASYLUM
for the Nervously Compromised
He remembered that night when wicked **Lord Canterville** was found choking with the **Knave of Diamonds** half-way down his throat and swore that the ghost had made him **swallow** it, for cheating....
Mumphh! Groooh..!!
All his **great achievements** came back to him again...
...from the **butler** who **shot himself...**
TAP TAP TAP!
...to Lady Stutfield, who drowned herself in the carp pond at the end of King's walk...
*Ah! The world is made for **men** and not for **women...!!***

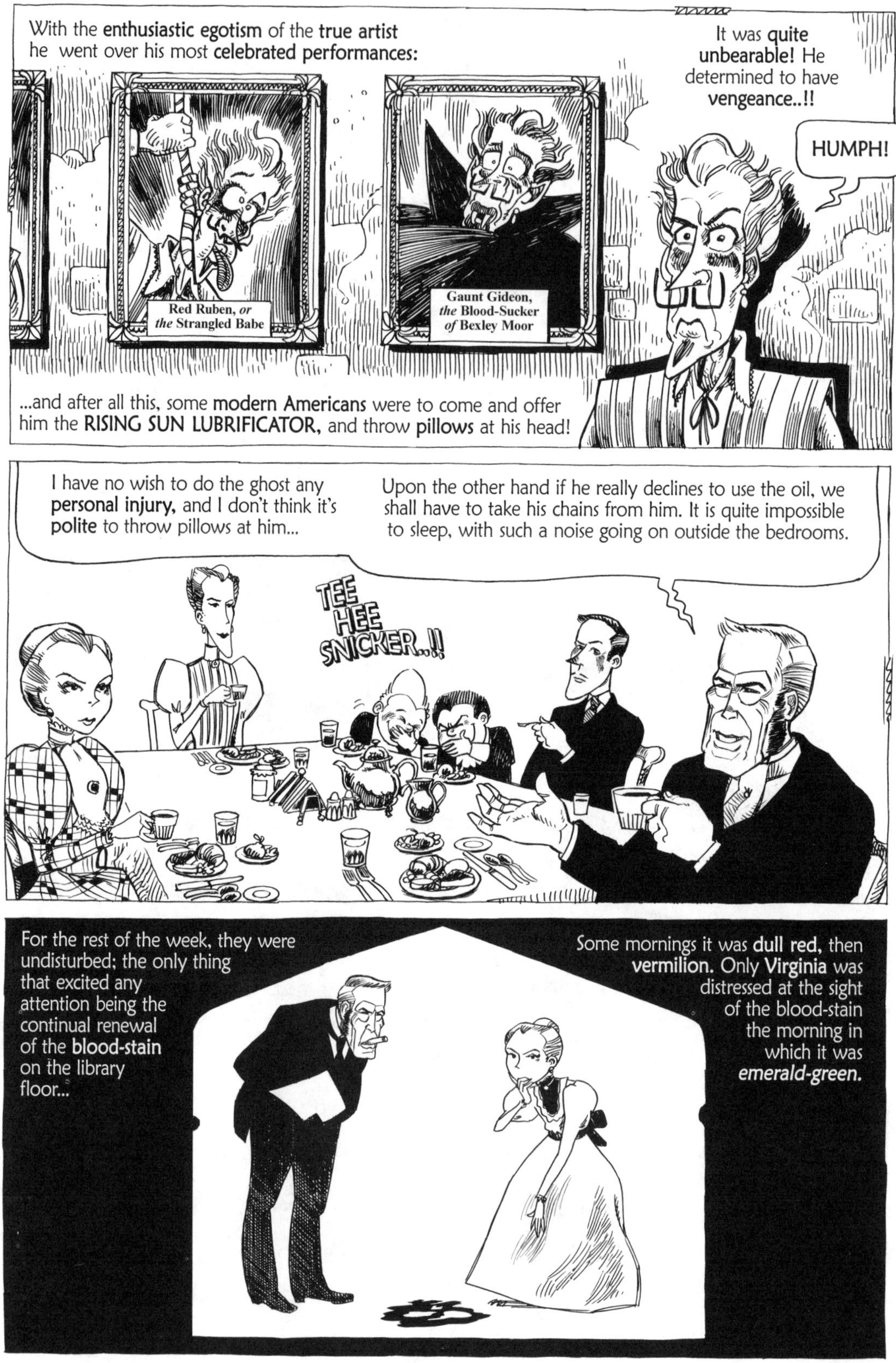
With the enthusiastic egotism of the true artist he went over his most celebrated performances:
Red Ruben, or the Strangled Babe
Gaunt Gideon, the Blood-Sucker of Bexley Moor
It was quite unbearable! He determined to have vengeance..!!
HUMPH!
...and after all this, some modern Americans were to come and offer him the RISING SUN LUBRIFICATOR, and throw pillows at his head!
I have no wish to do the ghost any personal injury, and I don't think it's polite to throw pillows at him...
Upon the other hand if he really declines to use the oil, we shall have to take his chains from him. It is quite impossible to sleep, with such a noise going on outside the bedrooms.
TEE HEE SNICKER...!!
For the rest of the week, they were undisturbed; the only thing that excited any attention being the continual renewal of the blood-stain on the library floor...
Some mornings it was dull red, then vermilion. Only Virginia was distressed at the sight of the blood-stain the morning in which it was emerald-green.

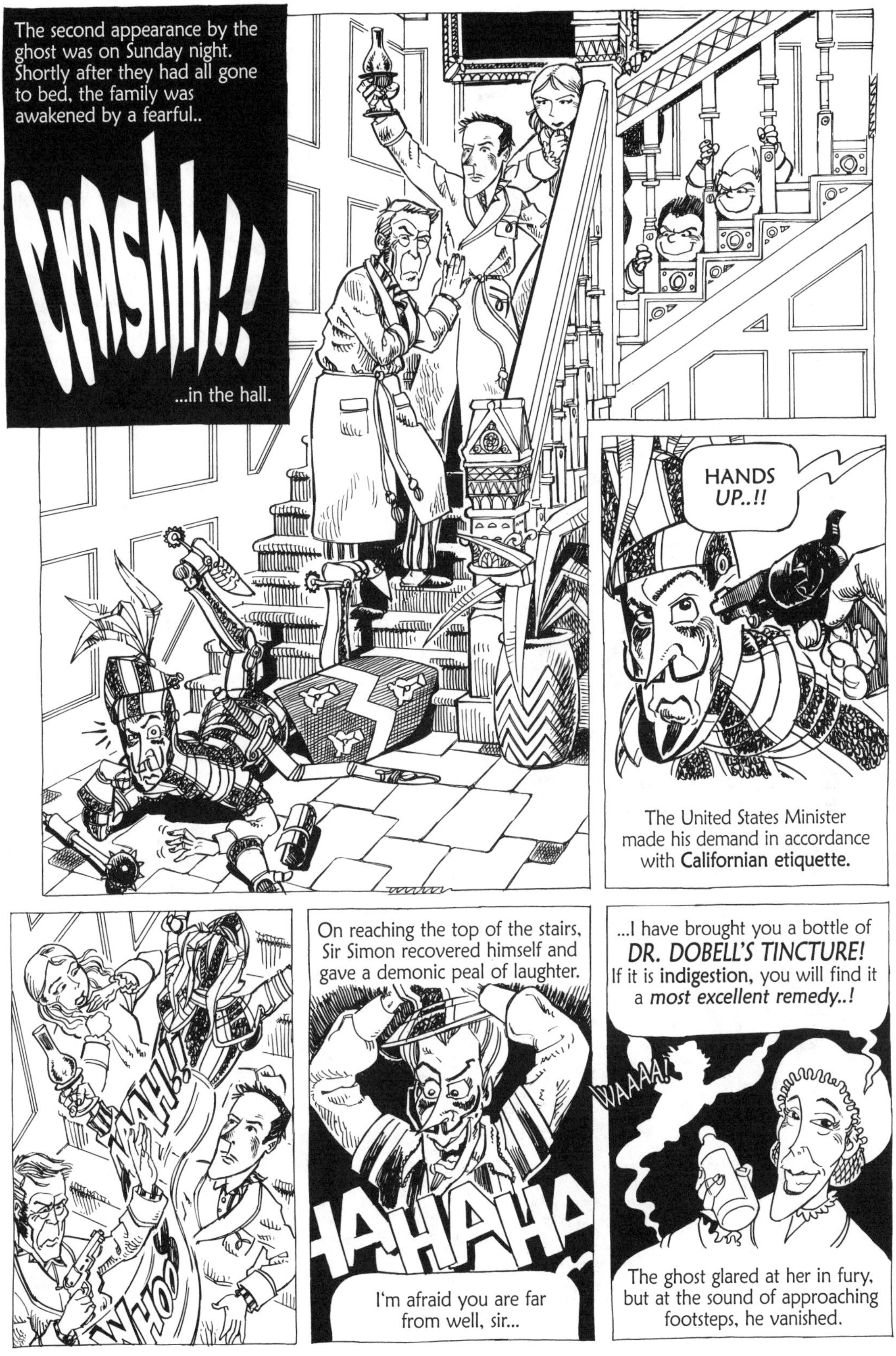
The second appearance by the ghost was on Sunday night. Shortly after they had all gone to bed, the family was awakened by a fearful..
Crashh!!
...in the hall.
HANDS UP..!!
The United States Minister made his demand in accordance with **Californian etiquette.**
WHOOSH
On reaching the top of the stairs, Sir Simon recovered himself and gave a demonic peal of laughter.
HAHAHAHA
I'm afraid you are far from well, sir...
...I have brought you a bottle of **DR. DOBELL'S TINCTURE!** If it is **indigestion,** you will find it a *most excellent remedy..!*
WAAAA!
The ghost glared at her in fury, but at the sound of approaching footsteps, he vanished.

On reaching his room he entirely broke down. The vulgarity of the twins and the materialism of Mrs. Otis were extremely annoying, but what had distressed him most was that he had been unable to wear the suit of mail...

He had hoped the Americans would be thrilled by the sight of a spectre in armor. Besides, it was his own suit. He had worn it at the Kenilworth Tournament, and had been complimented on it by the Virgin Queen herself.

Yet when he put it on, he had been overpowered by the weight of it and had fallen on the stone pavement.

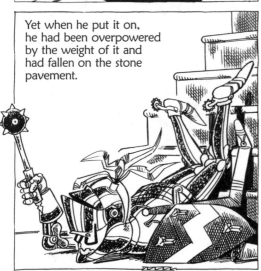

For some days after this he was ill, and hardly stirred out of his room except to keep the blood-stain in proper repair. However, he resolved to make a third attempt to frighten the United States Minister and his family.

He selected Friday 17th August for his appearance. Towards the evening a violent rainstorm came.

In fact, it was just such weather as he loved.

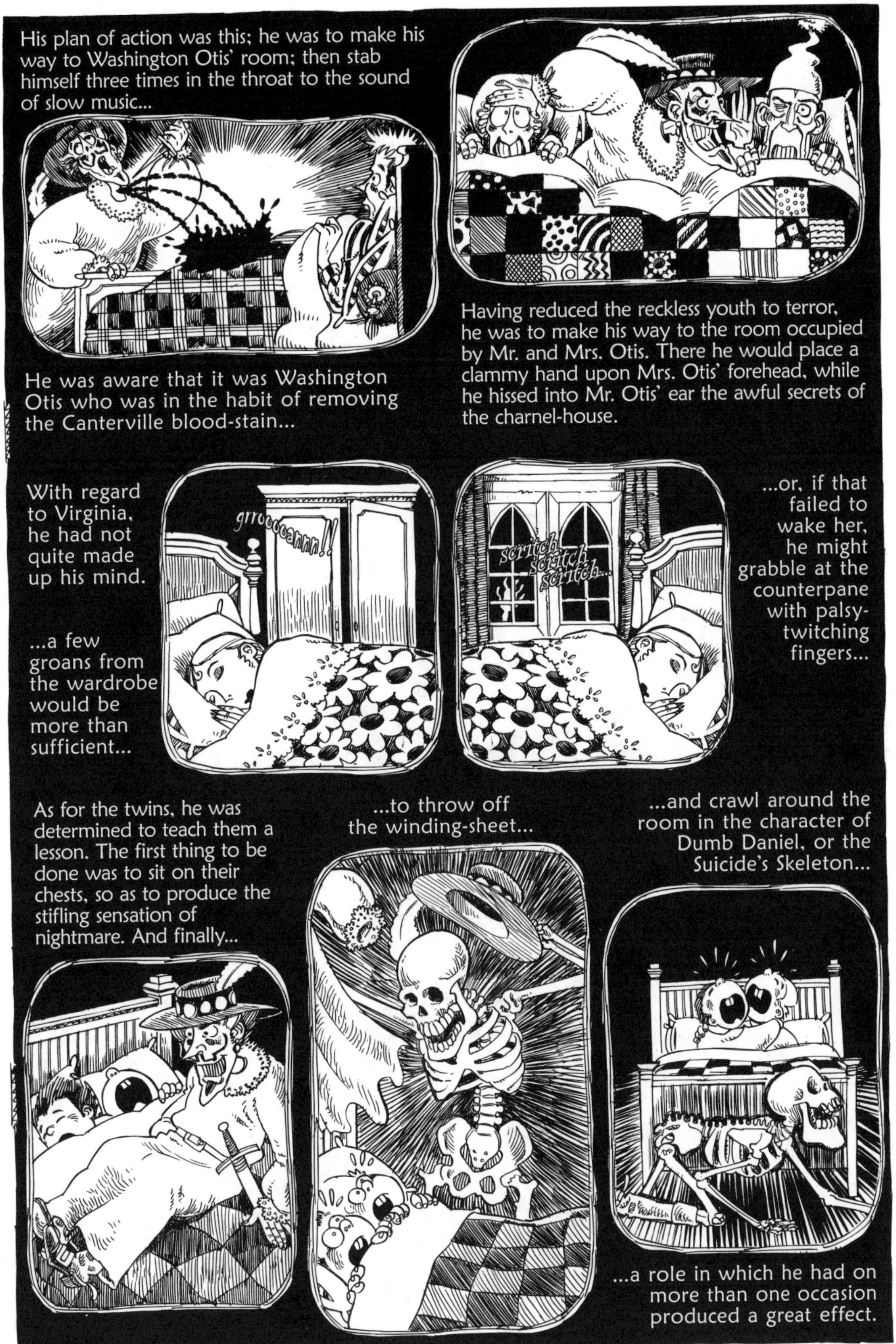
His plan of action was this; he was to make his way to Washington Otis' room; then stab himself three times in the throat to the sound of slow music...
He was aware that it was Washington Otis who was in the habit of removing the Canterville blood-stain...
Having reduced the reckless youth to terror, he was to make his way to the room occupied by Mr. and Mrs. Otis. There he would place a clammy hand upon Mrs. Otis' forehead, while he hissed into Mr. Otis' ear the awful secrets of the charnel-house.
With regard to Virginia, he had not quite made up his mind.
...a few groans from the wardrobe would be more than sufficient...
grroooooannn!!
scritch scritch scritch...
...or, if that failed to wake her, he might grabble at the counterpane with palsy-twitching fingers...
As for the twins, he was determined to teach them a lesson. The first thing to be done was to sit on their chests, so as to produce the stifling sensation of nightmare. And finally...
...to throw off the winding-sheet...
...and crawl around the room in the character of Dumb Daniel, or the Suicide's Skeleton...
...a role in which he had on more than one occasion produced a great effect.

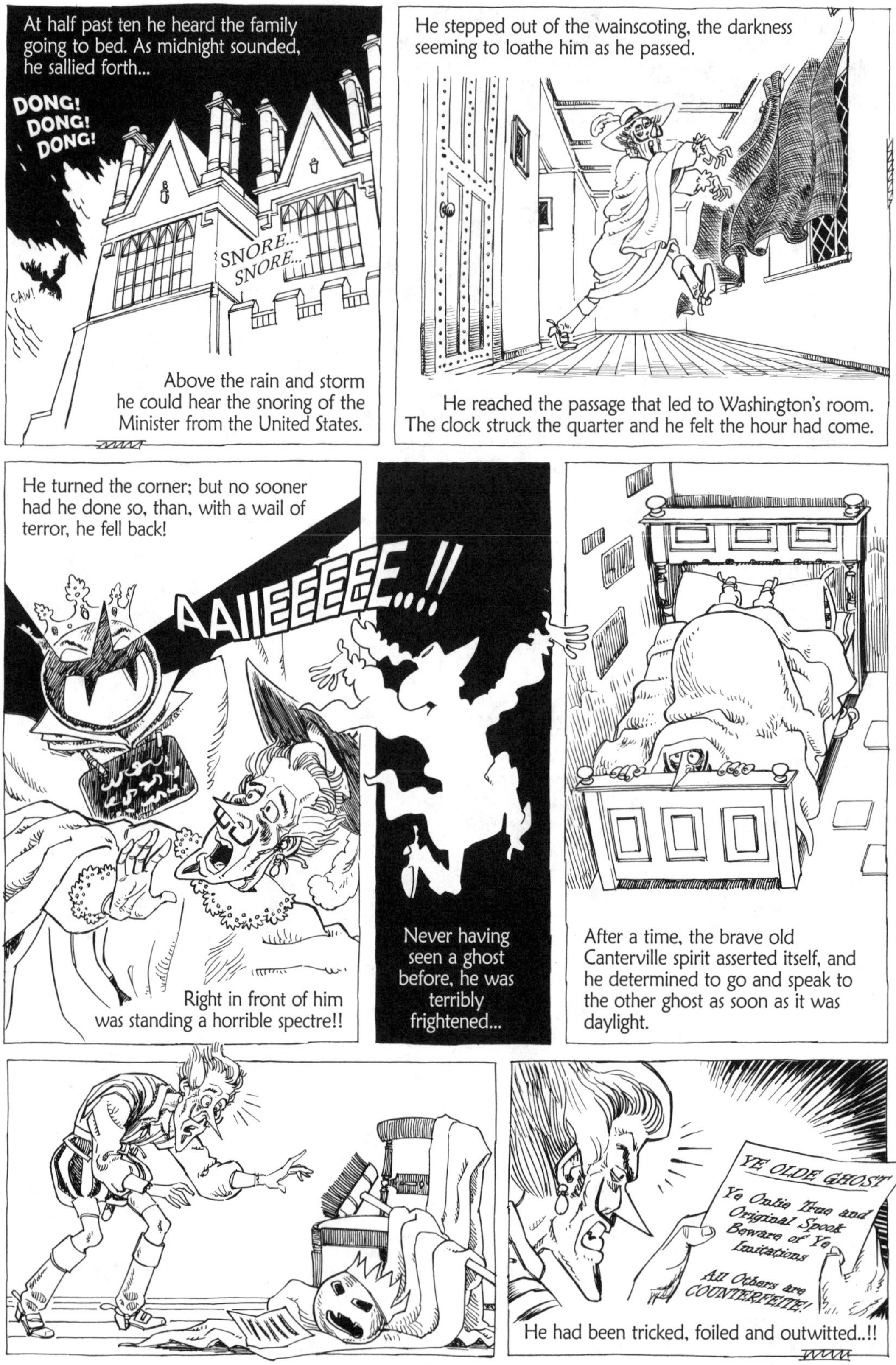
At half past ten he heard the family going to bed. As midnight sounded, he sallied forth...
DONG! DONG! DONG!
CAW!
SNORE... SNORE...
Above the rain and storm he could hear the snoring of the Minister from the United States.
He stepped out of the wainscoting, the darkness seeming to loathe him as he passed.
He reached the passage that led to Washington's room. The clock struck the quarter and he felt the hour had come.
He turned the corner; but no sooner had he done so, than, with a wail of terror, he fell back!
AAIIEEEEE..!!
Right in front of him was standing a horrible spectre!!
Never having seen a ghost before, he was terribly frightened...
After a time, the brave old Canterville spirit asserted itself, and he determined to go and speak to the other ghost as soon as it was daylight.
YE OLDE GHOST
Ye Onlie True and Original Spook
Beware of Ye Imitations
All Others are COUNTERFEITE!
He had been tricked, foiled and outwitted..!!

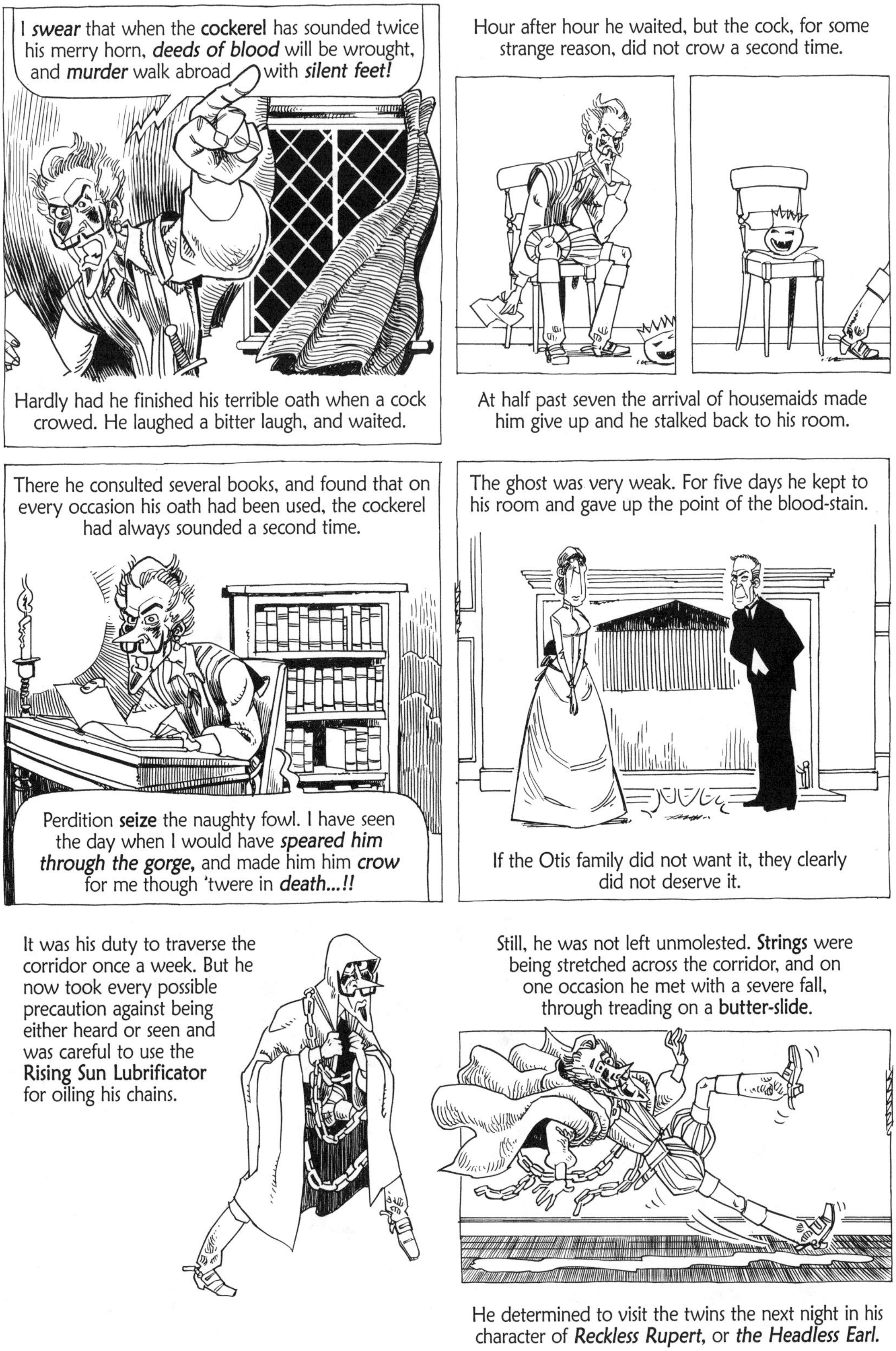
I swear that when the cockerel has sounded twice his merry horn, deeds of blood will be wrought, and murder walk abroad with silent feet!
Hardly had he finished his terrible oath when a cock crowed. He laughed a bitter laugh, and waited.
Hour after hour he waited, but the cock, for some strange reason, did not crow a second time.
At half past seven the arrival of housemaids made him give up and he stalked back to his room.
There he consulted several books, and found that on every occasion his oath had been used, the cockerel had always sounded a second time.
Perdition seize the naughty fowl. I have seen the day when I would have speared him through the gorge, and made him him crow for me though 'twere in death...!!
The ghost was very weak. For five days he kept to his room and gave up the point of the blood-stain.
If the Otis family did not want it, they clearly did not deserve it.
It was his duty to traverse the corridor once a week. But he now took every possible precaution against being either heard or seen and was careful to use the Rising Sun Lubrificator for oiling his chains.
Still, he was not left unmolested. Strings were being stretched across the corridor, and on one occasion he met with a severe fall, through treading on a butter-slide.
He determined to visit the twins the next night in his character of Reckless Rupert, or the Headless Earl.

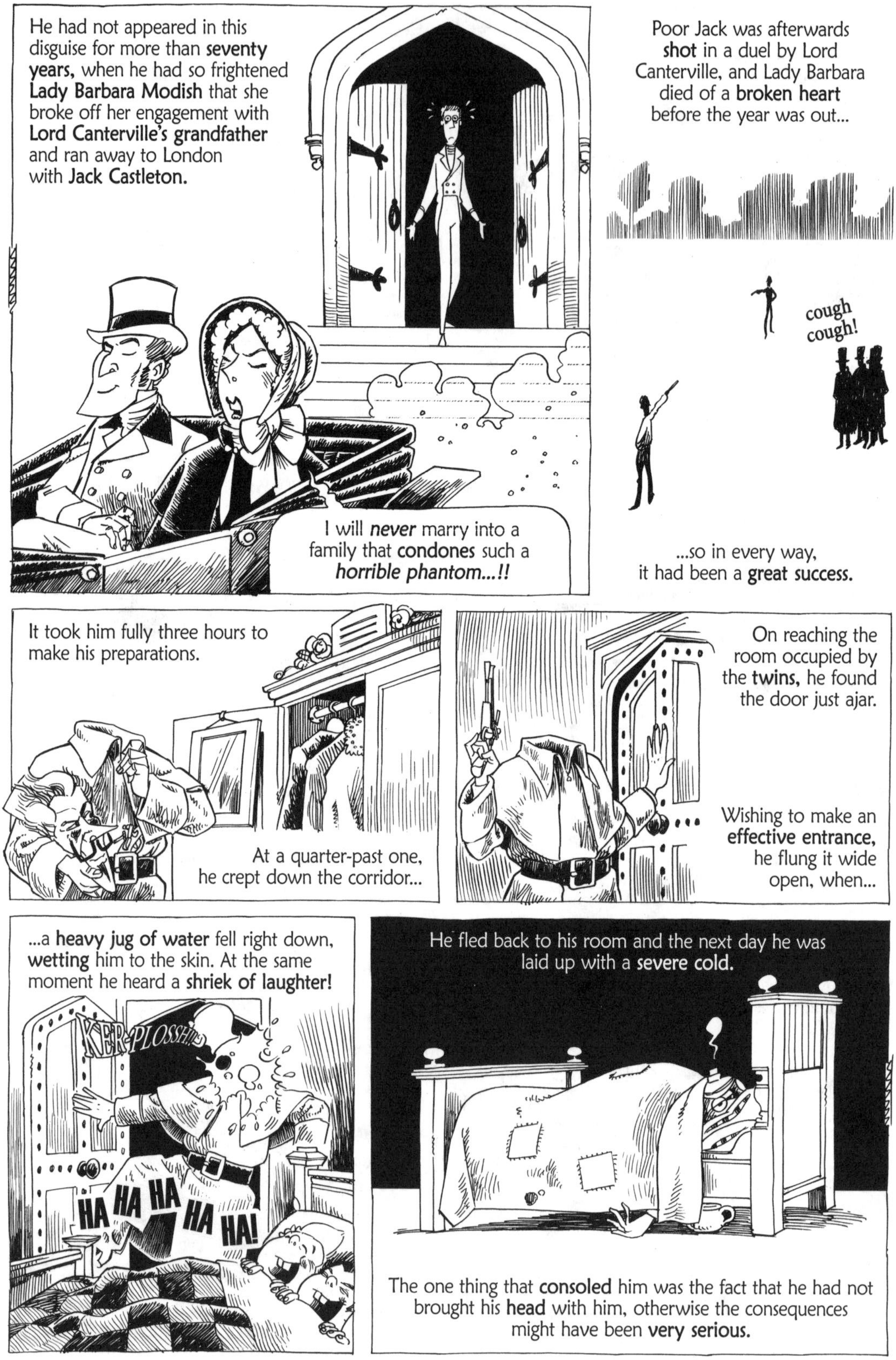
He had not appeared in this disguise for more than **seventy years,** when he had so frightened **Lady Barbara Modish** that she broke off her engagement with **Lord Canterville's grandfather** and ran away to London with **Jack Castleton.**
I will ***never*** marry into a family that **condones** such a ***horrible phantom...!!***
Poor Jack was afterwards **shot** in a duel by Lord Canterville, and Lady Barbara died of a **broken heart** before the year was out...
cough cough!
...so in every way, it had been a **great success.**
It took him fully three hours to make his preparations.
At a quarter-past one, he crept down the corridor...
On reaching the room occupied by the **twins,** he found the door just ajar.
Wishing to make an **effective entrance,** he flung it wide open, when...
...a **heavy jug of water** fell right down, **wetting** him to the skin. At the same moment he heard a **shriek of laughter!**
KER-PLOSSH
HA HA HA HA HA!
He fled back to his room and the next day he was laid up with a **severe cold.**
The one thing that **consoled** him was the fact that he had not brought his **head** with him, otherwise the consequences might have been **very serious.**

He now gave up all hope of frightening the rude American family.

The final blow he received occurred on the 19th of September.

He was amusing himself by making satirical remarks on the large Saroni photograph of the United States Minister and his wife.

He was dressed for the character of *Jonas the Graveless,* one of his most remarkable impersonations.

He was strolling towards the library to see if there were any traces of the blood-stain, when suddenly two figures *leaped* out at him from a corner...

Seized with panic he rushed for the staircase, but found **Washington Otis** waiting for him there with the **big garden syringe.**

Being **hemmed in** by his **enemies** on every side, he vanished into the **great iron stove,** and had to make his way home through the **chimneys,** arriving at his own room in **despair.**

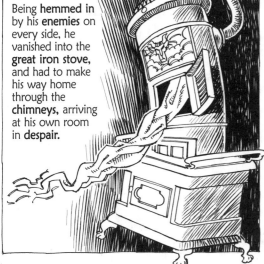

After this he was not seen again. The twins lay in wait for him on several occasions, but it was to no avail. It was evident that he would not appear...

Phooey!

69

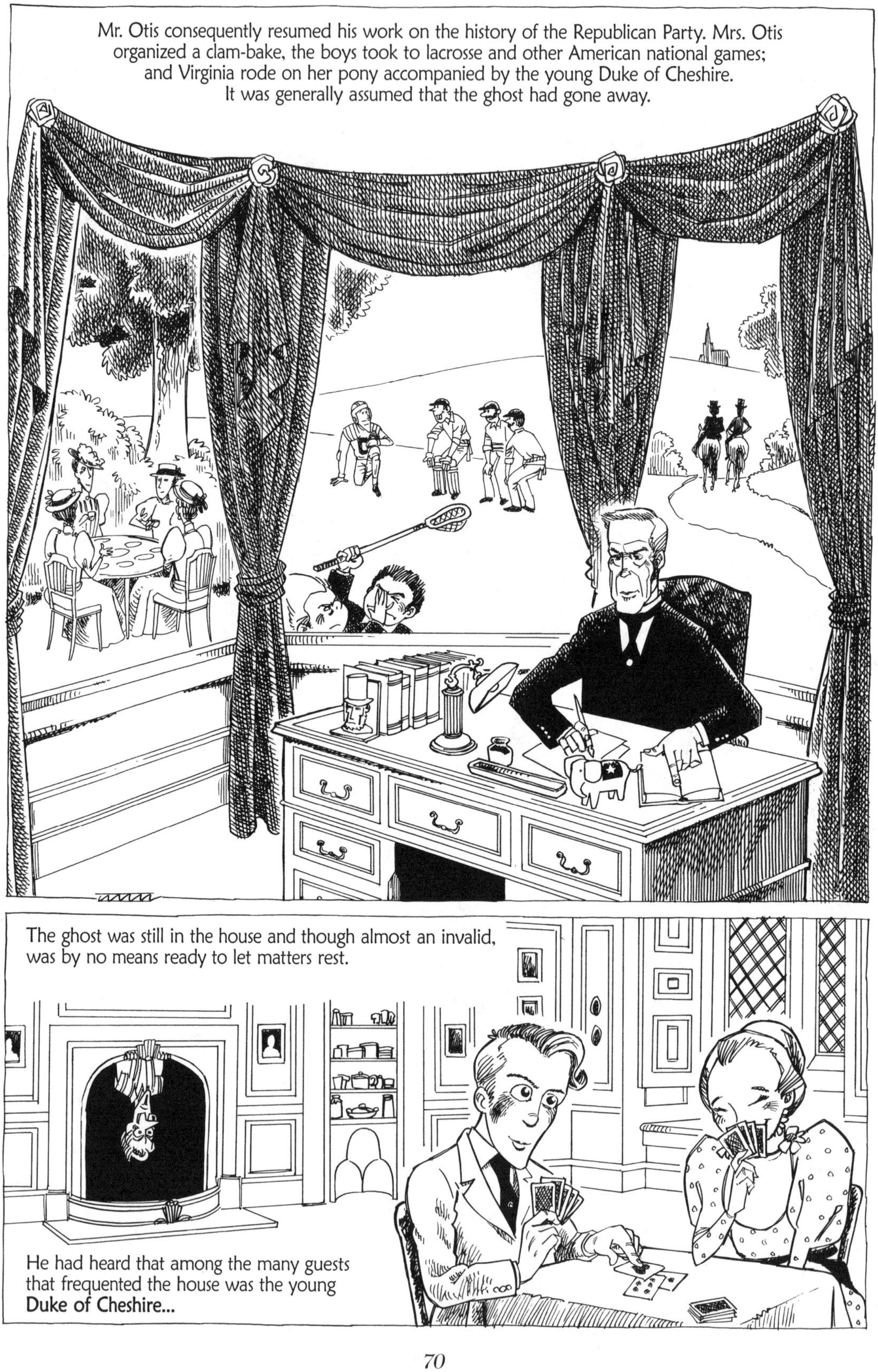
Mr. Otis consequently resumed his work on the history of the Republican Party. Mrs. Otis organized a clam-bake, the boys took to lacrosse and other American national games; and Virginia rode on her pony accompanied by the young Duke of Cheshire. It was generally assumed that the ghost had gone away.
The ghost was still in the house and though almost an invalid, was by no means ready to let matters rest.
He had heard that among the many guests that frequented the house was the young **Duke of Cheshire...**

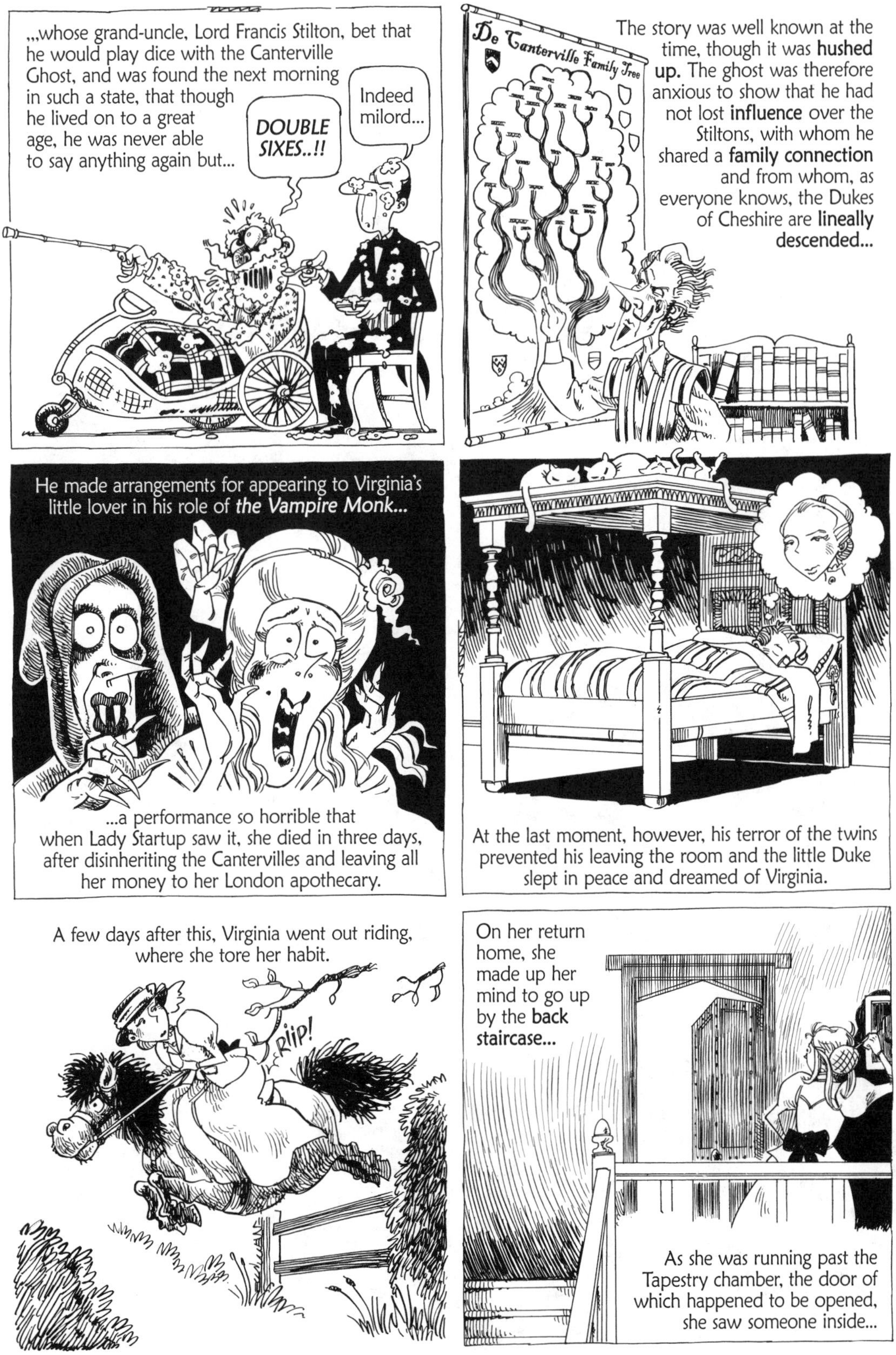
,,,whose grand-uncle, Lord Francis Stilton, bet that he would play dice with the Canterville Ghost, and was found the next morning in such a state, that though he lived on to a great age, he was never able to say anything again but...
DOUBLE SIXES..!!
Indeed milord...
De Canterville Family Tree
The story was well known at the time, though it was **hushed up.** The ghost was therefore anxious to show that he had not lost **influence** over the Stiltons, with whom he shared a **family connection** and from whom, as everyone knows, the Dukes of Cheshire are **lineally descended...**
He made arrangements for appearing to Virginia's little lover in his role of *the Vampire Monk...*
...a performance so horrible that when Lady Startup saw it, she died in three days, after disinheriting the Cantervilles and leaving all her money to her London apothecary.
At the last moment, however, his terror of the twins prevented his leaving the room and the little Duke slept in peace and dreamed of Virginia.
A few days after this, Virginia went out riding, where she tore her habit.
RIIP!
On her return home, she made up her mind to go up by the **back staircase...**
As she was running past the Tapestry chamber, the door of which happened to be opened, she saw someone inside...

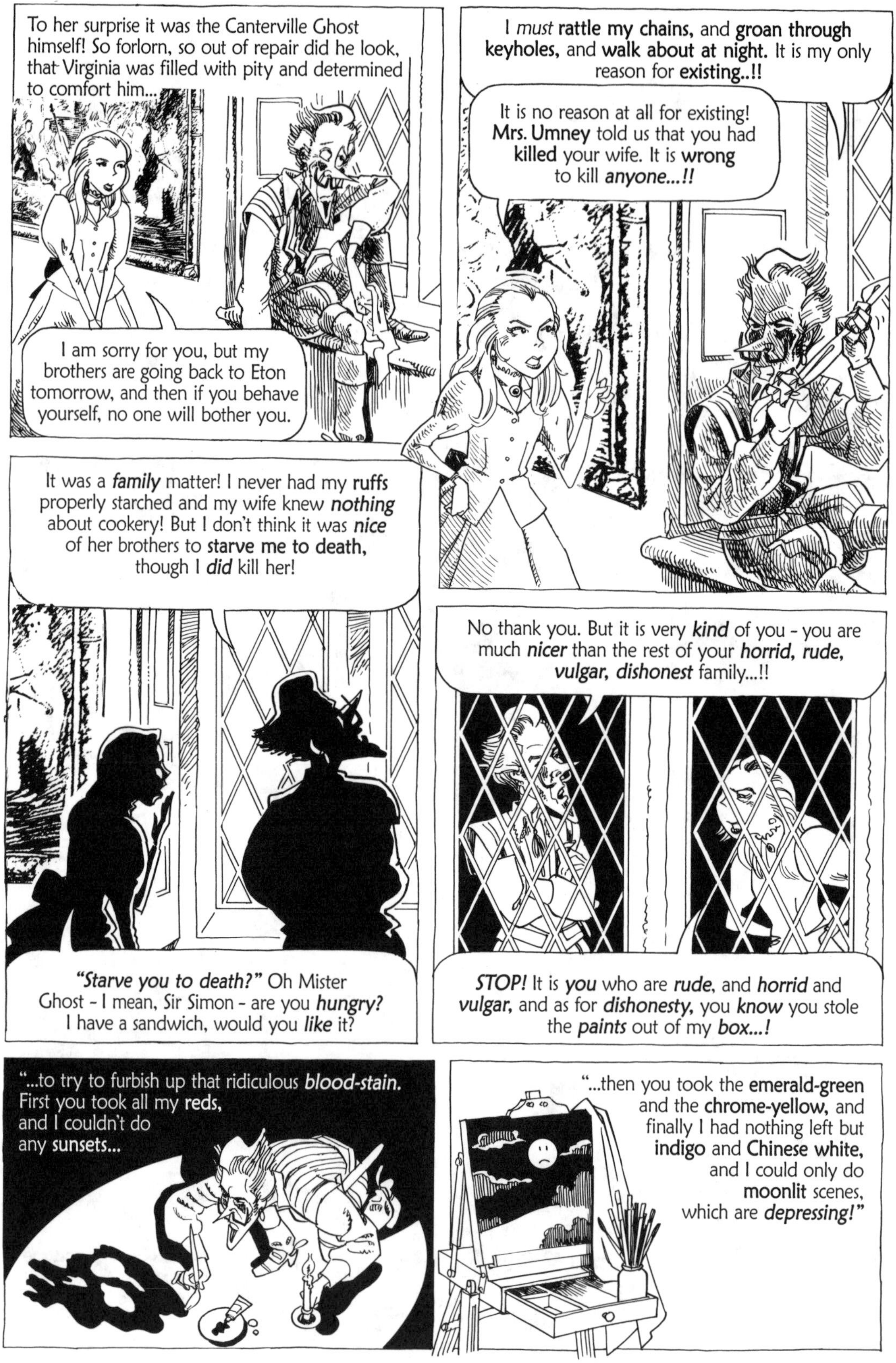
To her surprise it was the Canterville Ghost himself! So forlorn, so out of repair did he look, that Virginia was filled with pity and determined to comfort him...
I am sorry for you, but my brothers are going back to Eton tomorrow, and then if you behave yourself, no one will bother you.
I *must* **rattle my chains,** and **groan through keyholes,** and **walk about at night.** It is my only reason for **existing..!!**
It is no reason at all for existing! **Mrs. Umney** told us that you had **killed** your wife. It is **wrong** to kill ***anyone...!!***
It was a ***family*** matter! I never had my **ruffs** properly starched and my wife knew ***nothing*** about cookery! But I don't think it was ***nice*** of her brothers to **starve me to death,** though I ***did*** kill her!
"Starve you to death?" Oh Mister Ghost - I mean, Sir Simon - are you ***hungry?*** I have a sandwich, would you ***like*** it?
No thank you. But it is very ***kind*** of you - you are much ***nicer*** than the rest of your ***horrid, rude, vulgar, dishonest*** family...!!
STOP! It is ***you*** who are ***rude,*** and ***horrid*** and ***vulgar,*** and as for ***dishonesty,*** you ***know*** you stole the ***paints*** out of my ***box...!***
"...to try to furbish up that ridiculous ***blood-stain.*** First you took all my **reds,** and I couldn't do any **sunsets...**
"...then you took the **emerald-green** and the **chrome-yellow,** and finally I had nothing left but **indigo** and **Chinese white,** and I could only do **moonlit** scenes, which are ***depressing!"***

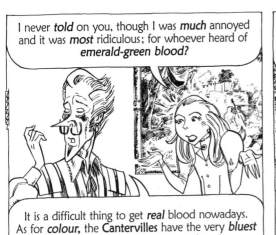

I never **told** on you, though I was **much** annoyed and it was **most** ridiculous; for whoever heard of **emerald-green blood?**

It is a difficult thing to get **real** blood nowadays. As for **colour**, the **Cantervilles** have the very **bluest** blood in England; but I know you Americans don't **care** for things of this kind!

You know **nothing** about it! The best thing you can do is to **emigrate** and **improve your mind!** My father will be **happy** to give you a **free passage!**

Once in **New York,** I know **lots** of people who would pay a **hundred thousand dollars** to have a **grandfather,** let alone a family ghost..!!

I don't think I should **like** America!

I suppose it must be because we have no **ruins...**

I will go and ask Papa to get the twins an extra week's holiday...

Please don't go, Miss Virginia! I have not slept for **three hundred years!** I **want** to sleep and I **cannot.** And I am so **tired...**

Virginia **trembled,** and for a few moments there was **silence.** She felt as if she was in a **terrible dream.**

Have you ever read the **old prophecy** on the library window?

Oh, **often,** I know it quite well...

Far away beyond the **pine-woods,** there is a little **garden.** There the **grass** grows long and deep, and the **nightingale** sings all night long. The cold, crystal **moon** looks down, and the **yew-tree** spreads out its **giant arms** over the sleepers...

You mean the garden of **Death...**

Yes! You can open for me the portal of **Death's** house, for **love** is always with you, and **love** is stronger than **Death** is...

When a golden girl can win
Prayer from out the lips of sin
When the barren almond bears
And the little child gives away
its tears
Then shall all the house be still
And peace come to Canterville

"...there are only six lines, but I don't know what they mean..."

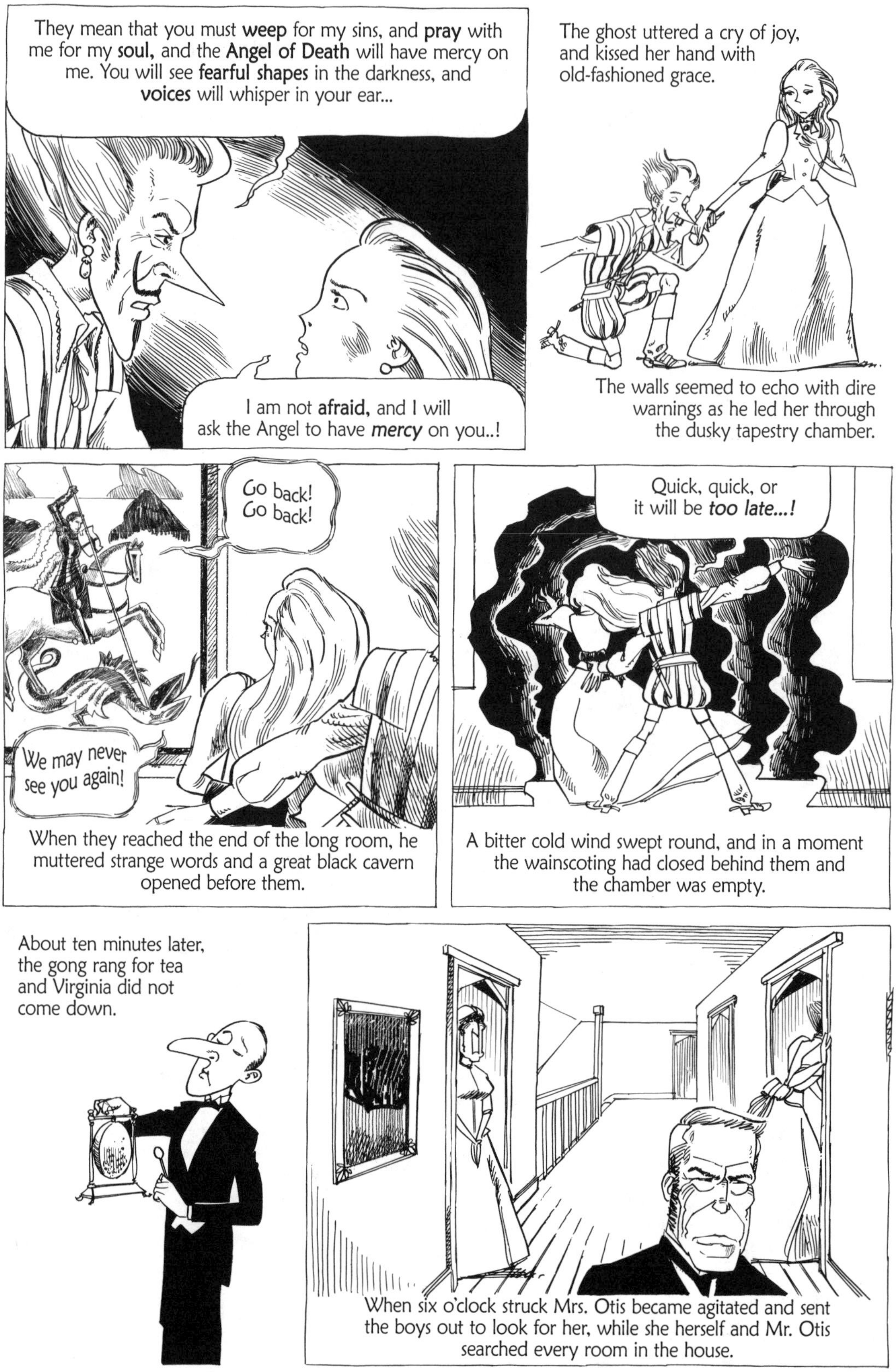
They mean that you must **weep** for my sins, and **pray** with me for my **soul**, and the **Angel of Death** will have mercy on me. You will see **fearful shapes** in the darkness, and **voices** will whisper in your ear...
I am not **afraid**, and I will ask the Angel to have ***mercy*** on you..!
The ghost uttered a cry of joy, and kissed her hand with old-fashioned grace.
The walls seemed to echo with dire warnings as he led her through the dusky tapestry chamber.
Go back! Go back!
We may never see you again!
When they reached the end of the long room, he muttered strange words and a great black cavern opened before them.
Quick, quick, or it will be ***too late...!***
A bitter cold wind swept round, and in a moment the wainscoting had closed behind them and the chamber was empty.
About ten minutes later, the gong rang for tea and Virginia did not come down.
When six o'clock struck Mrs. Otis became agitated and sent the boys out to look for her, while she herself and Mr. Otis searched every room in the house.

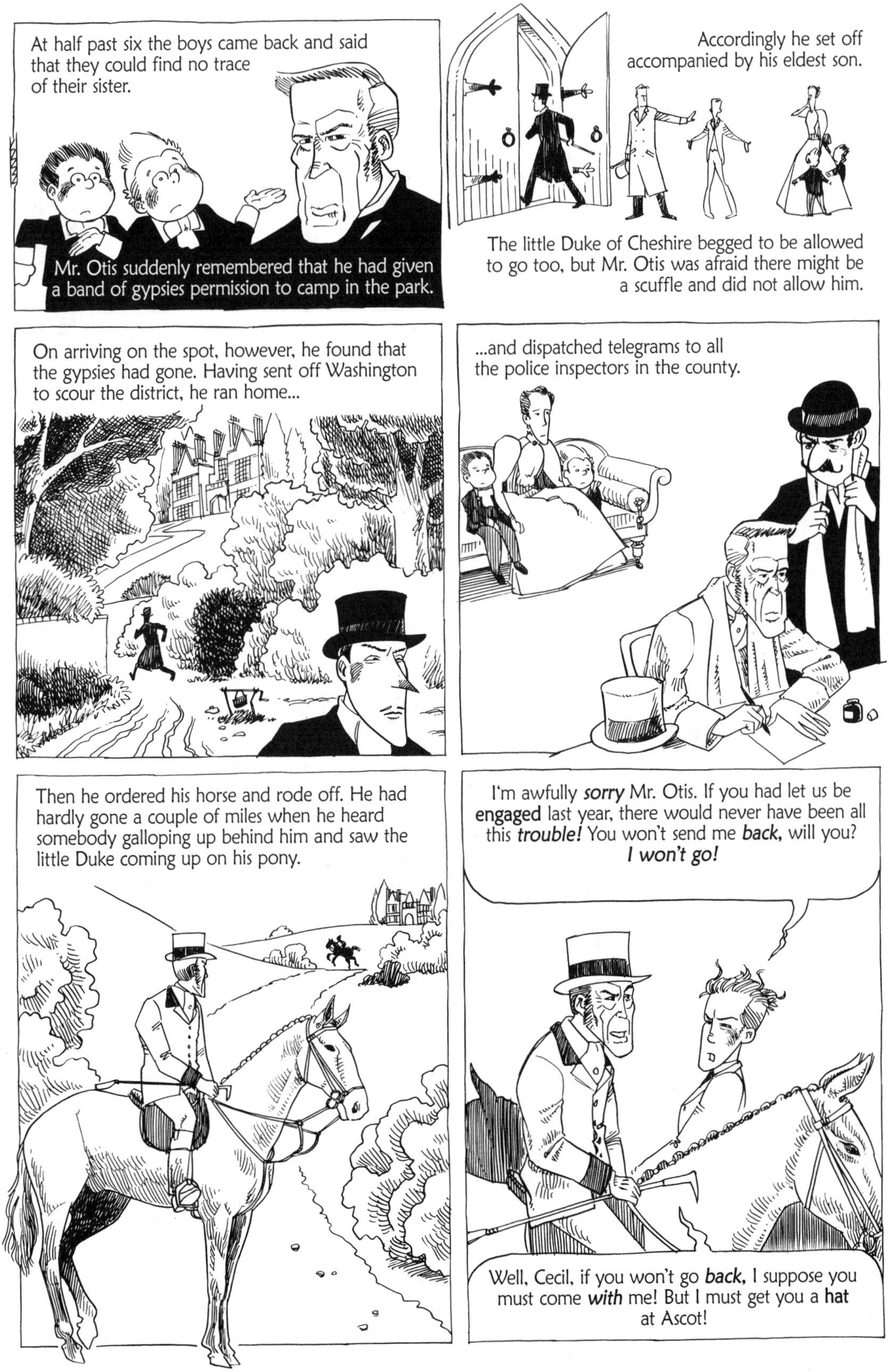
At half past six the boys came back and said that they could find no trace of their sister.
Mr. Otis suddenly remembered that he had given a band of gypsies permission to camp in the park.
Accordingly he set off accompanied by his eldest son.
The little Duke of Cheshire begged to be allowed to go too, but Mr. Otis was afraid there might be a scuffle and did not allow him.
On arriving on the spot, however, he found that the gypsies had gone. Having sent off Washington to scour the district, he ran home...
...and dispatched telegrams to all the police inspectors in the county.
Then he ordered his horse and rode off. He had hardly gone a couple of miles when he heard somebody galloping up behind him and saw the little Duke coming up on his pony.
I'm awfully *sorry* Mr. Otis. If you had let us be **engaged** last year, there would never have been all this ***trouble!*** You won't send me ***back,*** will you? ***I won't go!***
Well, Cecil, if you won't go ***back,*** I suppose you must come ***with*** me! But I must get you a **hat** at Ascot!

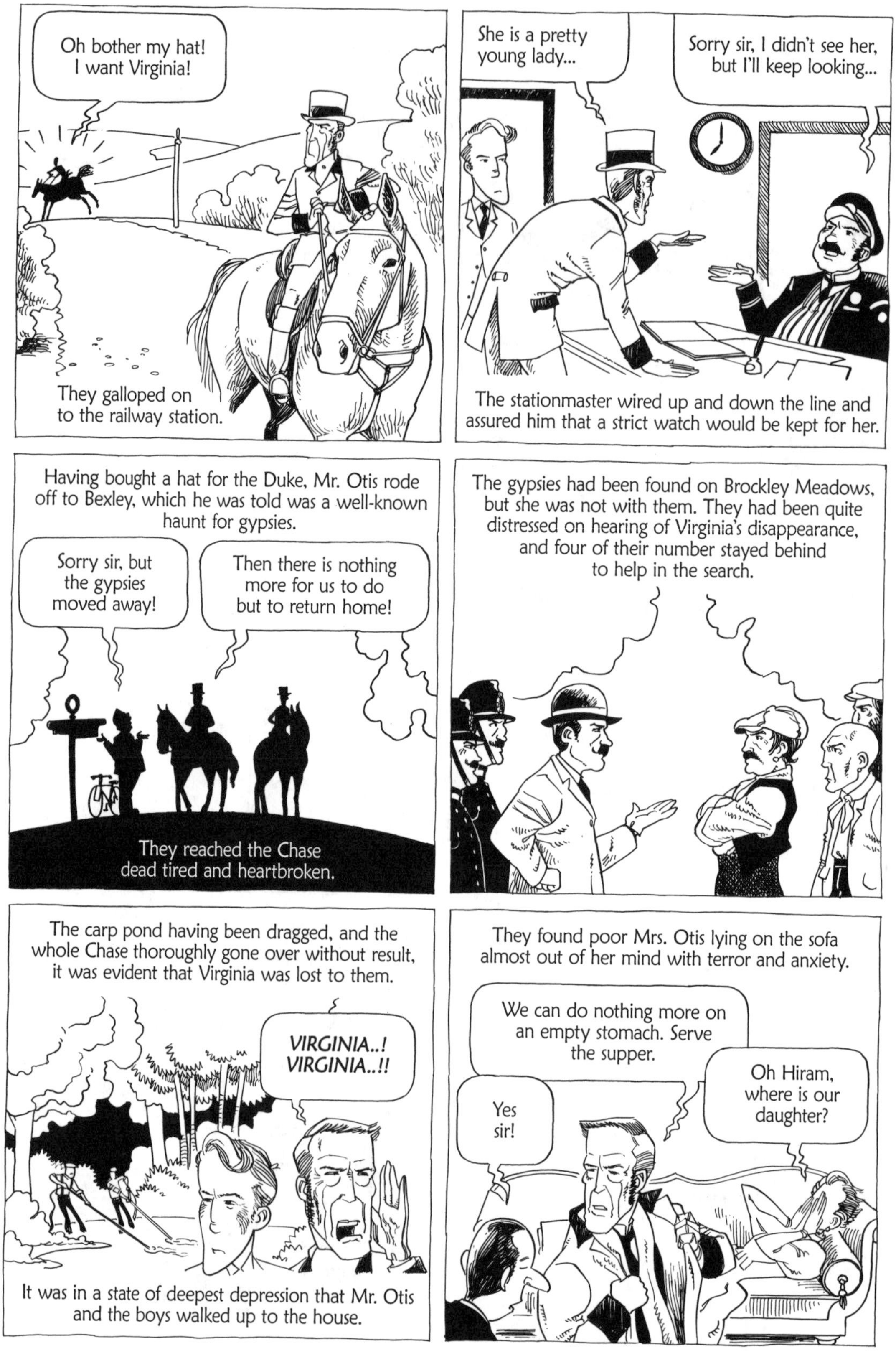
Oh bother my hat! I want Virginia!
They galloped on to the railway station.
She is a pretty young lady...
Sorry sir, I didn't see her, but I'll keep looking...
The stationmaster wired up and down the line and assured him that a strict watch would be kept for her.
Having bought a hat for the Duke, Mr. Otis rode off to Bexley, which he was told was a well-known haunt for gypsies.
Sorry sir, but the gypsies moved away!
Then there is nothing more for us to do but to return home!
They reached the Chase dead tired and heartbroken.
The gypsies had been found on Brockley Meadows, but she was not with them. They had been quite distressed on hearing of Virginia's disappearance, and four of their number stayed behind to help in the search.
The carp pond having been dragged, and the whole Chase thoroughly gone over without result, it was evident that Virginia was lost to them.
VIRGINIA..! VIRGINIA..!!
It was in a state of deepest depression that Mr. Otis and the boys walked up to the house.
They found poor Mrs. Otis lying on the sofa almost out of her mind with terror and anxiety.
We can do nothing more on an empty stomach. Serve the supper.
Yes sir!
Oh Hiram, where is our daughter?

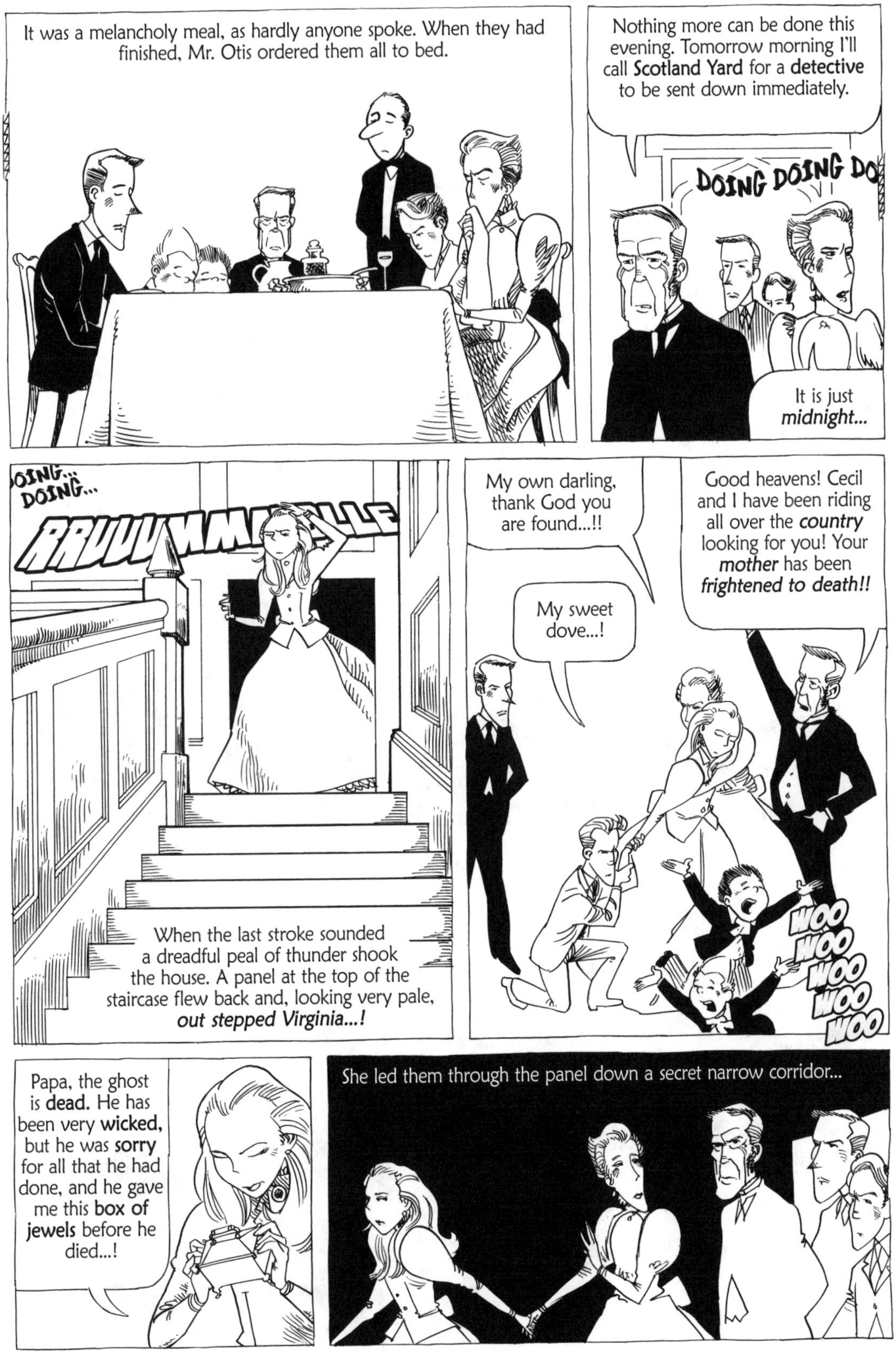
It was a melancholy meal, as hardly anyone spoke. When they had finished, Mr. Otis ordered them all to bed.
Nothing more can be done this evening. Tomorrow morning I'll call **Scotland Yard** for a **detective** to be sent down immediately.
DOING DOING DO
It is just ***midnight...***
DOING... DOING...
RRUUUMMBLLE
When the last stroke sounded a dreadful peal of thunder shook the house. A panel at the top of the staircase flew back and, looking very pale, ***out stepped Virginia...!***
My own darling, thank God you are found...!!
Good heavens! Cecil and I have been riding all over the ***country*** looking for you! Your ***mother*** has been ***frightened to death!!***
My sweet dove...!
WOO WOO WOO WOO WOO
Papa, the ghost is **dead.** He has been very **wicked,** but he was **sorry** for all that he had done, and he gave me this **box of jewels** before he died...!
She led them through the panel down a secret narrow corridor...

Finally they came to a door. They looked on in wonder at the terrible tragedy whose secret was now disclosed to them.

Hallo hallo! The old almond tree has blossomed!

I can see the **flowers** in the moonlight...!

God has *forgiven* him...

What an *angel* you are...!

Four days after a funeral started from Canterville Chase at about eleven o'clock at night. A deep grave had been dug under the old yew tree.

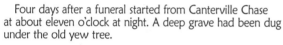

As the coffin was being lowered into the grave, Virginia laid on it a large cross made of almond blossoms.

As she did so the moon came out and she thought of the ghost's description of the garden of death.

My Lord, I am informed that these gems are of **great monetary worth.** I'm sure that you will recognize how *impossible* it would be for me to allow them to remain in the possession of any member of my family, who have all been brought up on the principles of **Republican simplicity.**

I return them to you, though **Virginia** is very anxious that you should allow her to retain the **box** as a memento of your unfortunate ancestor!

My dear sir, your charming daughter has rendered my ancestor an important service. The jewels are **hers!** Besides, you forget that you took the furniture and the ghost at a valuation, and anything that belonged to the **ghost** passed at once into your possession!

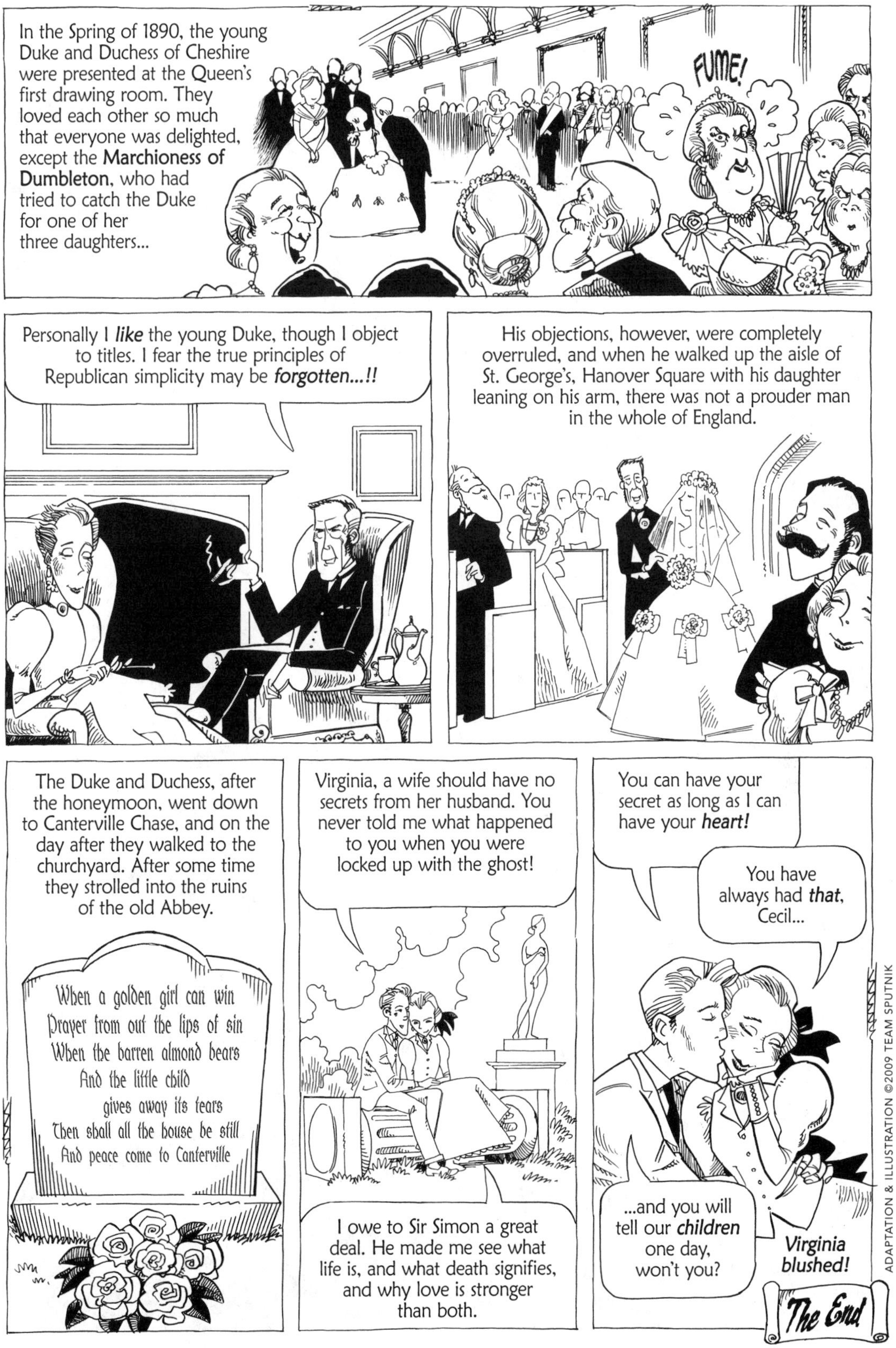
In the Spring of 1890, the young Duke and Duchess of Cheshire were presented at the Queen's first drawing room. They loved each other so much that everyone was delighted, except the **Marchioness of Dumbleton**, who had tried to catch the Duke for one of her three daughters...
FUME!
Personally I *like* the young Duke, though I object to titles. I fear the true principles of Republican simplicity may be ***forgotten...!!***
His objections, however, were completely overruled, and when he walked up the aisle of St. George's, Hanover Square with his daughter leaning on his arm, there was not a prouder man in the whole of England.
The Duke and Duchess, after the honeymoon, went down to Canterville Chase, and on the day after they walked to the churchyard. After some time they strolled into the ruins of the old Abbey.
When a golden girl can win
Prayer from out the lips of sin
When the barren almond bears
And the little child
gives away its tears
Then shall all the house be still
And peace come to Canterville
Virginia, a wife should have no secrets from her husband. You never told me what happened to you when you were locked up with the ghost!
I owe to Sir Simon a great deal. He made me see what life is, and what death signifies, and why love is stronger than both.
You can have your secret as long as I can have your ***heart!***
You have always had ***that***, Cecil...
...and you will tell our ***children*** one day, won't you?
Virginia blushed!
The End
ADAPTATION & ILLUSTRATION ©2009 TEAM SPUTNIK

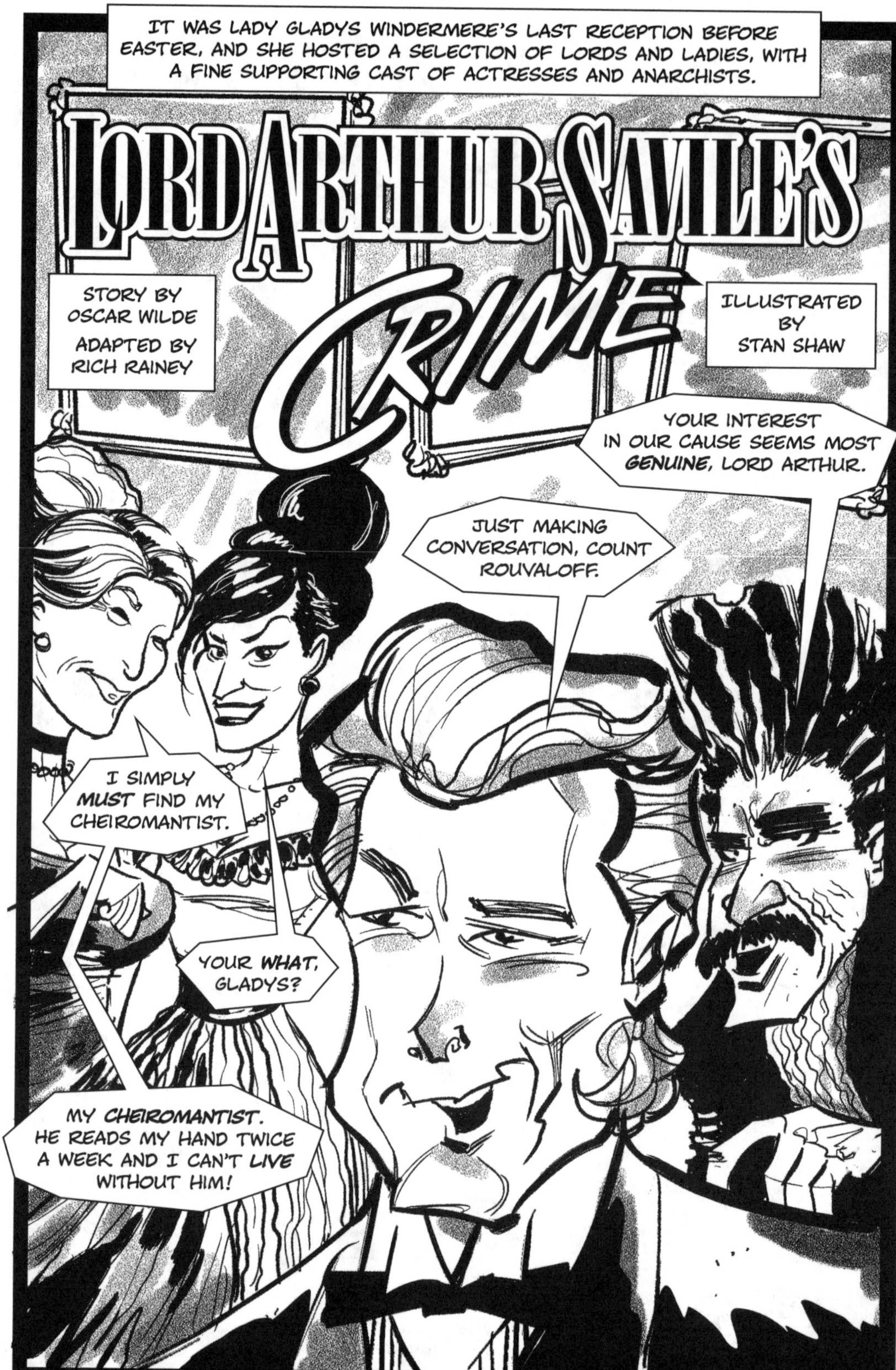
IT WAS LADY GLADYS WINDERMERE'S LAST RECEPTION BEFORE EASTER, AND SHE HOSTED A SELECTION OF LORDS AND LADIES, WITH A FINE SUPPORTING CAST OF ACTRESSES AND ANARCHISTS.
LORD ARTHUR SAVILE'S CRIME
STORY BY OSCAR WILDE
ADAPTED BY RICH RAINEY
ILLUSTRATED BY STAN SHAW
YOUR INTEREST IN OUR CAUSE SEEMS MOST GENUINE, LORD ARTHUR.
JUST MAKING CONVERSATION, COUNT ROUVALOFF.
I SIMPLY MUST FIND MY CHEIROMANTIST.
YOUR WHAT, GLADYS?
MY CHEIROMANTIST. HE READS MY HAND TWICE A WEEK AND I CAN'T LIVE WITHOUT HIM!

OH, I SEE. HE TELLS FORTUNES.
AND MISFORTUNES. HE THINKS I'M IN GREAT DANGER- ON BOTH LAND AND SEA.
I MAY HAVE TO LIVE IN A BALLOON AND HAVE MY DINNER DRAWN UP IN A BASKET EVERY EVENING.
SURELY, YOU DON'T TAKE HIM SERIOUSLY.
WHERE HAS MY PET CHEIROMANTIST WANDERED OFF TO?
SEE FOR YOURSELF- I'LL INTRODUCE YOU.
IF SOMEONE DOESN'T FETCH MR. PODGERS AT ONCE, I MUST GO MYSELF.
ALLOW ME, LADY WINDERMERE.
HOW GALLANT, LORD ARTHUR BUT...
...YOU DON'T KNOW WHAT HE LOOKS LIKE.
SUCH A MAN SHOULDN'T BE TOO HARD TO FIND. I IMAGINE HE'S-
-MYSTERIOUS LOOKING? POETIC? DARK AND DANGEROUS?
SO I GATHER.
WELL, BEFORE YOU GATHER ANYONE, YOU SHOULD KNOW MY FORTUNE TELLER LOOKS...

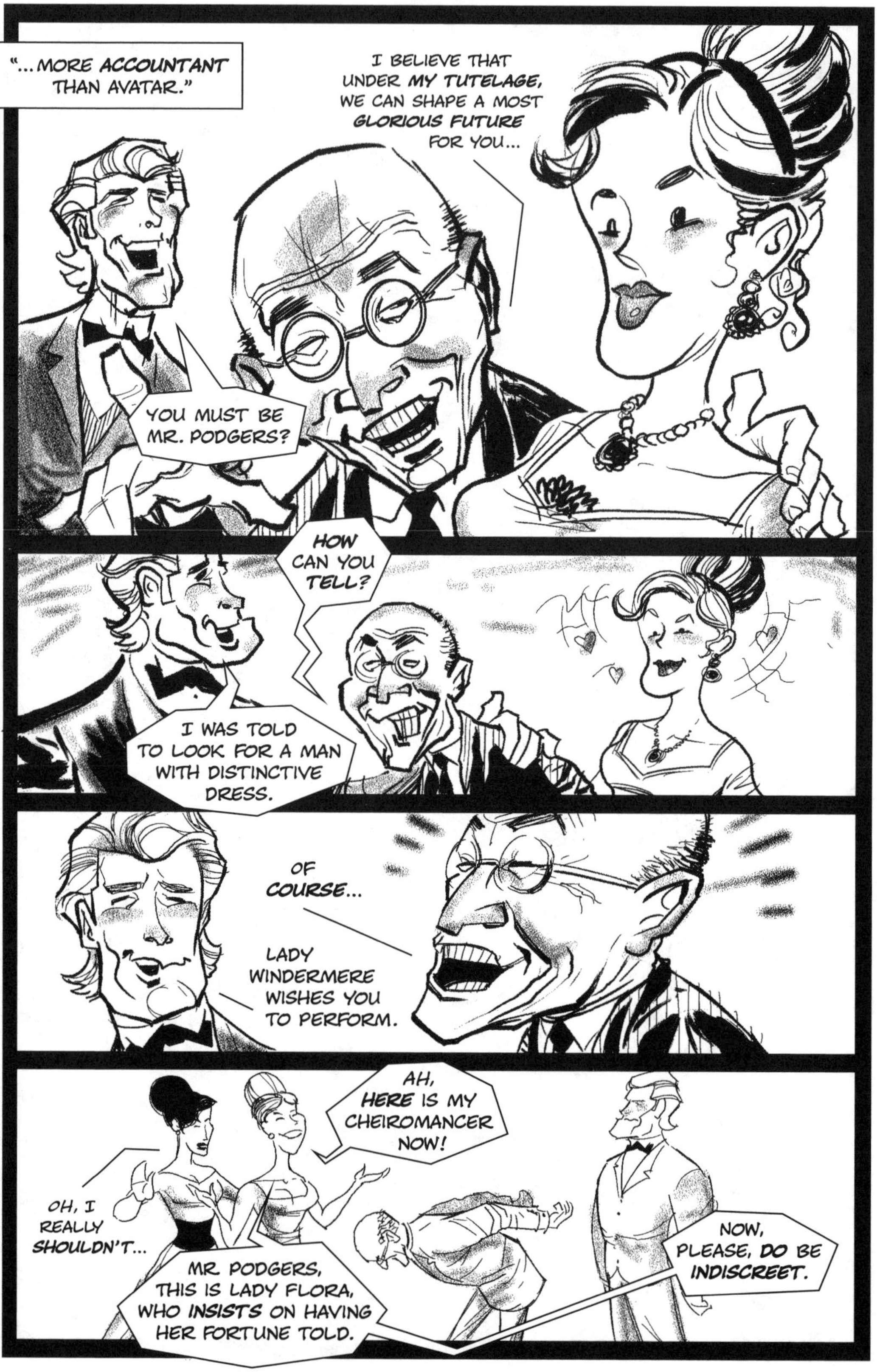
"...MORE ACCOUNTANT THAN AVATAR."
I BELIEVE THAT UNDER MY TUTELAGE, WE CAN SHAPE A MOST GLORIOUS FUTURE FOR YOU...
YOU MUST BE MR. PODGERS?
HOW CAN YOU TELL?
I WAS TOLD TO LOOK FOR A MAN WITH DISTINCTIVE DRESS.
OF COURSE...
LADY WINDERMERE WISHES YOU TO PERFORM.
AH, HERE IS MY CHEIROMANCER NOW!
OH, I REALLY SHOULDN'T...
MR. PODGERS, THIS IS LADY FLORA, WHO INSISTS ON HAVING HER FORTUNE TOLD.
NOW, PLEASE, DO BE INDISCREET.

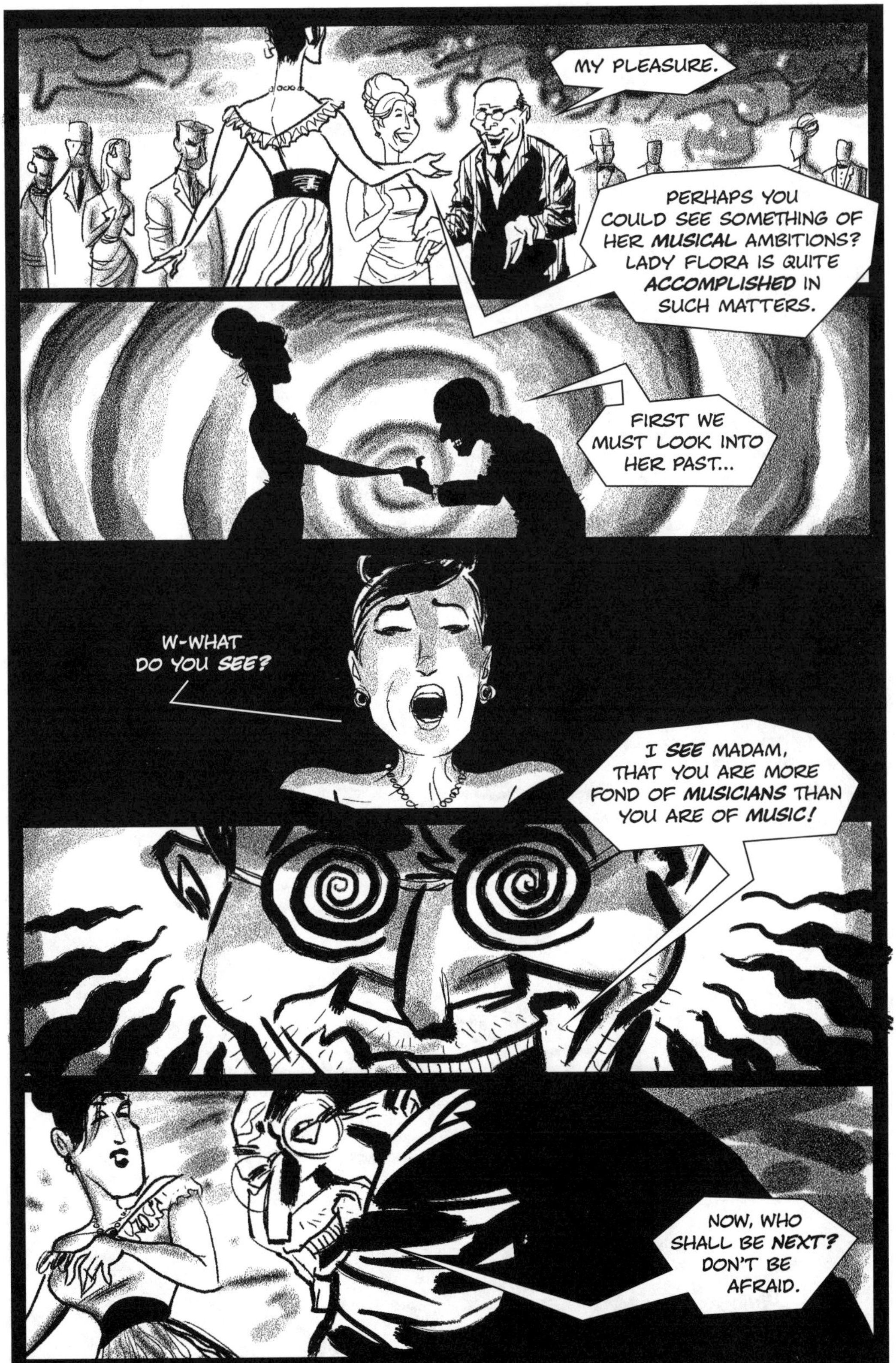
MY PLEASURE.
PERHAPS YOU COULD SEE SOMETHING OF HER MUSICAL AMBITIONS? LADY FLORA IS QUITE ACCOMPLISHED IN SUCH MATTERS.
FIRST WE MUST LOOK INTO HER PAST...
W-WHAT DO YOU SEE?
I SEE MADAM, THAT YOU ARE MORE FOND OF MUSICIANS THAN YOU ARE OF MUSIC!
NOW, WHO SHALL BE NEXT? DON'T BE AFRAID.

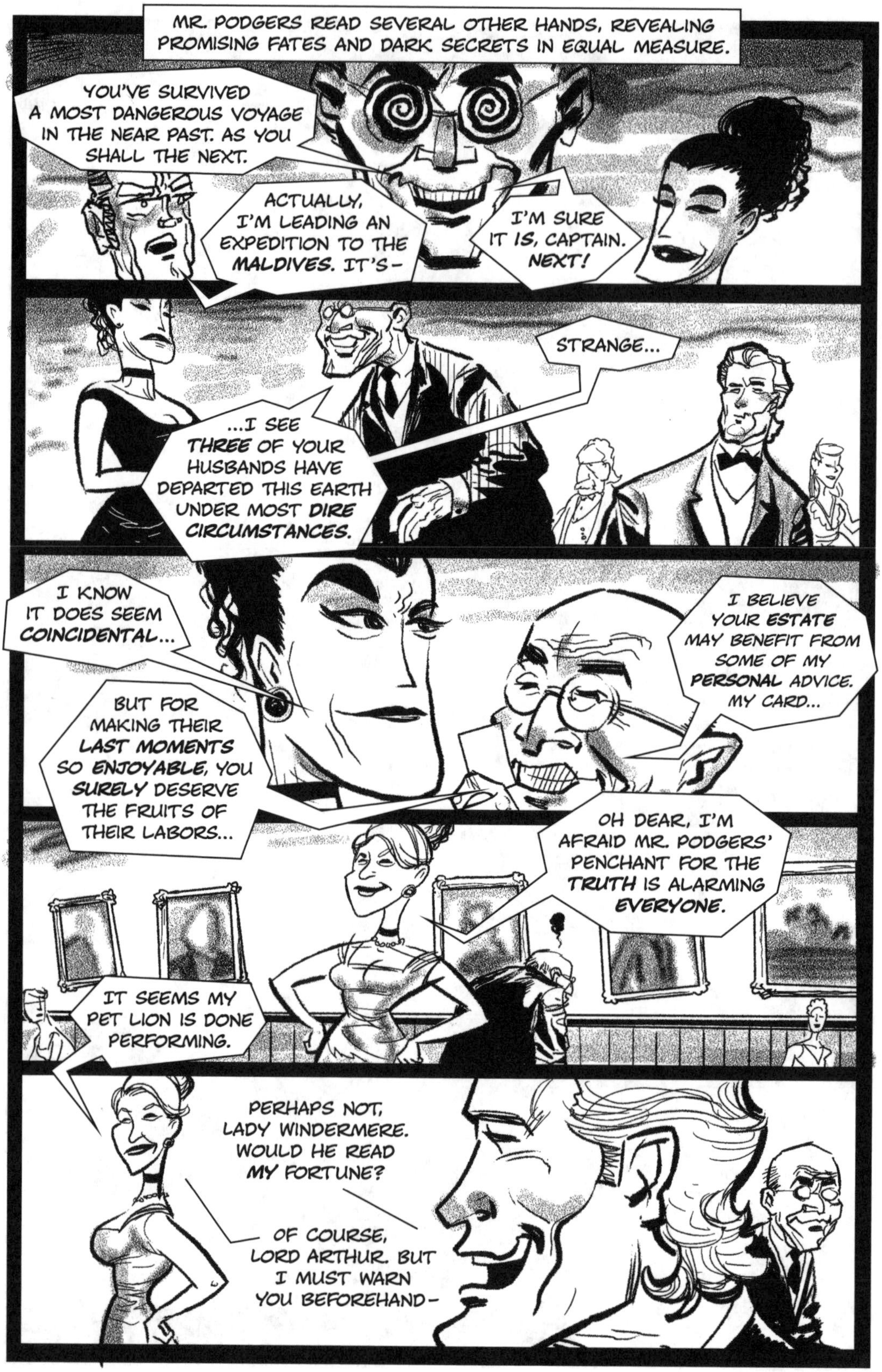
MR. PODGERS READ SEVERAL OTHER HANDS, REVEALING PROMISING FATES AND DARK SECRETS IN EQUAL MEASURE.
YOU'VE SURVIVED A MOST DANGEROUS VOYAGE IN THE NEAR PAST. AS YOU SHALL THE NEXT.
ACTUALLY, I'M LEADING AN EXPEDITION TO THE MALDIVES. IT'S-
I'M SURE IT IS, CAPTAIN. NEXT!
STRANGE...
...I SEE THREE OF YOUR HUSBANDS HAVE DEPARTED THIS EARTH UNDER MOST DIRE CIRCUMSTANCES.
I KNOW IT DOES SEEM COINCIDENTAL...
BUT FOR MAKING THEIR LAST MOMENTS SO ENJOYABLE, YOU SURELY DESERVE THE FRUITS OF THEIR LABORS...
I BELIEVE YOUR ESTATE MAY BENEFIT FROM SOME OF MY PERSONAL ADVICE. MY CARD...
OH DEAR, I'M AFRAID MR. PODGERS' PENCHANT FOR THE TRUTH IS ALARMING EVERYONE.
IT SEEMS MY PET LION IS DONE PERFORMING.
PERHAPS NOT, LADY WINDERMERE. WOULD HE READ MY FORTUNE?
OF COURSE, LORD ARTHUR. BUT I MUST WARN YOU BEFOREHAND-

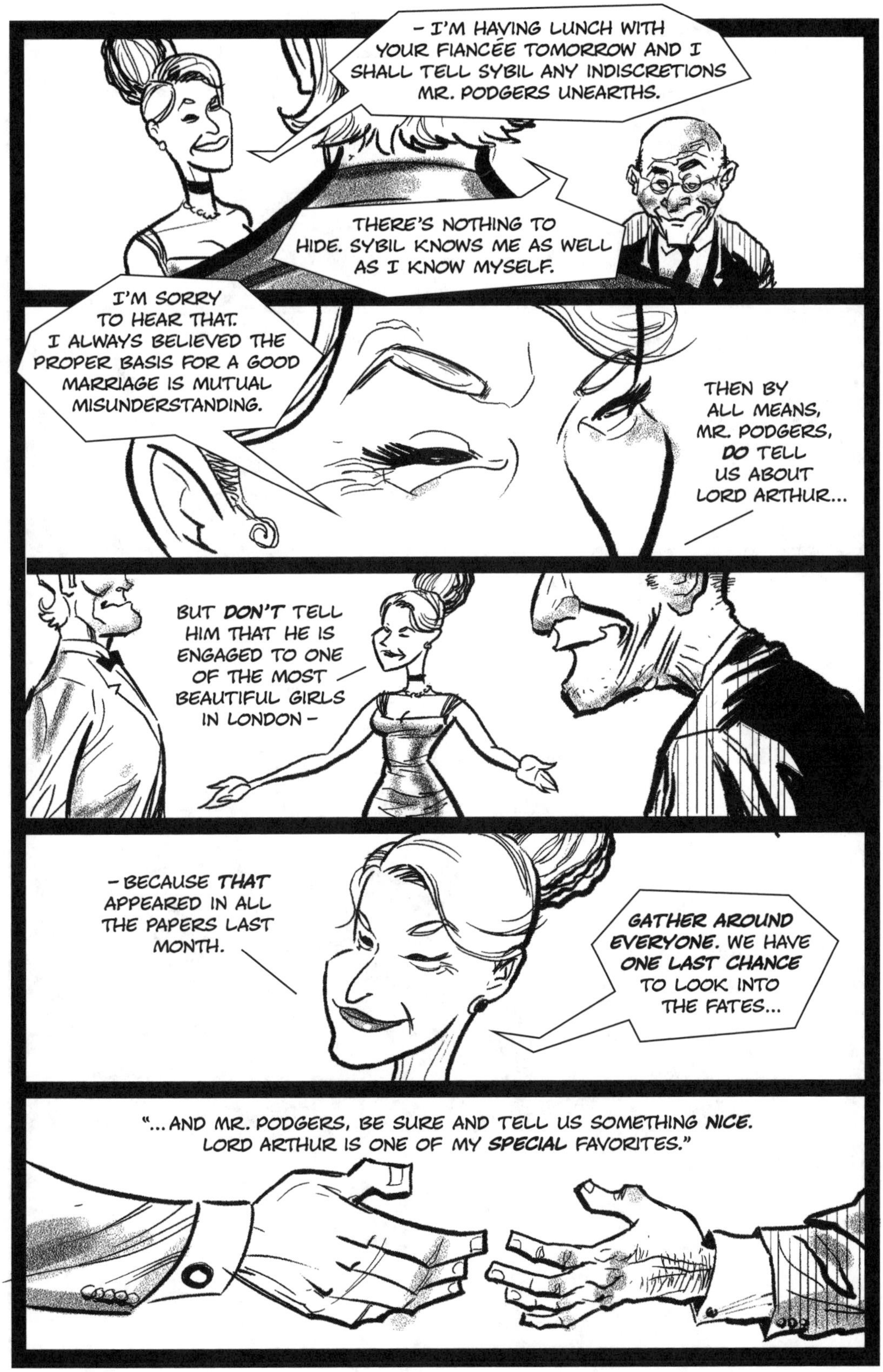
– I'M HAVING LUNCH WITH YOUR FIANCÉE TOMORROW AND I SHALL TELL SYBIL ANY INDISCRETIONS MR. PODGERS UNEARTHS.
THERE'S NOTHING TO HIDE. SYBIL KNOWS ME AS WELL AS I KNOW MYSELF.
I'M SORRY TO HEAR THAT. I ALWAYS BELIEVED THE PROPER BASIS FOR A GOOD MARRIAGE IS MUTUAL MISUNDERSTANDING.
THEN BY ALL MEANS, MR. PODGERS, DO TELL US ABOUT LORD ARTHUR...
BUT DON'T TELL HIM THAT HE IS ENGAGED TO ONE OF THE MOST BEAUTIFUL GIRLS IN LONDON –
– BECAUSE THAT APPEARED IN ALL THE PAPERS LAST MONTH.
GATHER AROUND EVERYONE. WE HAVE ONE LAST CHANCE TO LOOK INTO THE FATES...
"...AND MR. PODGERS, BE SURE AND TELL US SOMETHING NICE. LORD ARTHUR IS ONE OF MY SPECIAL FAVORITES."

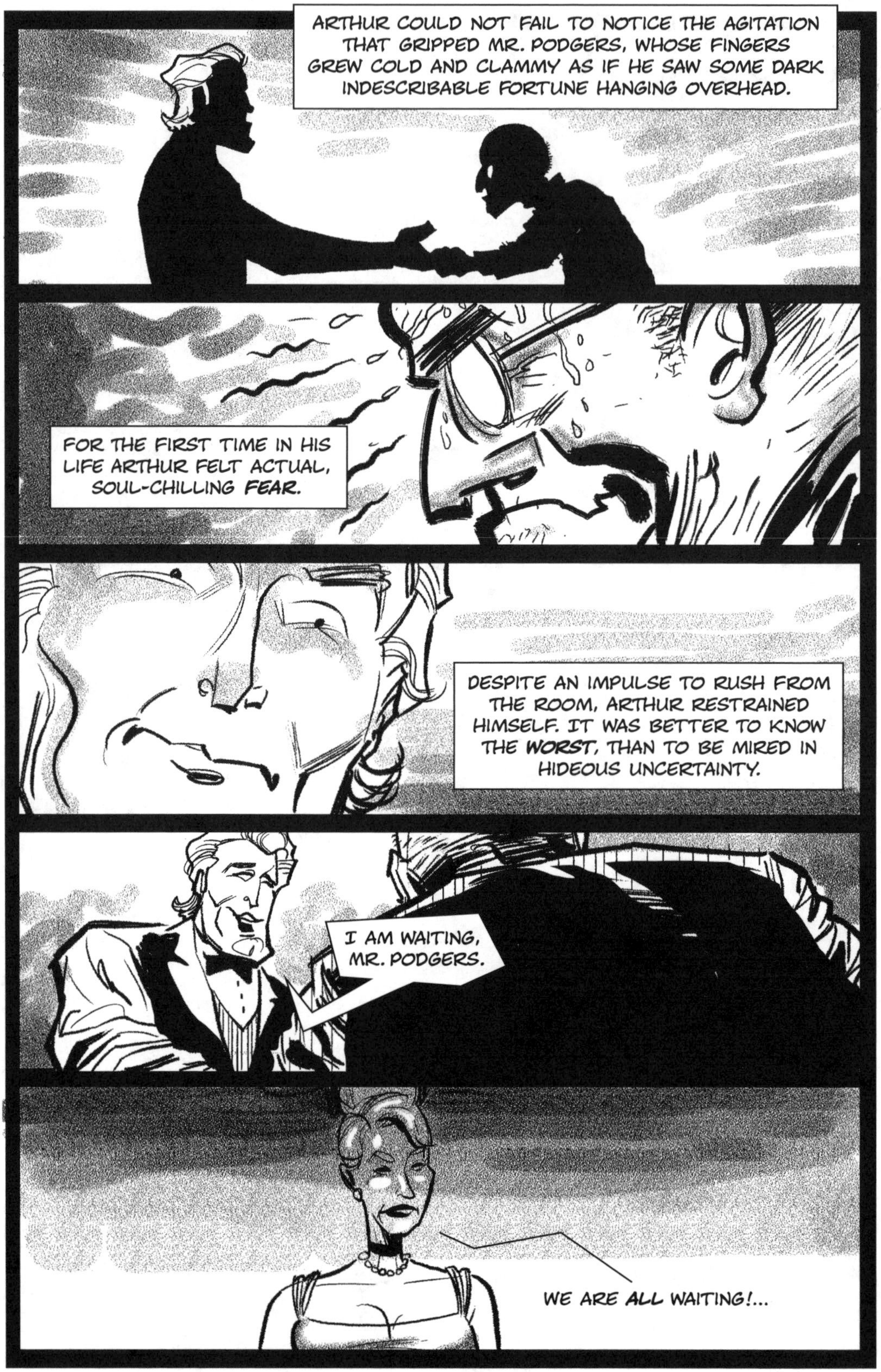
ARTHUR COULD NOT FAIL TO NOTICE THE AGITATION THAT GRIPPED MR. PODGERS, WHOSE FINGERS GREW COLD AND CLAMMY AS IF HE SAW SOME DARK INDESCRIBABLE FORTUNE HANGING OVERHEAD.
FOR THE FIRST TIME IN HIS LIFE ARTHUR FELT ACTUAL, SOUL-CHILLING FEAR.
DESPITE AN IMPULSE TO RUSH FROM THE ROOM, ARTHUR RESTRAINED HIMSELF. IT WAS BETTER TO KNOW THE WORST, THAN TO BE MIRED IN HIDEOUS UNCERTAINTY.
I AM WAITING, MR. PODGERS.
WE ARE ALL WAITING!...

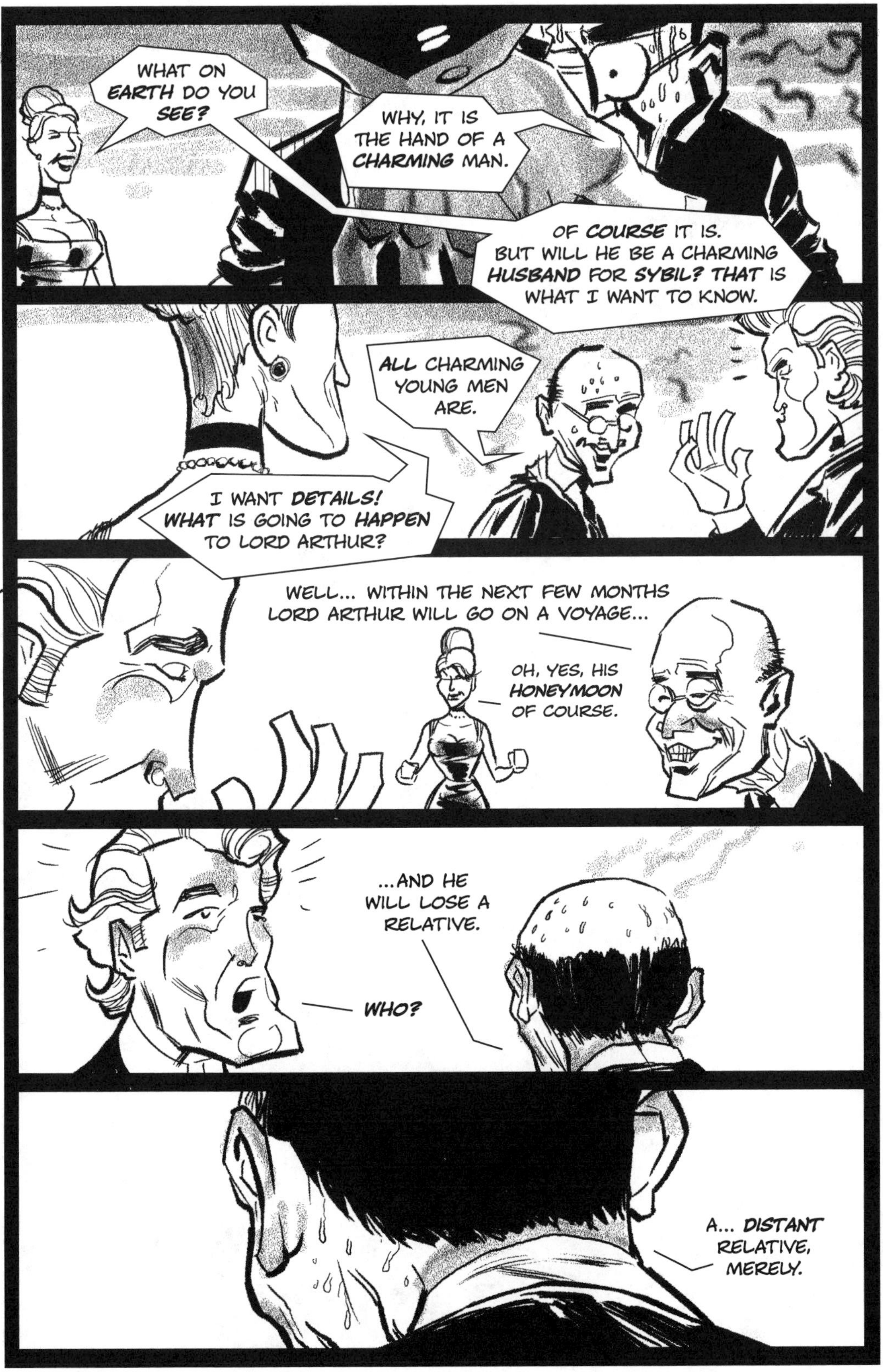
WHAT ON EARTH DO YOU SEE?
WHY, IT IS THE HAND OF A CHARMING MAN.
OF COURSE IT IS. BUT WILL HE BE A CHARMING HUSBAND FOR SYBIL? THAT IS WHAT I WANT TO KNOW.
ALL CHARMING YOUNG MEN ARE.
I WANT DETAILS! WHAT IS GOING TO HAPPEN TO LORD ARTHUR?
WELL... WITHIN THE NEXT FEW MONTHS LORD ARTHUR WILL GO ON A VOYAGE...
OH, YES, HIS HONEYMOON OF COURSE.
...AND HE WILL LOSE A RELATIVE.
WHO?
A... DISTANT RELATIVE, MERELY.

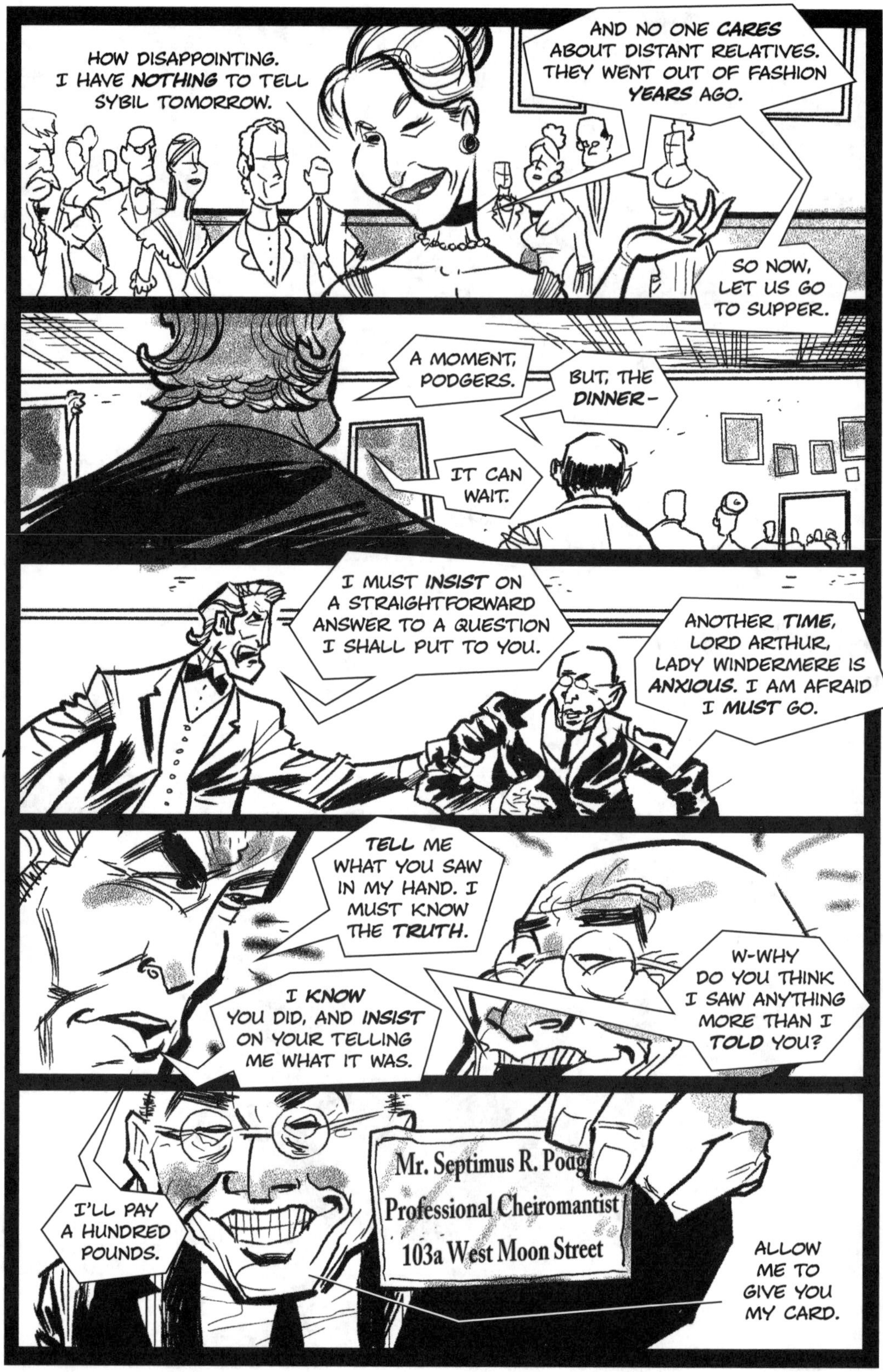
HOW DISAPPOINTING. I HAVE NOTHING TO TELL SYBIL TOMORROW.
AND NO ONE CARES ABOUT DISTANT RELATIVES. THEY WENT OUT OF FASHION YEARS AGO.
SO NOW, LET US GO TO SUPPER.
A MOMENT, PODGERS.
BUT, THE DINNER–
IT CAN WAIT.
I MUST INSIST ON A STRAIGHTFORWARD ANSWER TO A QUESTION I SHALL PUT TO YOU.
ANOTHER TIME, LORD ARTHUR, LADY WINDERMERE IS ANXIOUS. I AM AFRAID I MUST GO.
TELL ME WHAT YOU SAW IN MY HAND. I MUST KNOW THE TRUTH.
W-WHY DO YOU THINK I SAW ANYTHING MORE THAN I TOLD YOU?
I KNOW YOU DID, AND INSIST ON YOUR TELLING ME WHAT IT WAS.
I'LL PAY A HUNDRED POUNDS.
Mr. Septimus R. Podg
Professional Cheiromantist
103a West Moon Street
ALLOW ME TO GIVE YOU MY CARD.

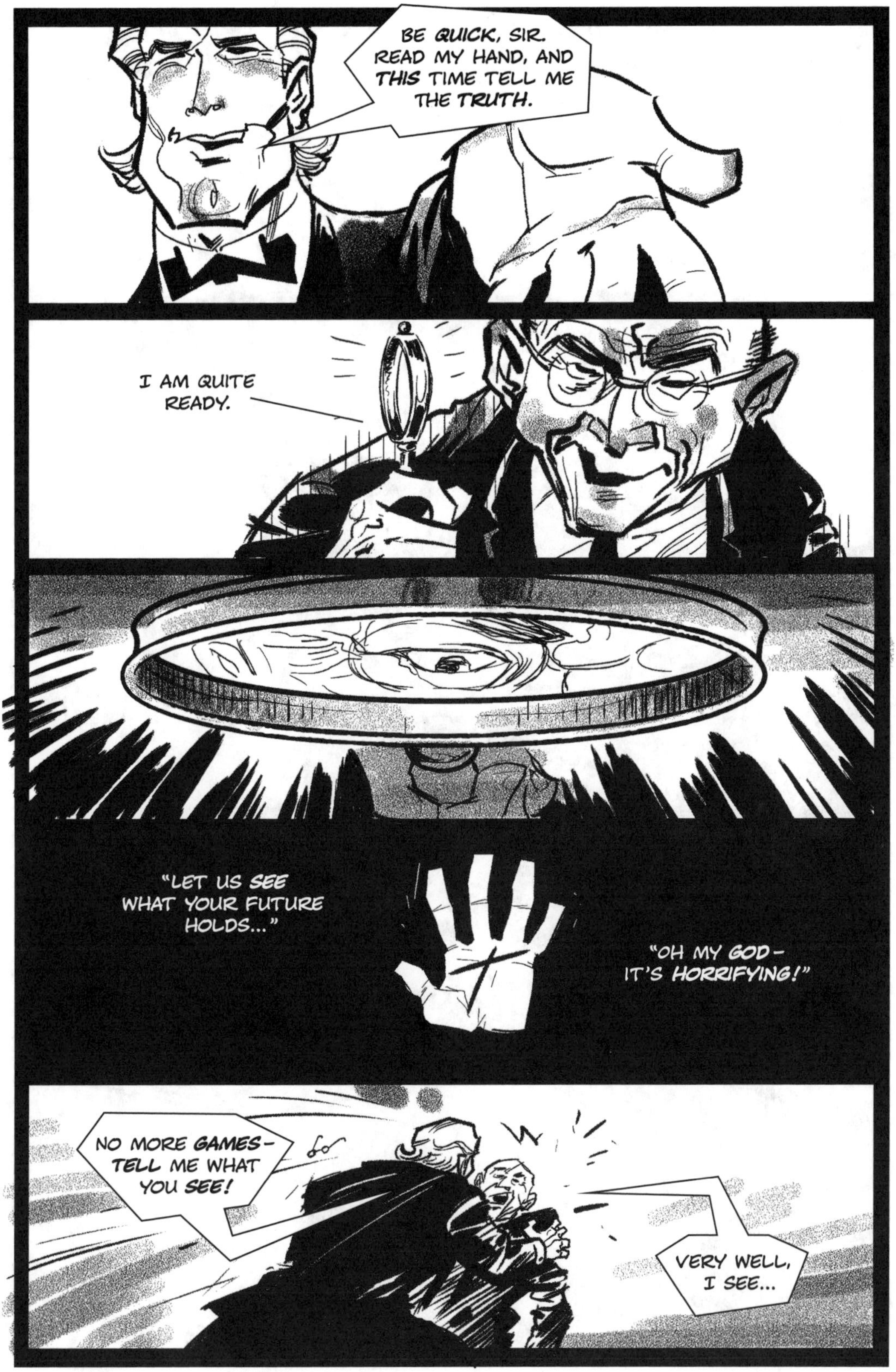
BE QUICK, SIR. READ MY HAND, AND THIS TIME TELL ME THE TRUTH.
I AM QUITE READY.
"LET US SEE WHAT YOUR FUTURE HOLDS..."
"OH MY GOD– IT'S HORRIFYING!"
NO MORE GAMES– TELL ME WHAT YOU SEE!
VERY WELL, I SEE...

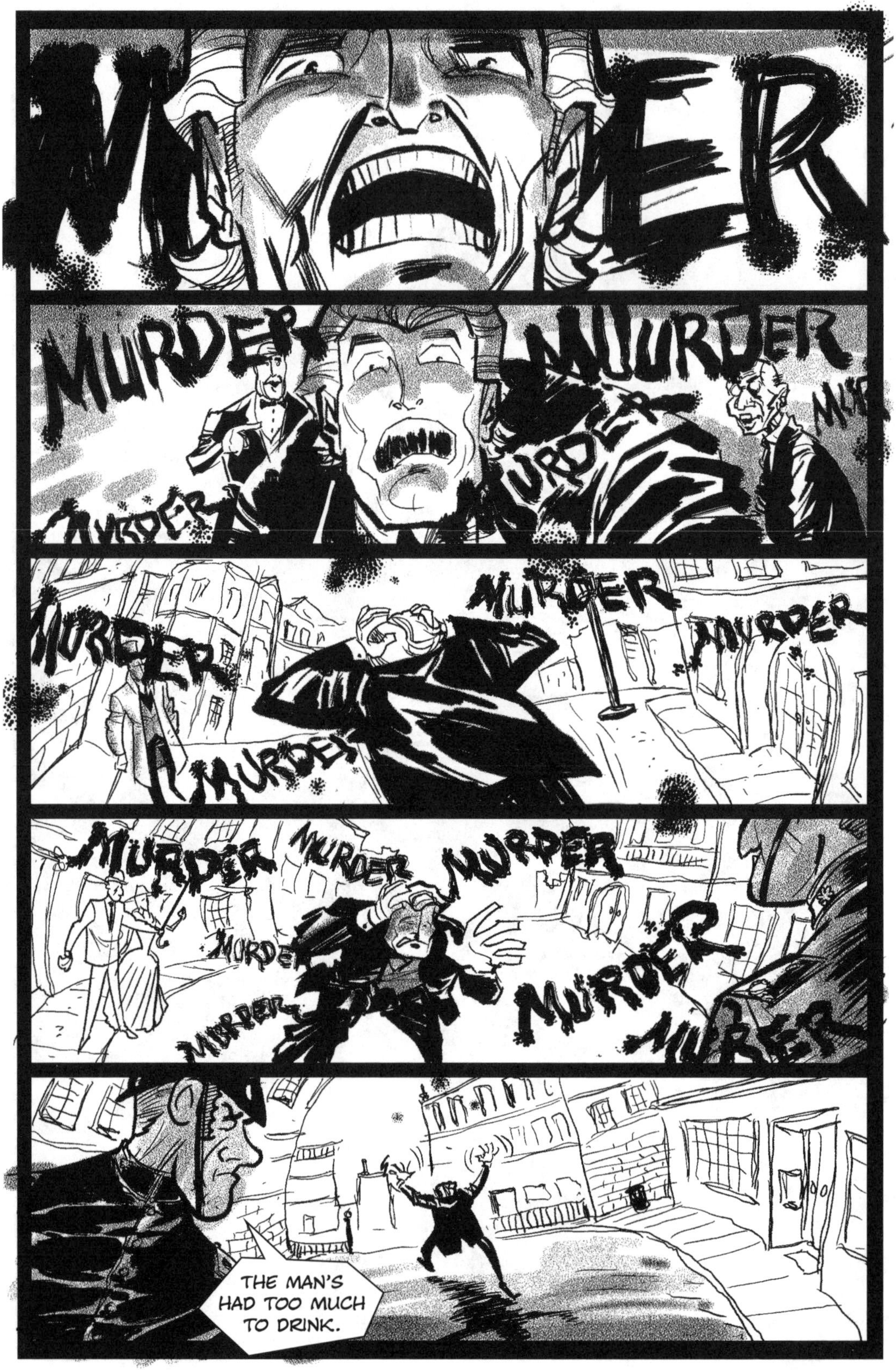
MURDER
MURDER
MURDER
MURDER
MURDER
MURDER
MURDER
MURDER
MURDER
MURDER
MURDER
MURDER
MURDER
MURDER
THE MAN'S HAD TOO MUCH TO DRINK.

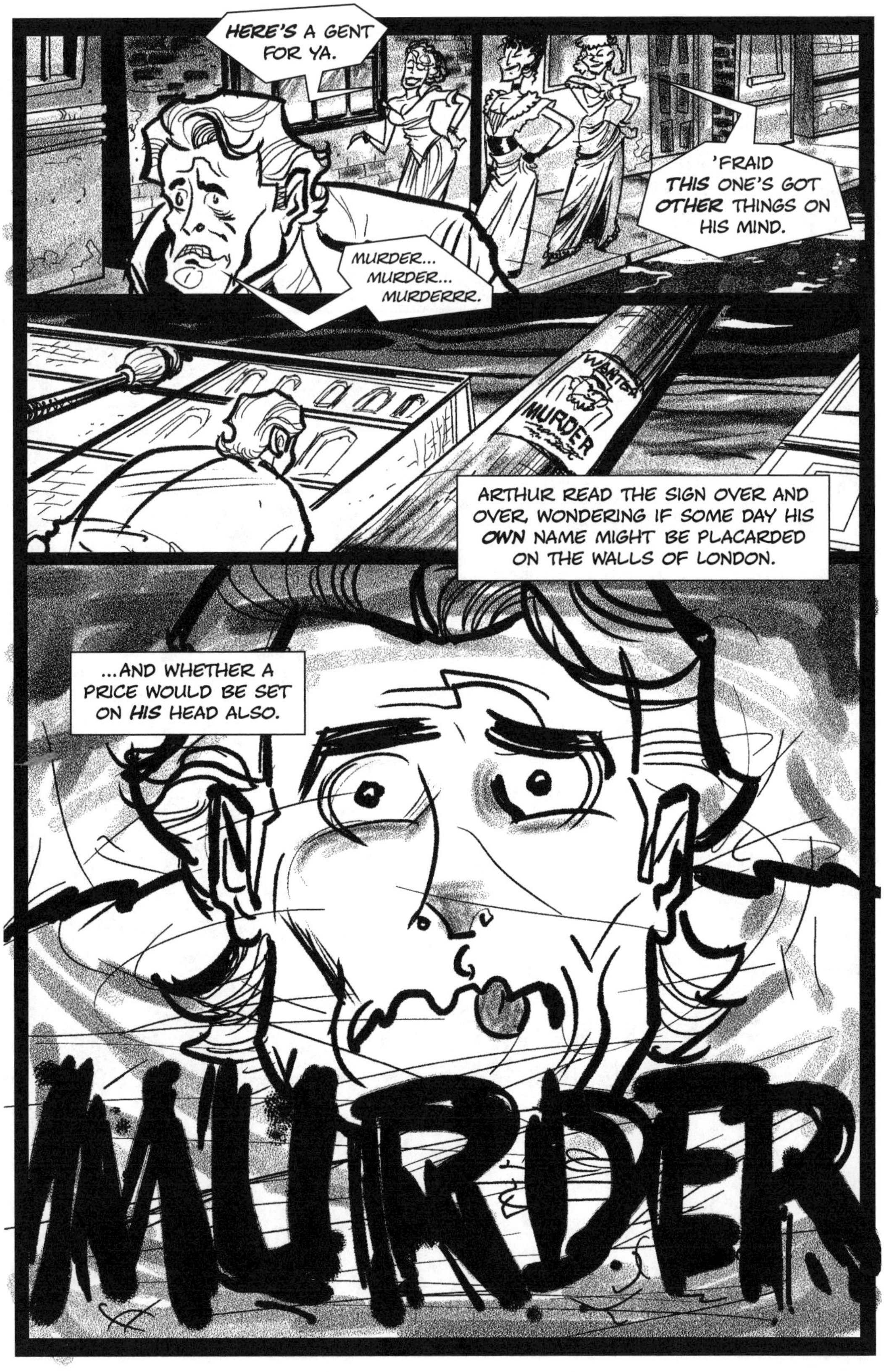
HERE'S A GENT FOR YA.
'FRAID THIS ONE'S GOT OTHER THINGS ON HIS MIND.
MURDER... MURDER... MURDERRR.
WANTED
MURDER
ARTHUR READ THE SIGN OVER AND OVER, WONDERING IF SOME DAY HIS OWN NAME MIGHT BE PLACARDED ON THE WALLS OF LONDON.
...AND WHETHER A PRICE WOULD BE SET ON HIS HEAD ALSO.
MURDER

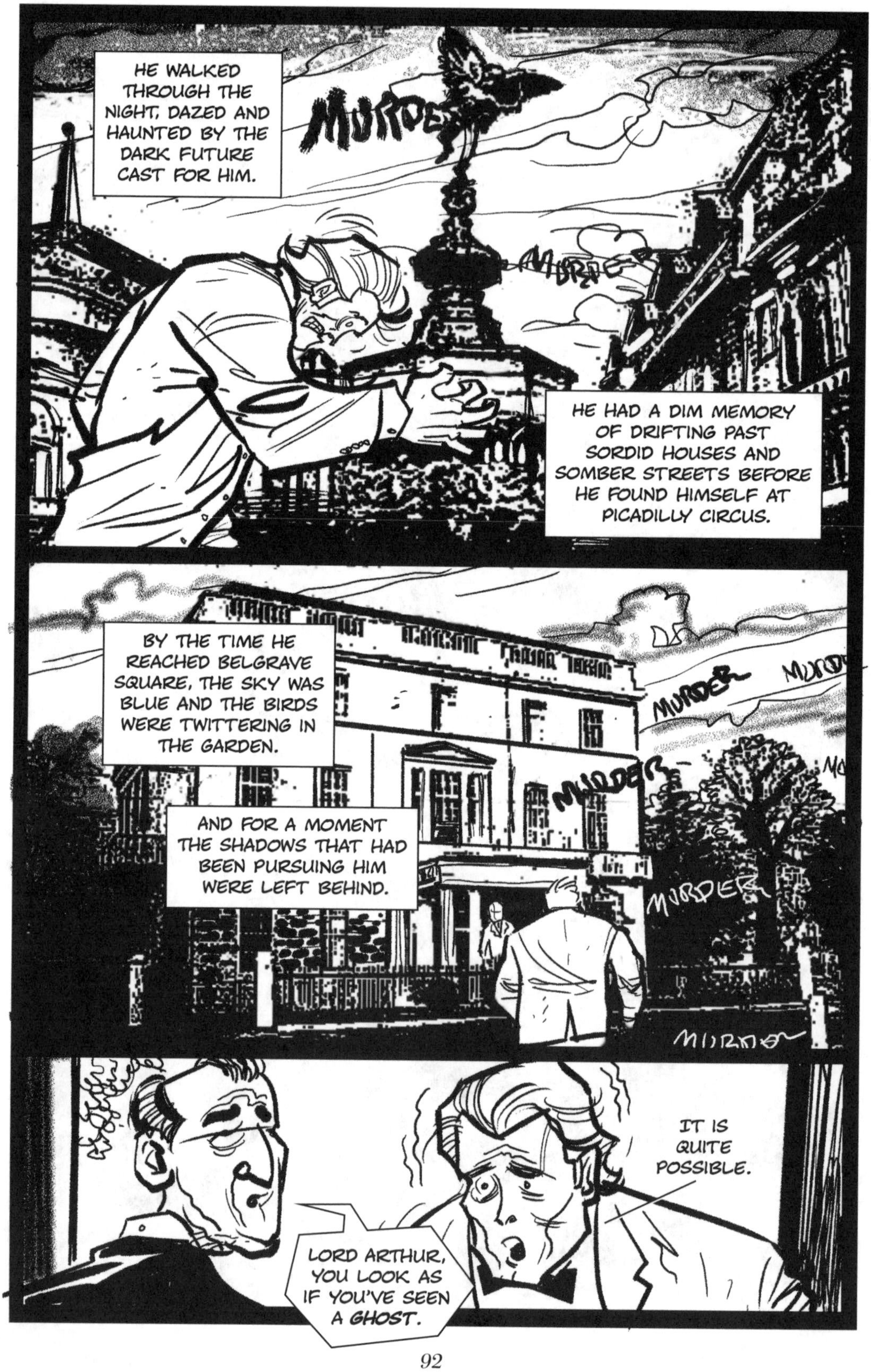
HE WALKED THROUGH THE NIGHT, DAZED AND HAUNTED BY THE DARK FUTURE CAST FOR HIM.
MURDER
HE HAD A DIM MEMORY OF DRIFTING PAST SORDID HOUSES AND SOMBER STREETS BEFORE HE FOUND HIMSELF AT PICADILLY CIRCUS.
BY THE TIME HE REACHED BELGRAVE SQUARE, THE SKY WAS BLUE AND THE BIRDS WERE TWITTERING IN THE GARDEN.
MURDER
MURDER
AND FOR A MOMENT THE SHADOWS THAT HAD BEEN PURSUING HIM WERE LEFT BEHIND.
LORD ARTHUR, YOU LOOK AS IF YOU'VE SEEN A GHOST.
IT IS QUITE POSSIBLE.

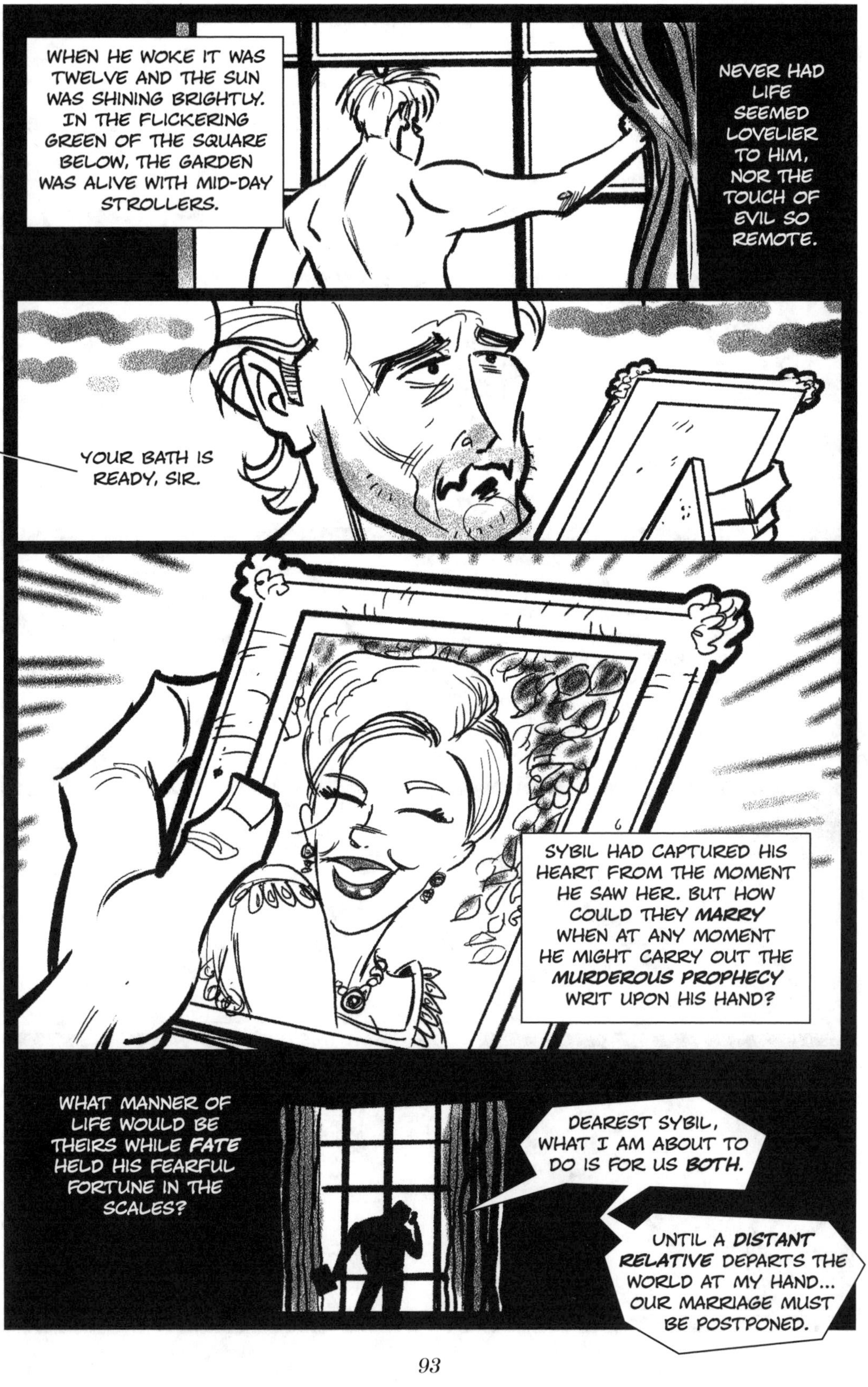
WHEN HE WOKE IT WAS TWELVE AND THE SUN WAS SHINING BRIGHTLY. IN THE FLICKERING GREEN OF THE SQUARE BELOW, THE GARDEN WAS ALIVE WITH MID-DAY STROLLERS.
NEVER HAD LIFE SEEMED LOVELIER TO HIM, NOR THE TOUCH OF EVIL SO REMOTE.
YOUR BATH IS READY, SIR.
SYBIL HAD CAPTURED HIS HEART FROM THE MOMENT HE SAW HER. BUT HOW COULD THEY MARRY WHEN AT ANY MOMENT HE MIGHT CARRY OUT THE MURDEROUS PROPHECY WRIT UPON HIS HAND?
WHAT MANNER OF LIFE WOULD BE THEIRS WHILE FATE HELD HIS FEARFUL FORTUNE IN THE SCALES?
DEAREST SYBIL, WHAT I AM ABOUT TO DO IS FOR US BOTH.
UNTIL A DISTANT RELATIVE DEPARTS THE WORLD AT MY HAND... OUR MARRIAGE MUST BE POSTPONED.

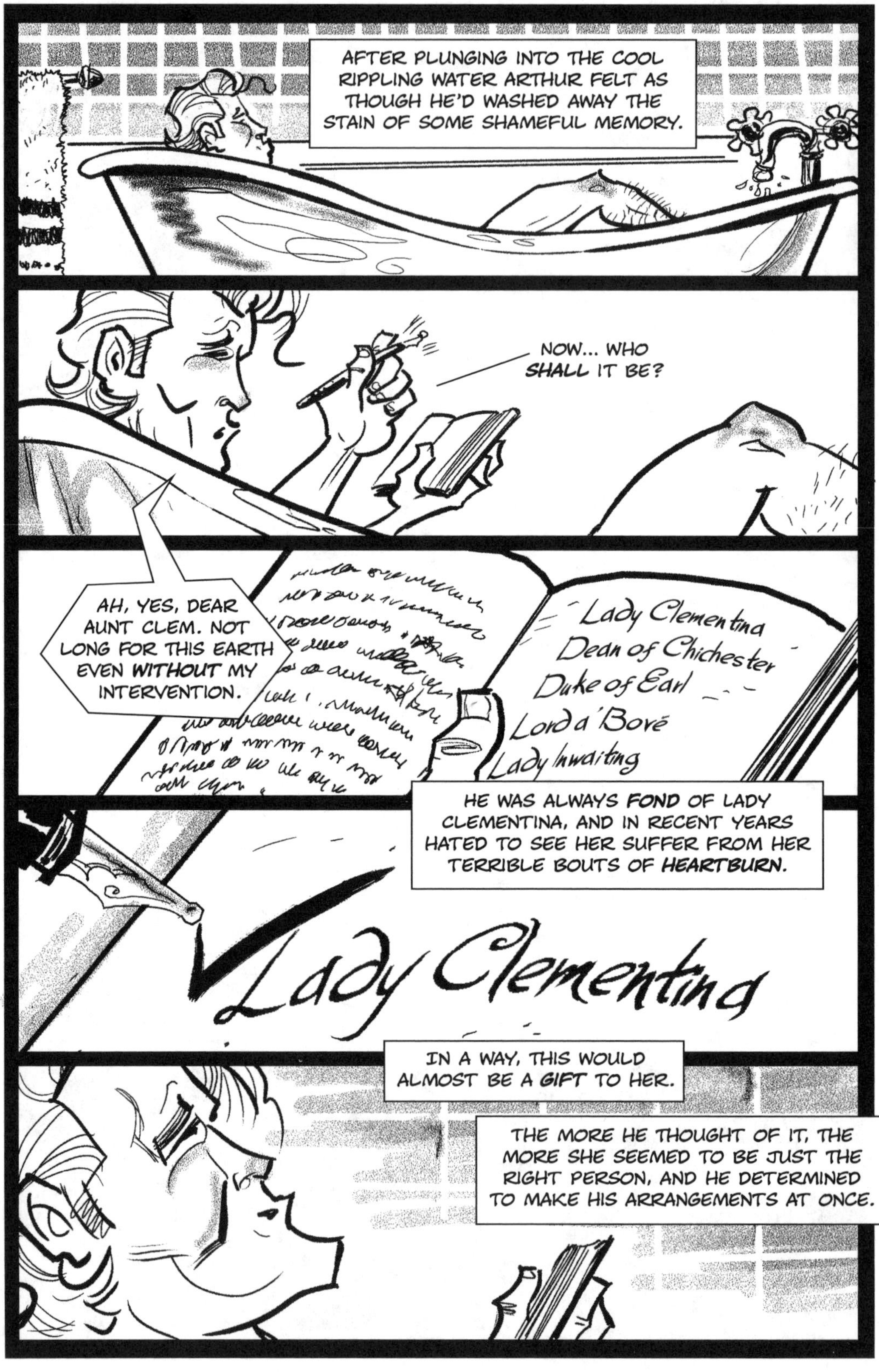
AFTER PLUNGING INTO THE COOL RIPPLING WATER ARTHUR FELT AS THOUGH HE'D WASHED AWAY THE STAIN OF SOME SHAMEFUL MEMORY.
NOW... WHO SHALL IT BE?
AH, YES, DEAR AUNT CLEM. NOT LONG FOR THIS EARTH EVEN WITHOUT MY INTERVENTION.
Lady Clementina
Dean of Chichester
Duke of Earl
Lord a'Boré
Lady Inwaiting
HE WAS ALWAYS FOND OF LADY CLEMENTINA, AND IN RECENT YEARS HATED TO SEE HER SUFFER FROM HER TERRIBLE BOUTS OF HEARTBURN.
Lady Clementina
IN A WAY, THIS WOULD ALMOST BE A GIFT TO HER.
THE MORE HE THOUGHT OF IT, THE MORE SHE SEEMED TO BE JUST THE RIGHT PERSON, AND HE DETERMINED TO MAKE HIS ARRANGEMENTS AT ONCE.

A SHORT HANSOM RIDE TOOK HIM TO HIS CLUB, WHICH HAD ONE OF THE BEST PRIVATE LIBRARIES IN LONDON.

WILL THERE BE ANYTHING ELSE, LORD ARTHUR?

NO, I BELIEVE I HAVE EVERYTHING I NEED...

...RIGHT HERE.

PHARMACOPEIA

Aconitine – Swift, and almost immediate in effect, this potent and painless drug is by no means unpalatable when taken in the form of a gelatin capsule. A dose of the root of the common Mon... and the drug is used in small d... ...odyne.

PHARMACO...

Arsenic – An extre... solid element, comm... insecticide or weed k... steel-gray, crystalline a... taste. Extreme caution... the storage and hand... ...d, as its solubili... ...can be prob...

HE TOOK NOTE OF THE AMOUNT REQUIRED FOR A FATAL DOSAGE AND THEN STROLLED UP ST. JAMES'S STREET TO THE CHEMIST'S SHOP.

PESTLE & HUMBR... PHARMACIE...

ACONITINE IS A DANGEROUS DRUG, LORD ARTHUR, I'M AFRAID ONE NEEDS A **MEDICAL CERTIFICATE**...

I'M WELL AWARE OF THE DANGER, MR. PESTLE. IT'S TO PUT DOWN A NORWEGIAN MASTIFF— THE HOUND MAY HAVE **RABIES** AND HAS ALREADY BITTEN THE COACHMAN **TWICE**.

I BELIEVE WE CAN MAKE AN **EXCEPTION** IN YOUR CASE, LORD ARTHUR. YOU SEEM **WELL-VERSED** IN TOXICOLOGY.

ONE TRIES TO BE **DILIGENT** IN SUCH MATTERS. IT'D BE A **CRIME** NOT TO.

DESPITE HIS SMALL VICTORY, ARTHUR WASN'T SATISFIED. HOW COULD HE MAKE THE POISON LOOK LIKE A GIFT?...

Le Chocolatier

AH— THERE'S JUST THE THING!

95

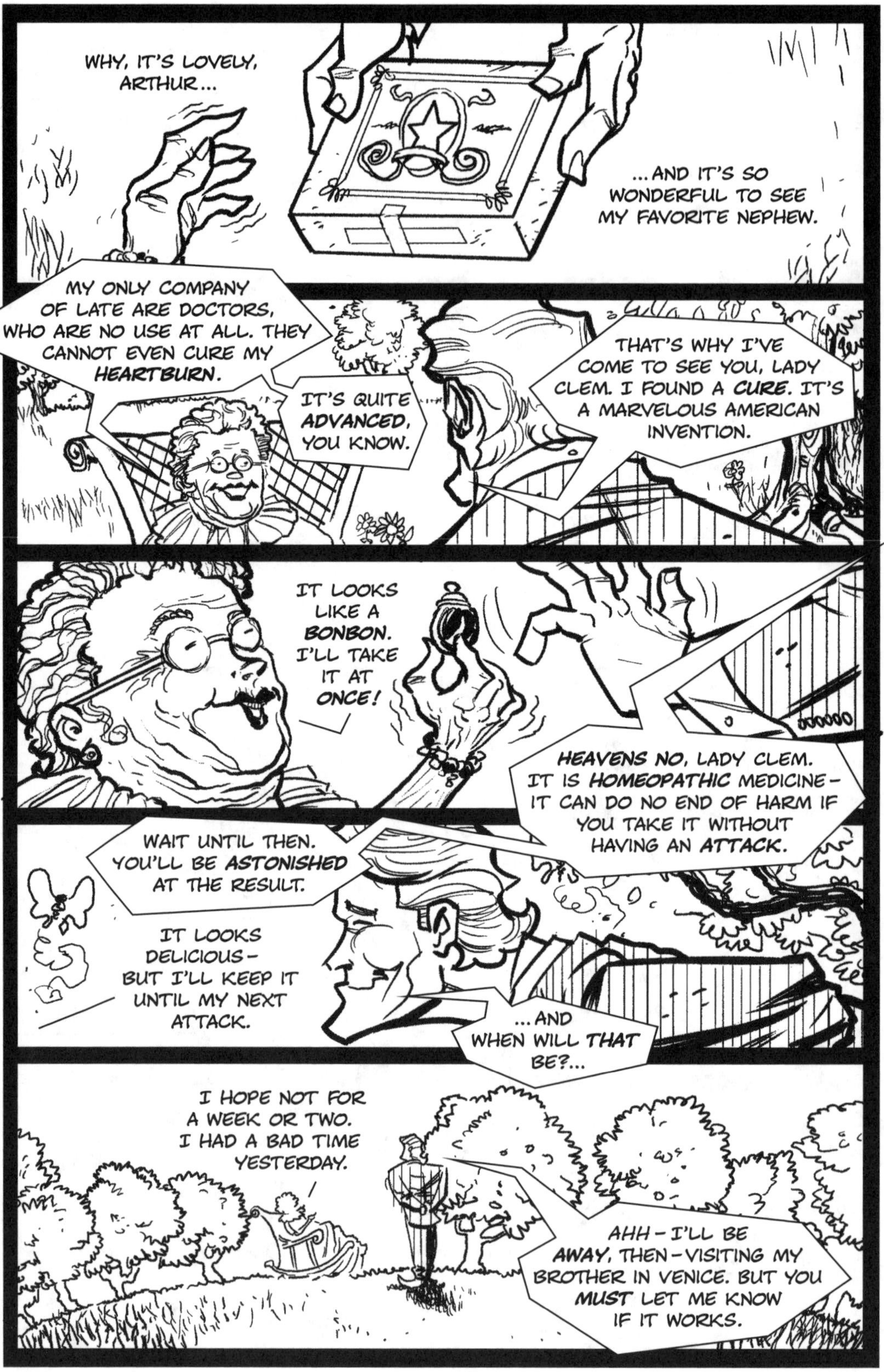
WHY, IT'S LOVELY, ARTHUR...
...AND IT'S SO WONDERFUL TO SEE MY FAVORITE NEPHEW.
MY ONLY COMPANY OF LATE ARE DOCTORS, WHO ARE NO USE AT ALL. THEY CANNOT EVEN CURE MY HEARTBURN.
THAT'S WHY I'VE COME TO SEE YOU, LADY CLEM. I FOUND A CURE. IT'S A MARVELOUS AMERICAN INVENTION.
IT'S QUITE ADVANCED, YOU KNOW.
IT LOOKS LIKE A BONBON. I'LL TAKE IT AT ONCE!
HEAVENS NO, LADY CLEM. IT IS HOMEOPATHIC MEDICINE– IT CAN DO NO END OF HARM IF YOU TAKE IT WITHOUT HAVING AN ATTACK.
WAIT UNTIL THEN. YOU'LL BE ASTONISHED AT THE RESULT.
IT LOOKS DELICIOUS– BUT I'LL KEEP IT UNTIL MY NEXT ATTACK.
...AND WHEN WILL THAT BE?...
I HOPE NOT FOR A WEEK OR TWO. I HAD A BAD TIME YESTERDAY.
AHH–I'LL BE AWAY, THEN–VISITING MY BROTHER IN VENICE. BUT YOU MUST LET ME KNOW IF IT WORKS.

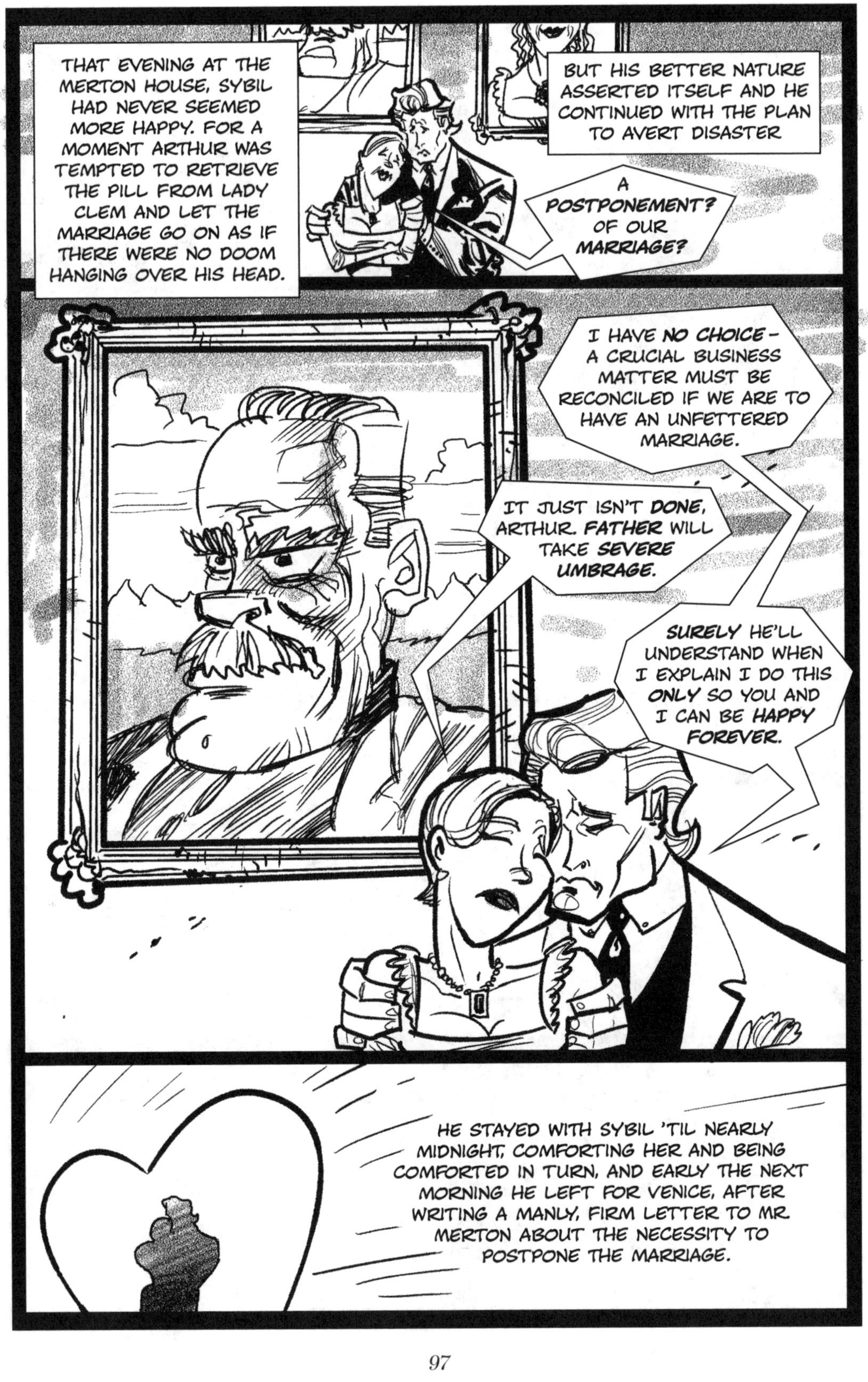
THAT EVENING AT THE MERTON HOUSE, SYBIL HAD NEVER SEEMED MORE HAPPY. FOR A MOMENT ARTHUR WAS TEMPTED TO RETRIEVE THE PILL FROM LADY CLEM AND LET THE MARRIAGE GO ON AS IF THERE WERE NO DOOM HANGING OVER HIS HEAD.
BUT HIS BETTER NATURE ASSERTED ITSELF AND HE CONTINUED WITH THE PLAN TO AVERT DISASTER
A POSTPONEMENT? OF OUR MARRIAGE?
I HAVE NO CHOICE – A CRUCIAL BUSINESS MATTER MUST BE RECONCILED IF WE ARE TO HAVE AN UNFETTERED MARRIAGE.
IT JUST ISN'T DONE, ARTHUR. FATHER WILL TAKE SEVERE UMBRAGE.
SURELY HE'LL UNDERSTAND WHEN I EXPLAIN I DO THIS ONLY SO YOU AND I CAN BE HAPPY FOREVER.
HE STAYED WITH SYBIL 'TIL NEARLY MIDNIGHT, COMFORTING HER AND BEING COMFORTED IN TURN, AND EARLY THE NEXT MORNING HE LEFT FOR VENICE, AFTER WRITING A MANLY, FIRM LETTER TO MR MERTON ABOUT THE NECESSITY TO POSTPONE THE MARRIAGE.

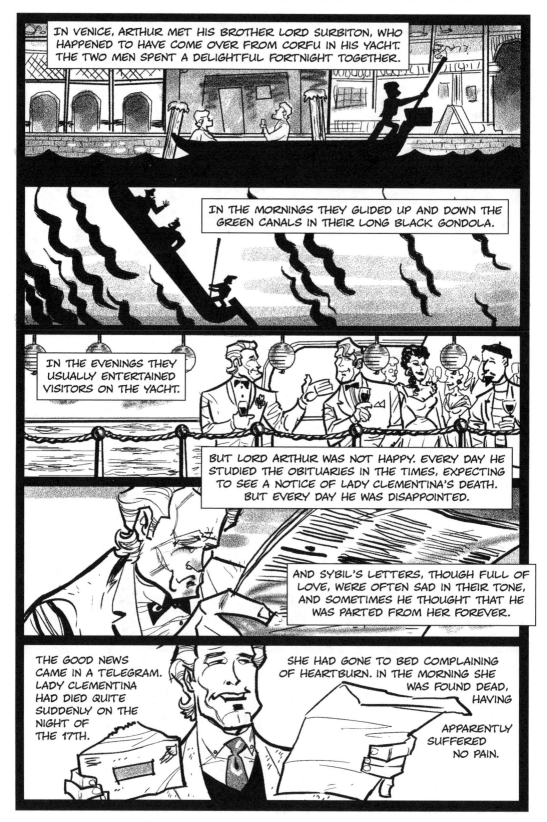

IN VENICE, ARTHUR MET HIS BROTHER LORD SURBITON, WHO HAPPENED TO HAVE COME OVER FROM CORFU IN HIS YACHT. THE TWO MEN SPENT A DELIGHTFUL FORTNIGHT TOGETHER.

IN THE MORNINGS THEY GLIDED UP AND DOWN THE GREEN CANALS IN THEIR LONG BLACK GONDOLA.

IN THE EVENINGS THEY USUALLY ENTERTAINED VISITORS ON THE YACHT.

BUT LORD ARTHUR WAS NOT HAPPY. EVERY DAY HE STUDIED THE OBITUARIES IN THE TIMES, EXPECTING TO SEE A NOTICE OF LADY CLEMENTINA'S DEATH. BUT EVERY DAY HE WAS DISAPPOINTED.

AND SYBIL'S LETTERS, THOUGH FULL OF LOVE, WERE OFTEN SAD IN THEIR TONE, AND SOMETIMES HE THOUGHT THAT HE WAS PARTED FROM HER FOREVER.

THE GOOD NEWS CAME IN A TELEGRAM. LADY CLEMENTINA HAD DIED QUITE SUDDENLY ON THE NIGHT OF THE 17TH.

SHE HAD GONE TO BED COMPLAINING OF HEARTBURN. IN THE MORNING SHE WAS FOUND DEAD, HAVING APPARENTLY SUFFERED NO PAIN.

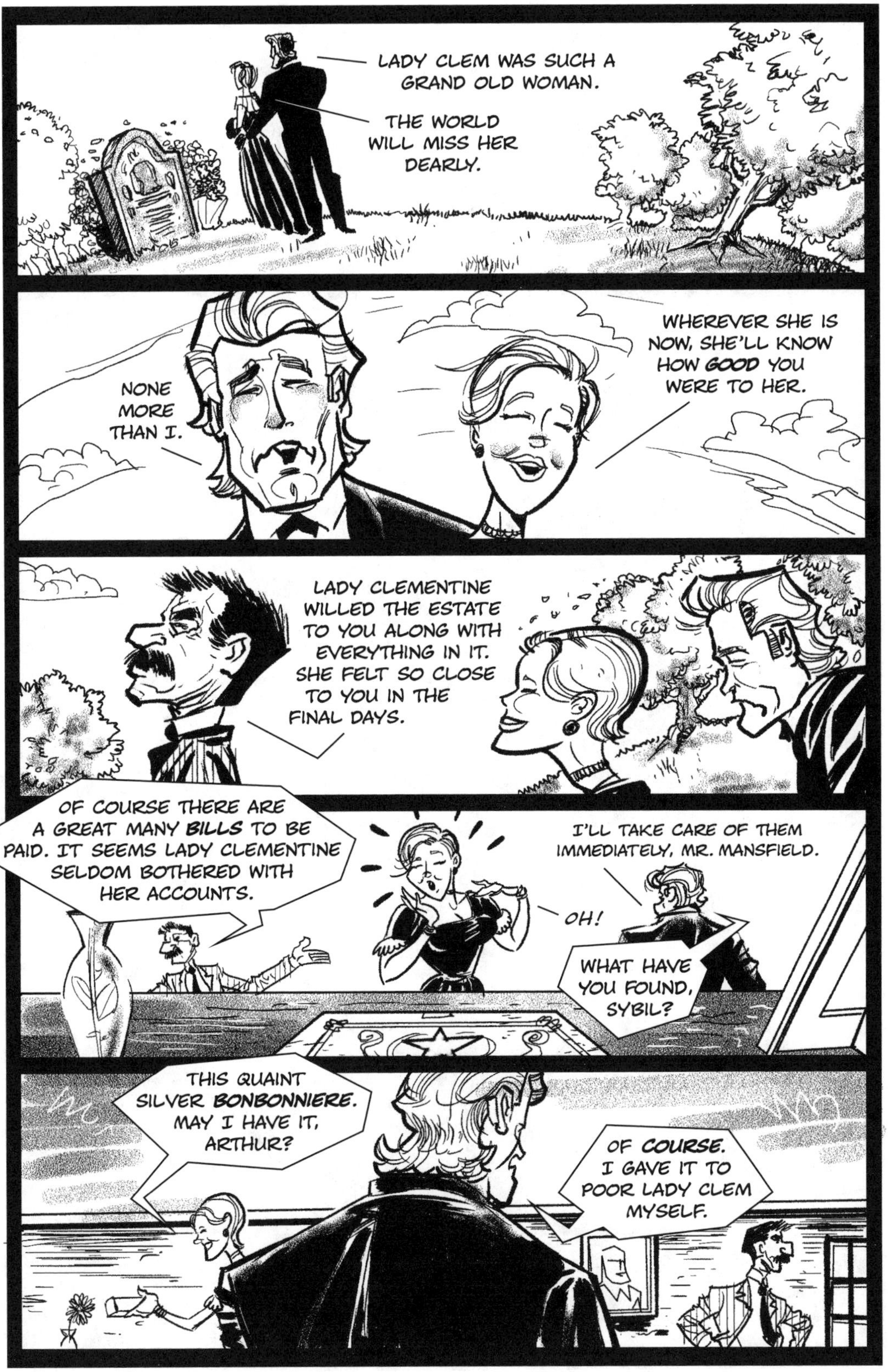
LADY CLEM WAS SUCH A GRAND OLD WOMAN.
THE WORLD WILL MISS HER DEARLY.
NONE MORE THAN I.
WHEREVER SHE IS NOW, SHE'LL KNOW HOW **GOOD** YOU WERE TO HER.
LADY CLEMENTINE WILLED THE ESTATE TO YOU ALONG WITH EVERYTHING IN IT. SHE FELT SO CLOSE TO YOU IN THE FINAL DAYS.
OF COURSE THERE ARE A GREAT MANY **BILLS** TO BE PAID. IT SEEMS LADY CLEMENTINE SELDOM BOTHERED WITH HER ACCOUNTS.
I'LL TAKE CARE OF THEM IMMEDIATELY, MR. MANSFIELD.
OH!
WHAT HAVE YOU FOUND, SYBIL?
THIS QUAINT SILVER **BONBONNIERE**. MAY I HAVE IT, ARTHUR?
OF **COURSE**. I GAVE IT TO POOR LADY CLEM MYSELF.

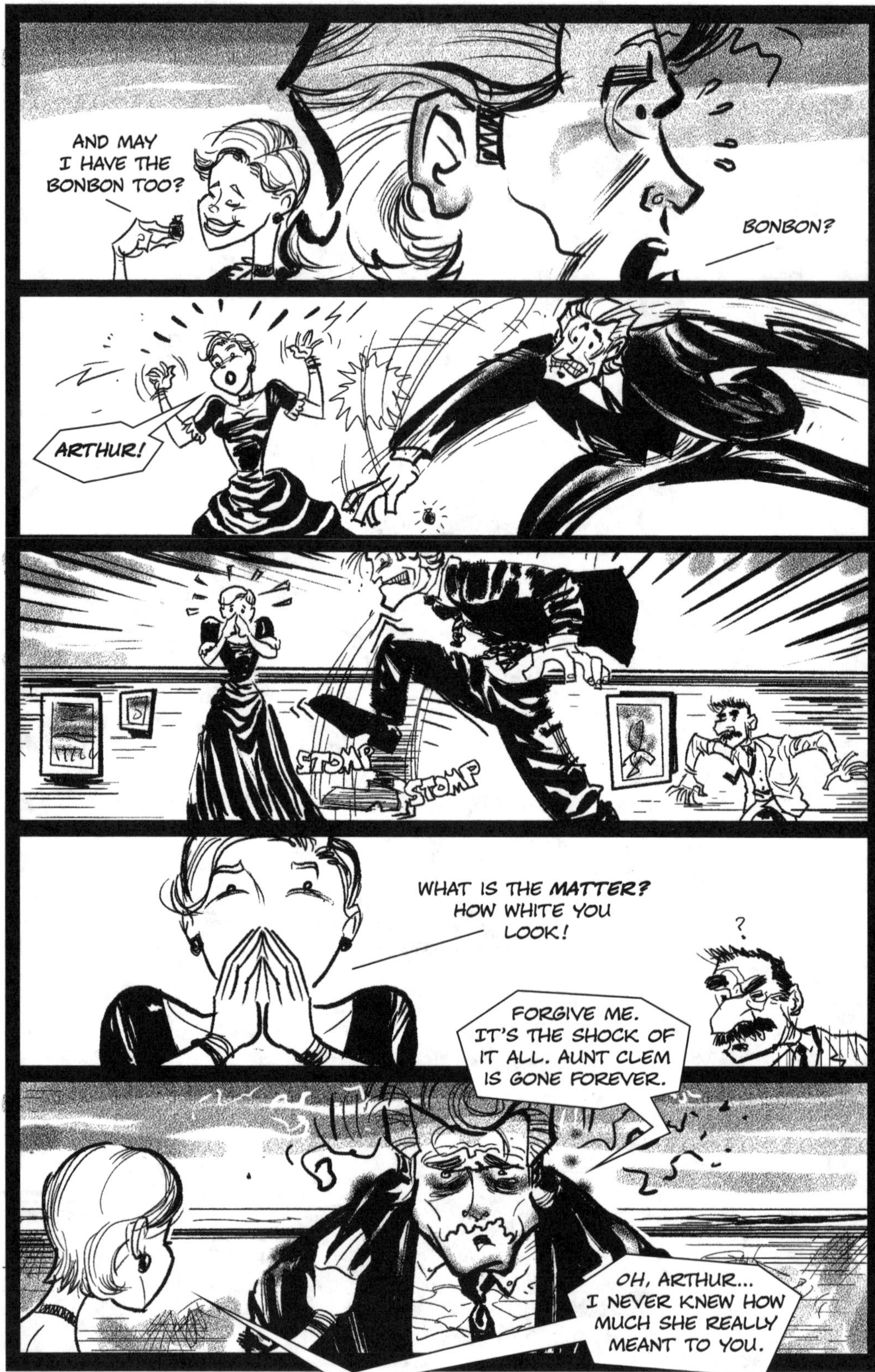
AND MAY I HAVE THE BONBON TOO?
BONBON?
ARTHUR!
STOMP
STOMP
WHAT IS THE MATTER? HOW WHITE YOU LOOK!
?
FORGIVE ME. IT'S THE SHOCK OF IT ALL. AUNT CLEM IS GONE FOREVER.
OH, ARTHUR... I NEVER KNEW HOW MUCH SHE REALLY MEANT TO YOU.

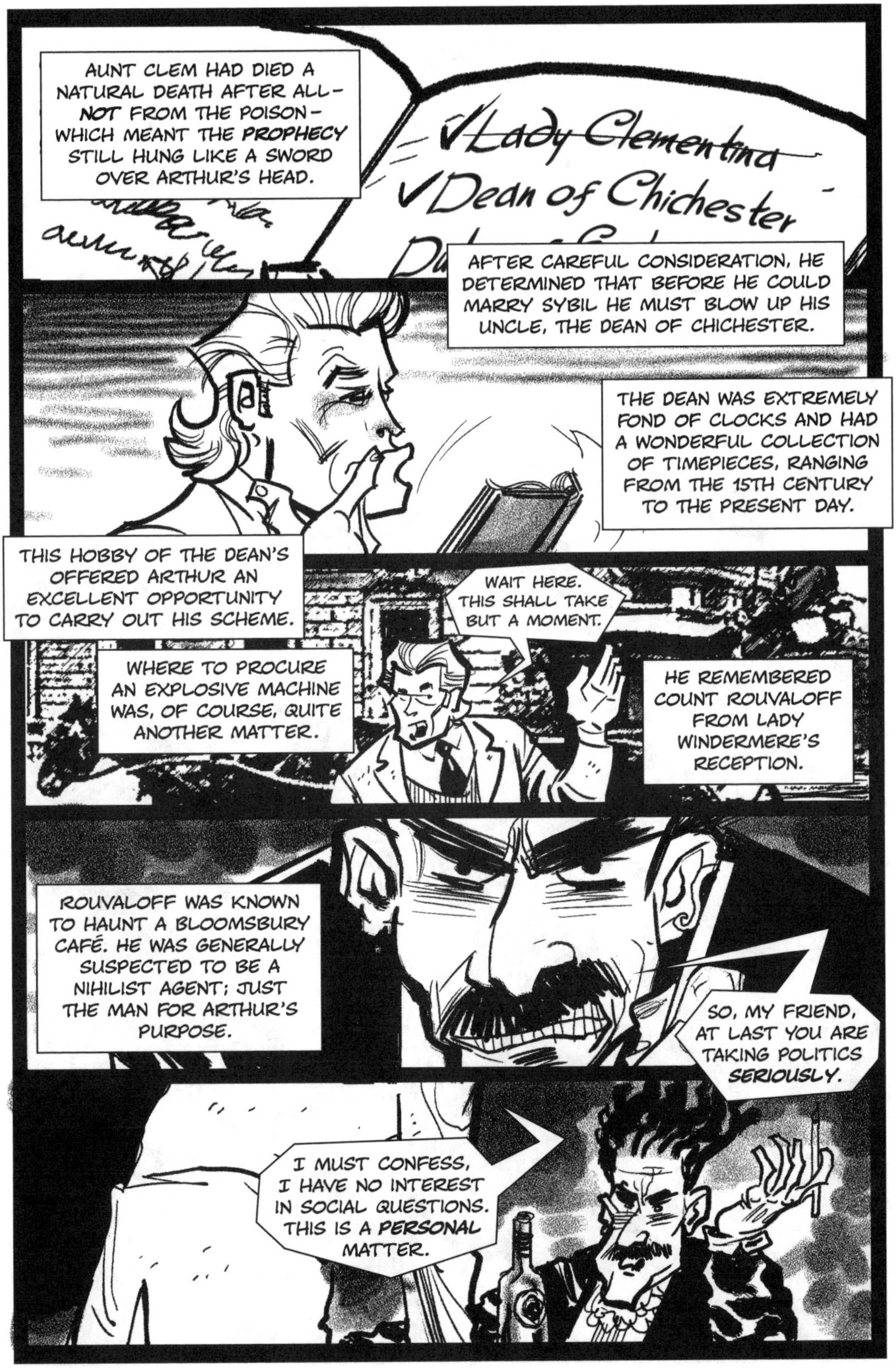
AUNT CLEM HAD DIED A NATURAL DEATH AFTER ALL– NOT FROM THE POISON– WHICH MEANT THE PROPHECY STILL HUNG LIKE A SWORD OVER ARTHUR'S HEAD.
√Lady Clementina
√Dean of Chichester
AFTER CAREFUL CONSIDERATION, HE DETERMINED THAT BEFORE HE COULD MARRY SYBIL HE MUST BLOW UP HIS UNCLE, THE DEAN OF CHICHESTER.
THE DEAN WAS EXTREMELY FOND OF CLOCKS AND HAD A WONDERFUL COLLECTION OF TIMEPIECES, RANGING FROM THE 15TH CENTURY TO THE PRESENT DAY.
THIS HOBBY OF THE DEAN'S OFFERED ARTHUR AN EXCELLENT OPPORTUNITY TO CARRY OUT HIS SCHEME.
WAIT HERE. THIS SHALL TAKE BUT A MOMENT.
WHERE TO PROCURE AN EXPLOSIVE MACHINE WAS, OF COURSE, QUITE ANOTHER MATTER.
HE REMEMBERED COUNT ROUVALOFF FROM LADY WINDERMERE'S RECEPTION.
ROUVALOFF WAS KNOWN TO HAUNT A BLOOMSBURY CAFÉ. HE WAS GENERALLY SUSPECTED TO BE A NIHILIST AGENT; JUST THE MAN FOR ARTHUR'S PURPOSE.
SO, MY FRIEND, AT LAST YOU ARE TAKING POLITICS SERIOUSLY.
I MUST CONFESS, I HAVE NO INTEREST IN SOCIAL QUESTIONS. THIS IS A PERSONAL MATTER.

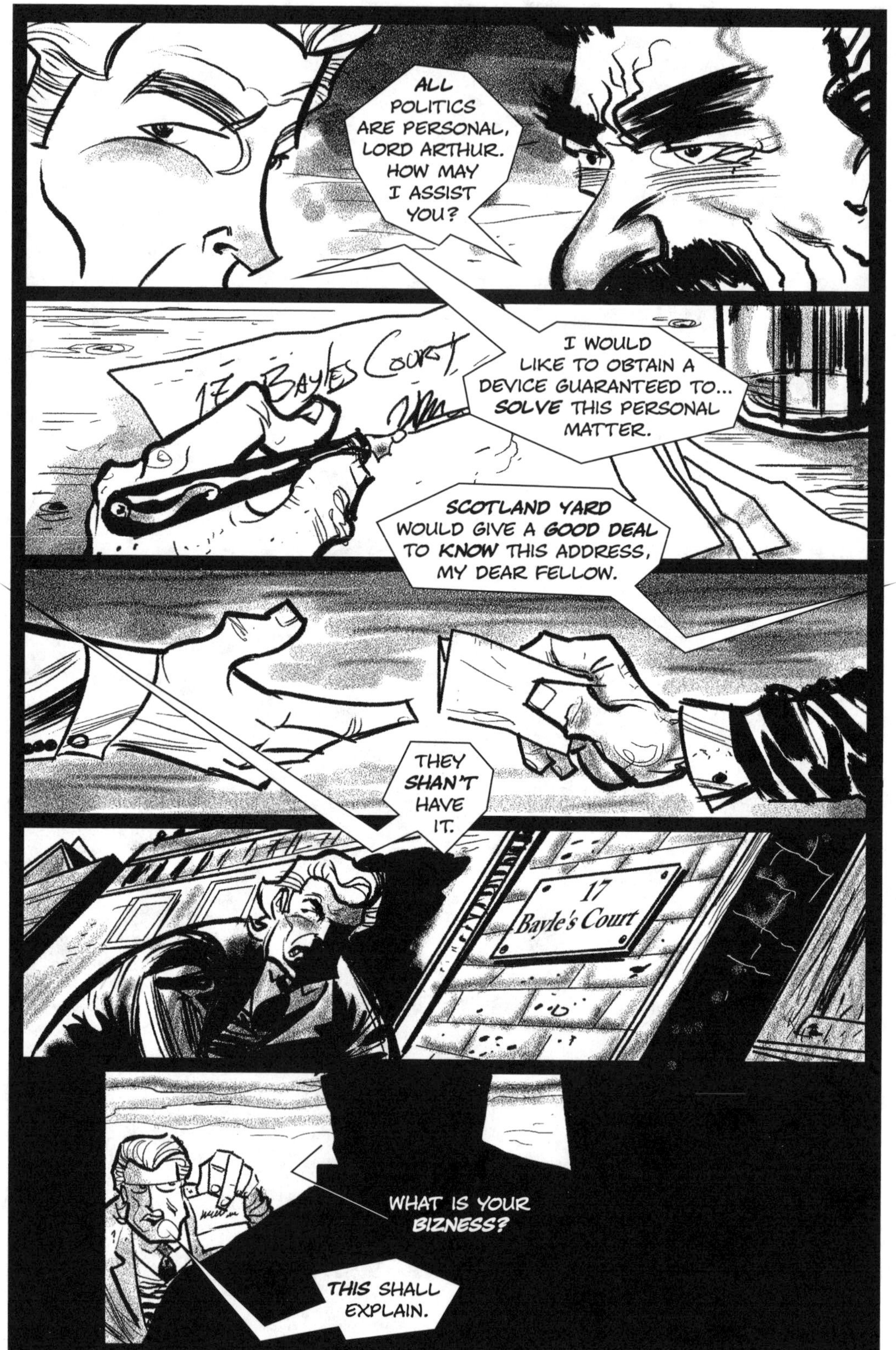
ALL POLITICS ARE PERSONAL, LORD ARTHUR. HOW MAY I ASSIST YOU?
17 Bayles Court
I WOULD LIKE TO OBTAIN A DEVICE GUARANTEED TO... SOLVE THIS PERSONAL MATTER.
SCOTLAND YARD WOULD GIVE A GOOD DEAL TO KNOW THIS ADDRESS, MY DEAR FELLOW.
THEY SHAN'T HAVE IT.
17 Bayle's Court
WHAT IS YOUR BIZNESS?
THIS SHALL EXPLAIN.

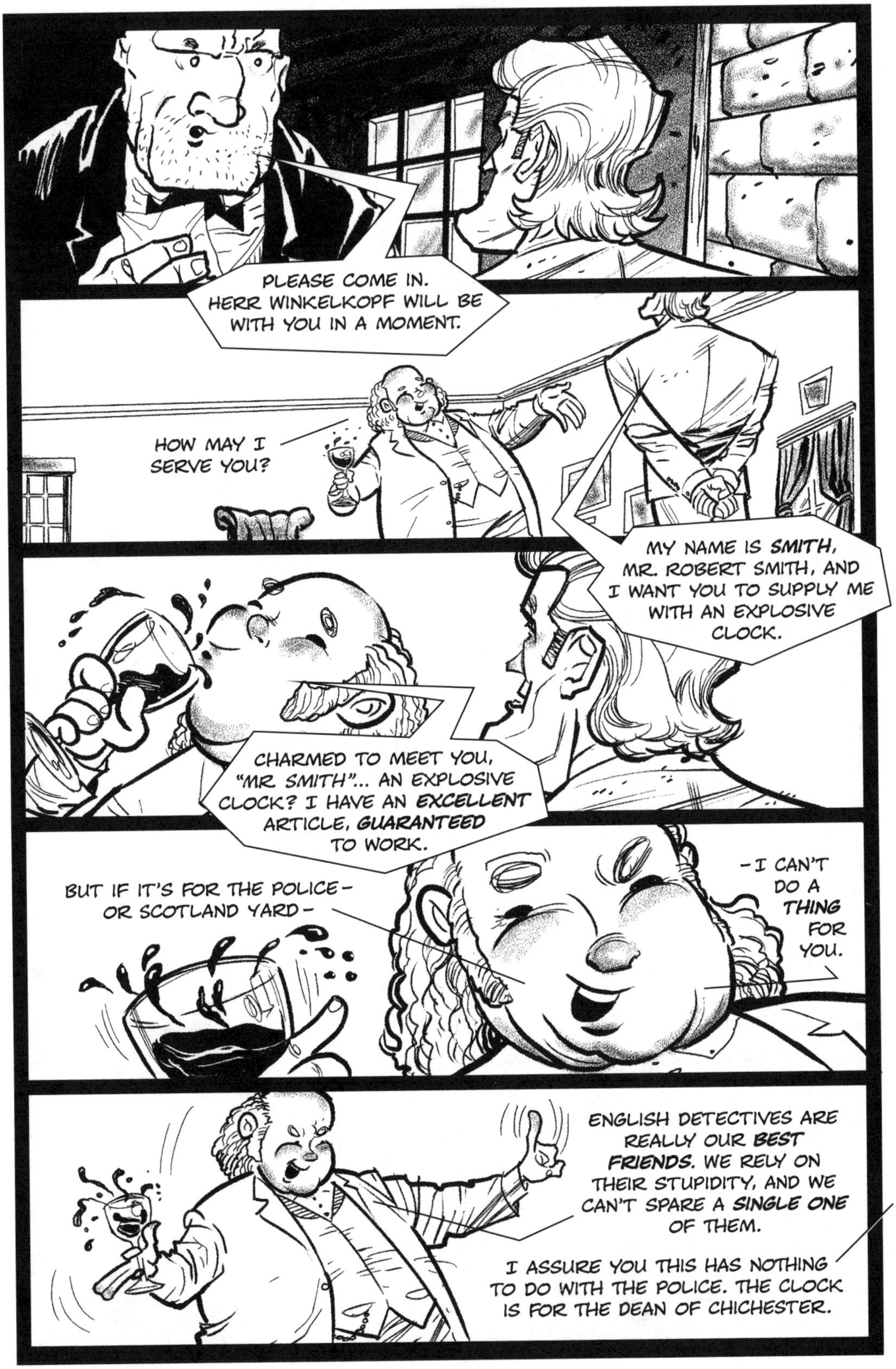
PLEASE COME IN. HERR WINKELKOPF WILL BE WITH YOU IN A MOMENT.
HOW MAY I SERVE YOU?
MY NAME IS **SMITH**, MR. ROBERT SMITH, AND I WANT YOU TO SUPPLY ME WITH AN EXPLOSIVE CLOCK.
CHARMED TO MEET YOU, "MR SMITH"... AN EXPLOSIVE CLOCK? I HAVE AN **EXCELLENT** ARTICLE, **GUARANTEED** TO WORK.
BUT IF IT'S FOR THE POLICE– OR SCOTLAND YARD–
–I CAN'T DO A **THING** FOR YOU.
ENGLISH DETECTIVES ARE REALLY OUR **BEST FRIENDS**. WE RELY ON THEIR STUPIDITY, AND WE CAN'T SPARE A **SINGLE ONE** OF THEM.
I ASSURE YOU THIS HAS NOTHING TO DO WITH THE POLICE. THE CLOCK IS FOR THE DEAN OF CHICHESTER.

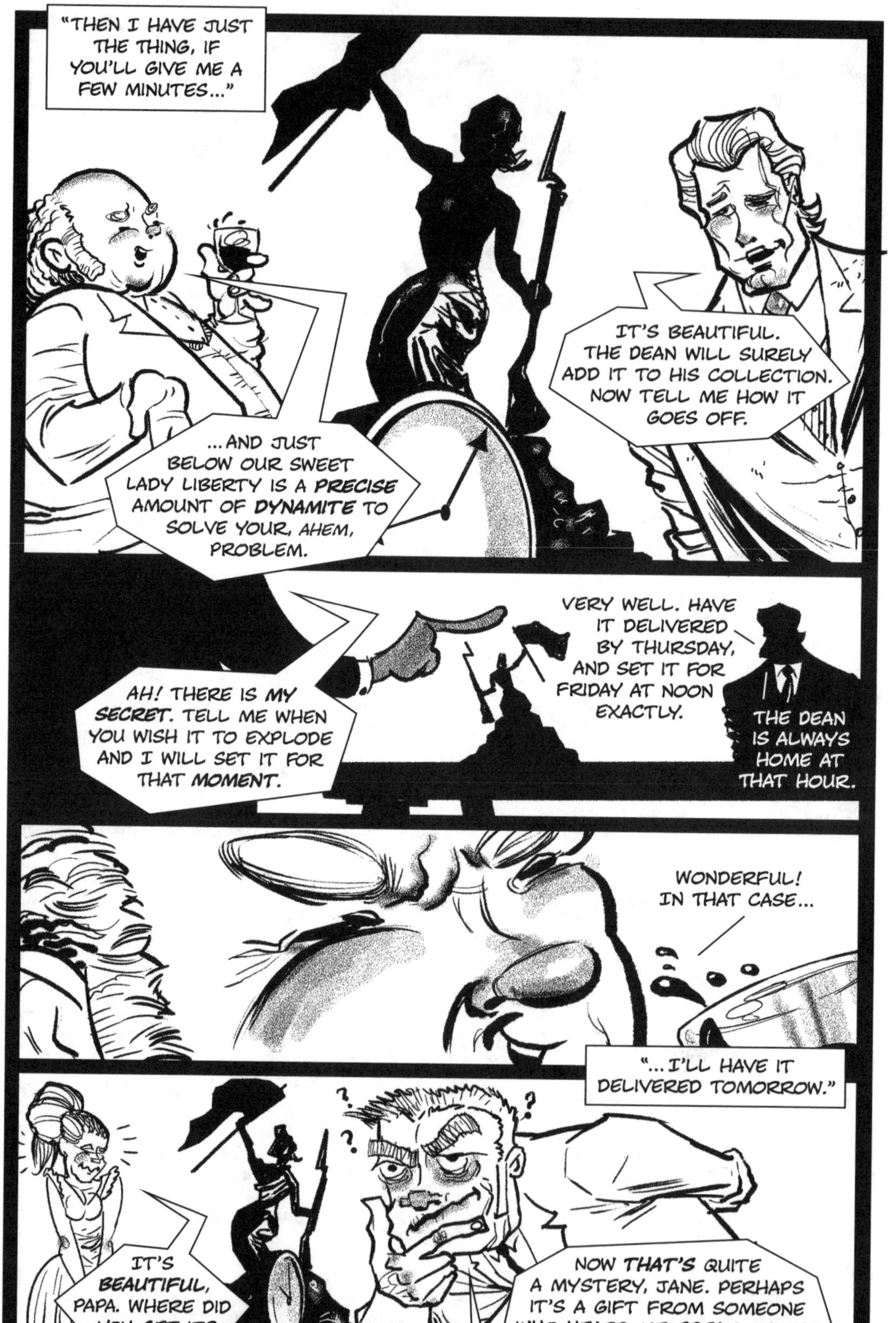
"THEN I HAVE JUST THE THING, IF YOU'LL GIVE ME A FEW MINUTES..."
IT'S BEAUTIFUL. THE DEAN WILL SURELY ADD IT TO HIS COLLECTION. NOW TELL ME HOW IT GOES OFF.
...AND JUST BELOW OUR SWEET LADY LIBERTY IS A PRECISE AMOUNT OF DYNAMITE TO SOLVE YOUR, AHEM, PROBLEM.
AH! THERE IS MY SECRET. TELL ME WHEN YOU WISH IT TO EXPLODE AND I WILL SET IT FOR THAT MOMENT.
VERY WELL. HAVE IT DELIVERED BY THURSDAY, AND SET IT FOR FRIDAY AT NOON EXACTLY.
THE DEAN IS ALWAYS HOME AT THAT HOUR.
WONDERFUL! IN THAT CASE...
"...I'LL HAVE IT DELIVERED TOMORROW."
IT'S BEAUTIFUL, PAPA. WHERE DID YOU GET IT?
NOW THAT'S QUITE A MYSTERY, JANE. PERHAPS IT'S A GIFT FROM SOMEONE WHO HEARD ME SPEAK ON THE POTENTIAL HAZARDS OF TOO MUCH LIBERTY.

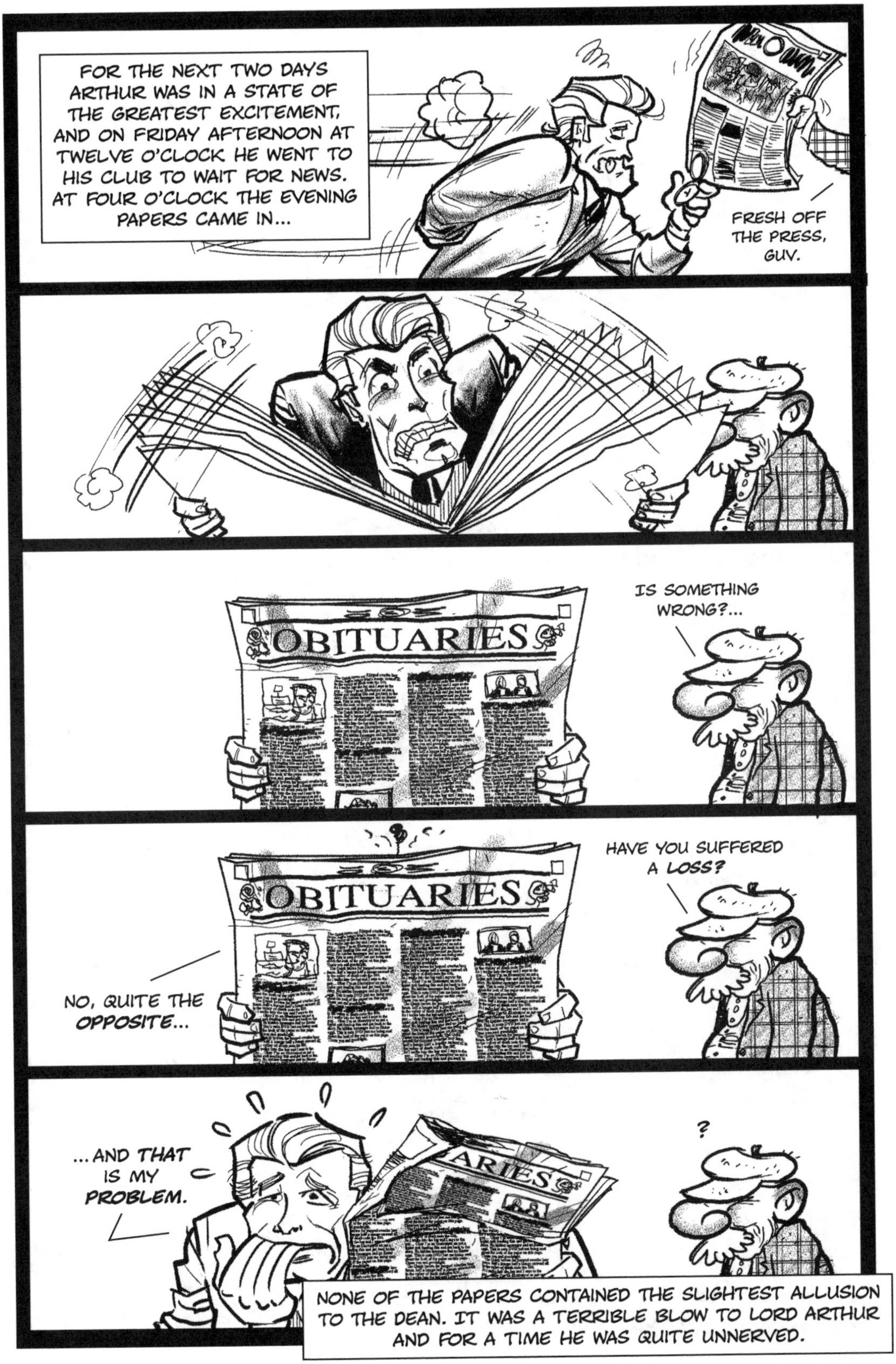
FOR THE NEXT TWO DAYS ARTHUR WAS IN A STATE OF THE GREATEST EXCITEMENT, AND ON FRIDAY AFTERNOON AT TWELVE O'CLOCK HE WENT TO HIS CLUB TO WAIT FOR NEWS. AT FOUR O'CLOCK THE EVENING PAPERS CAME IN...
FRESH OFF THE PRESS, GUV.
OBITUARIES
IS SOMETHING WRONG?...
OBITUARIES
HAVE YOU SUFFERED A LOSS?
NO, QUITE THE OPPOSITE...
?
...AND THAT IS MY PROBLEM.
ARIES
NONE OF THE PAPERS CONTAINED THE SLIGHTEST ALLUSION TO THE DEAN. IT WAS A TERRIBLE BLOW TO LORD ARTHUR AND FOR A TIME HE WAS QUITE UNNERVED.

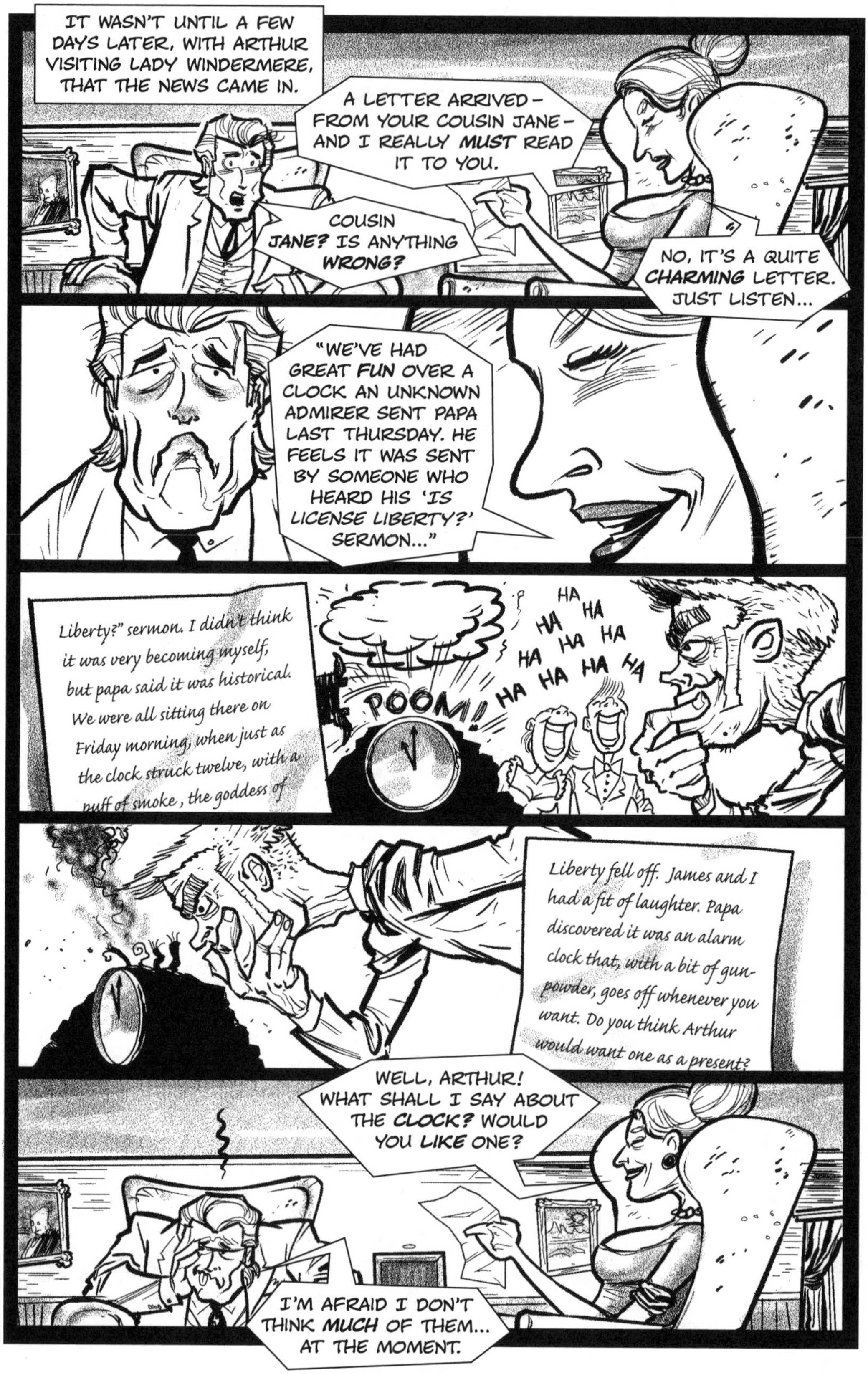
IT WASN'T UNTIL A FEW DAYS LATER, WITH ARTHUR VISITING LADY WINDERMERE, THAT THE NEWS CAME IN.
A LETTER ARRIVED—FROM YOUR COUSIN JANE—AND I REALLY MUST READ IT TO YOU.
COUSIN JANE? IS ANYTHING WRONG?
NO, IT'S A QUITE CHARMING LETTER. JUST LISTEN...
"WE'VE HAD GREAT FUN OVER A CLOCK AN UNKNOWN ADMIRER SENT PAPA LAST THURSDAY. HE FEELS IT WAS SENT BY SOMEONE WHO HEARD HIS 'IS LICENSE LIBERTY?' SERMON..."
Liberty?" sermon. I didn't think it was very becoming myself, but papa said it was historical. We were all sitting there on Friday morning, when just as the clock struck twelve, with a puff of smoke, the goddess of
POOM!
HA HA HA HA HA HA HA HA HA HA
Liberty fell off. James and I had a fit of laughter. Papa discovered it was an alarm clock that, with a bit of gun-powder, goes off whenever you want. Do you think Arthur would want one as a present?
WELL, ARTHUR! WHAT SHALL I SAY ABOUT THE CLOCK? WOULD YOU LIKE ONE?
I'M AFRAID I DON'T THINK MUCH OF THEM... AT THE MOMENT.

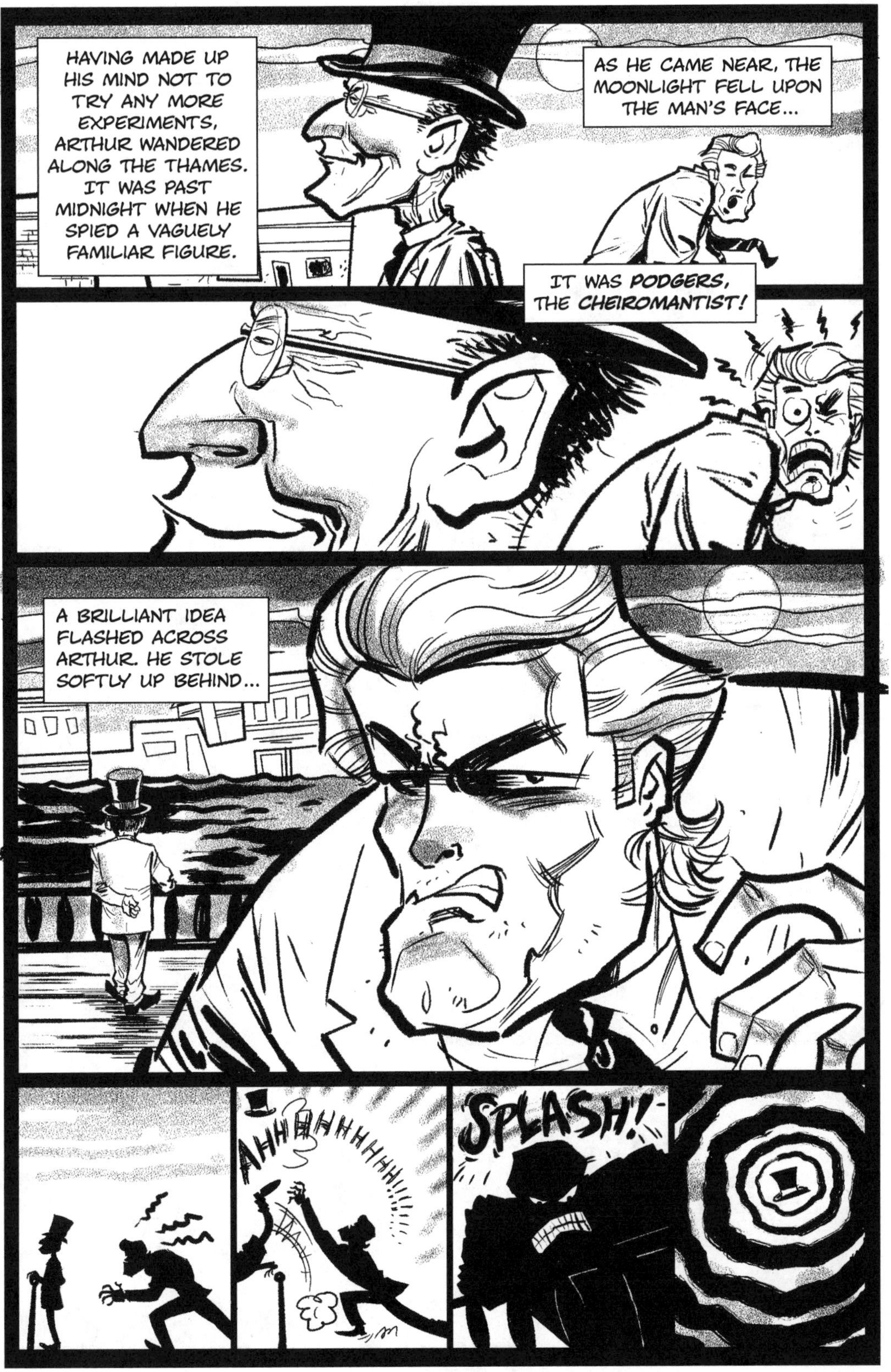
HAVING MADE UP HIS MIND NOT TO TRY ANY MORE EXPERIMENTS, ARTHUR WANDERED ALONG THE THAMES. IT WAS PAST MIDNIGHT WHEN HE SPIED A VAGUELY FAMILIAR FIGURE.
AS HE CAME NEAR, THE MOONLIGHT FELL UPON THE MAN'S FACE...
IT WAS PODGERS, THE CHEIROMANTIST!
A BRILLIANT IDEA FLASHED ACROSS ARTHUR. HE STOLE SOFTLY UP BEHIND...
AHHHHHHHHHH
SPLASH!

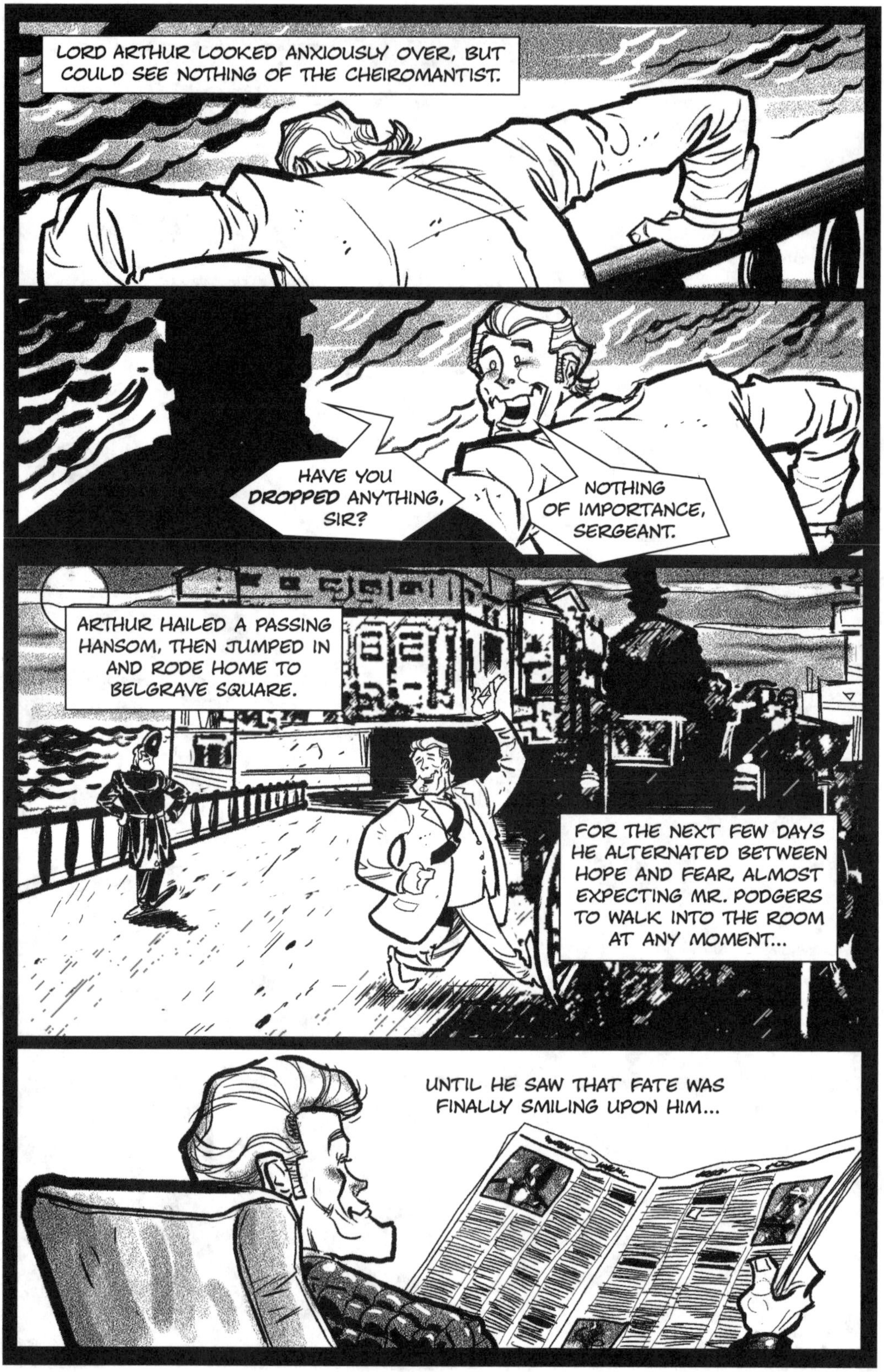
LORD ARTHUR LOOKED ANXIOUSLY OVER, BUT COULD SEE NOTHING OF THE CHEIROMANTIST.
HAVE YOU DROPPED ANYTHING, SIR?
NOTHING OF IMPORTANCE, SERGEANT.
ARTHUR HAILED A PASSING HANSOM, THEN JUMPED IN AND RODE HOME TO BELGRAVE SQUARE.
FOR THE NEXT FEW DAYS HE ALTERNATED BETWEEN HOPE AND FEAR, ALMOST EXPECTING MR. PODGERS TO WALK INTO THE ROOM AT ANY MOMENT...
UNTIL HE SAW THAT FATE WAS FINALLY SMILING UPON HIM...

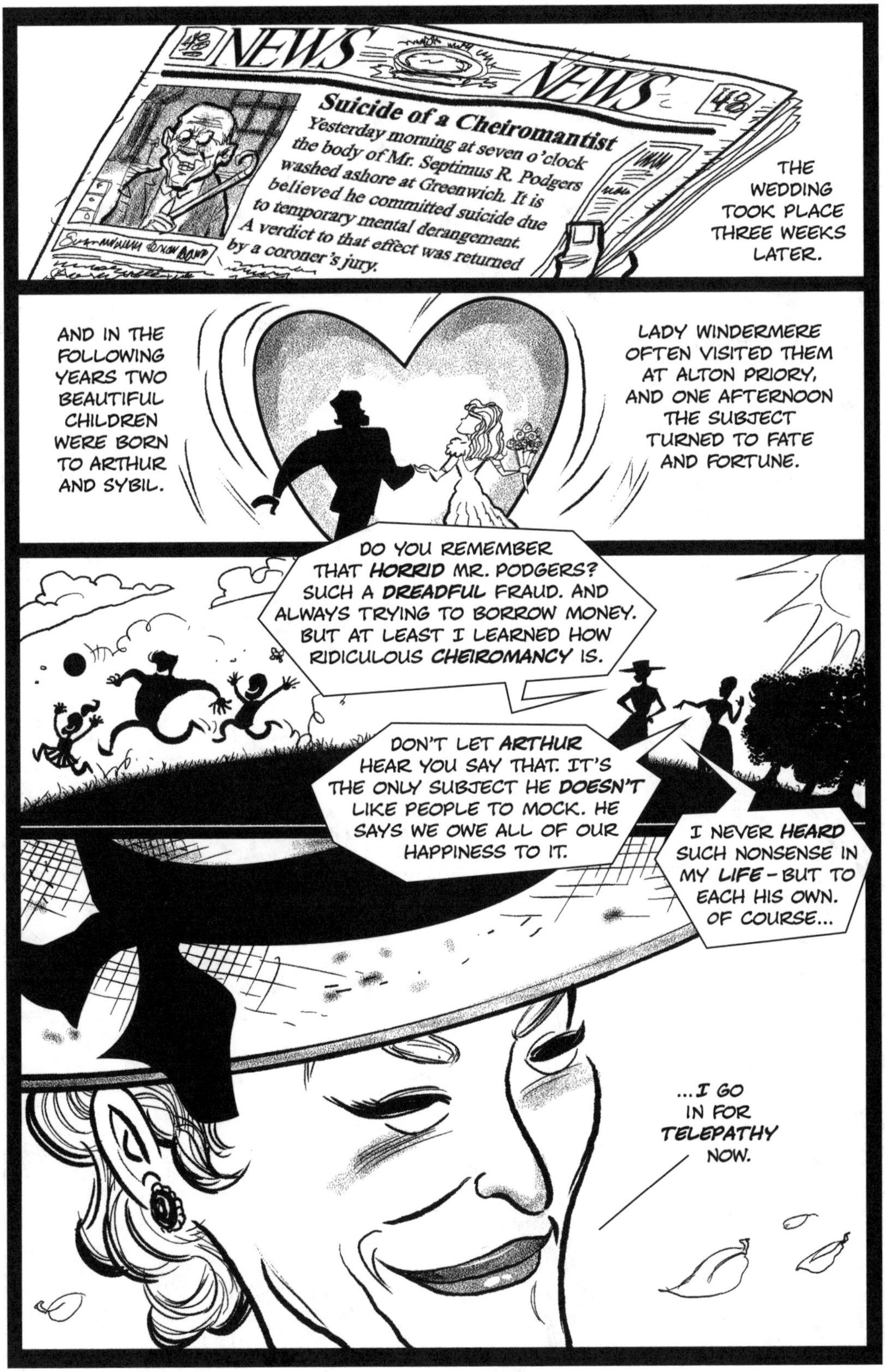
NEWS
NEWS
Suicide of a Cheiromantist
Yesterday morning at seven o'clock the body of Mr. Septimus R. Podgers washed ashore at Greenwich. It is believed he committed suicide due to temporary mental derangement. A verdict to that effect was returned by a coroner's jury.
THE WEDDING TOOK PLACE THREE WEEKS LATER.
AND IN THE FOLLOWING YEARS TWO BEAUTIFUL CHILDREN WERE BORN TO ARTHUR AND SYBIL.
LADY WINDERMERE OFTEN VISITED THEM AT ALTON PRIORY, AND ONE AFTERNOON THE SUBJECT TURNED TO FATE AND FORTUNE.
DO YOU REMEMBER THAT HORRID MR. PODGERS? SUCH A DREADFUL FRAUD. AND ALWAYS TRYING TO BORROW MONEY. BUT AT LEAST I LEARNED HOW RIDICULOUS CHEIROMANCY IS.
DON'T LET ARTHUR HEAR YOU SAY THAT. IT'S THE ONLY SUBJECT HE DOESN'T LIKE PEOPLE TO MOCK. HE SAYS WE OWE ALL OF OUR HAPPINESS TO IT.
I NEVER HEARD SUCH NONSENSE IN MY LIFE - BUT TO EACH HIS OWN. OF COURSE...
...I GO IN FOR TELEPATHY NOW.

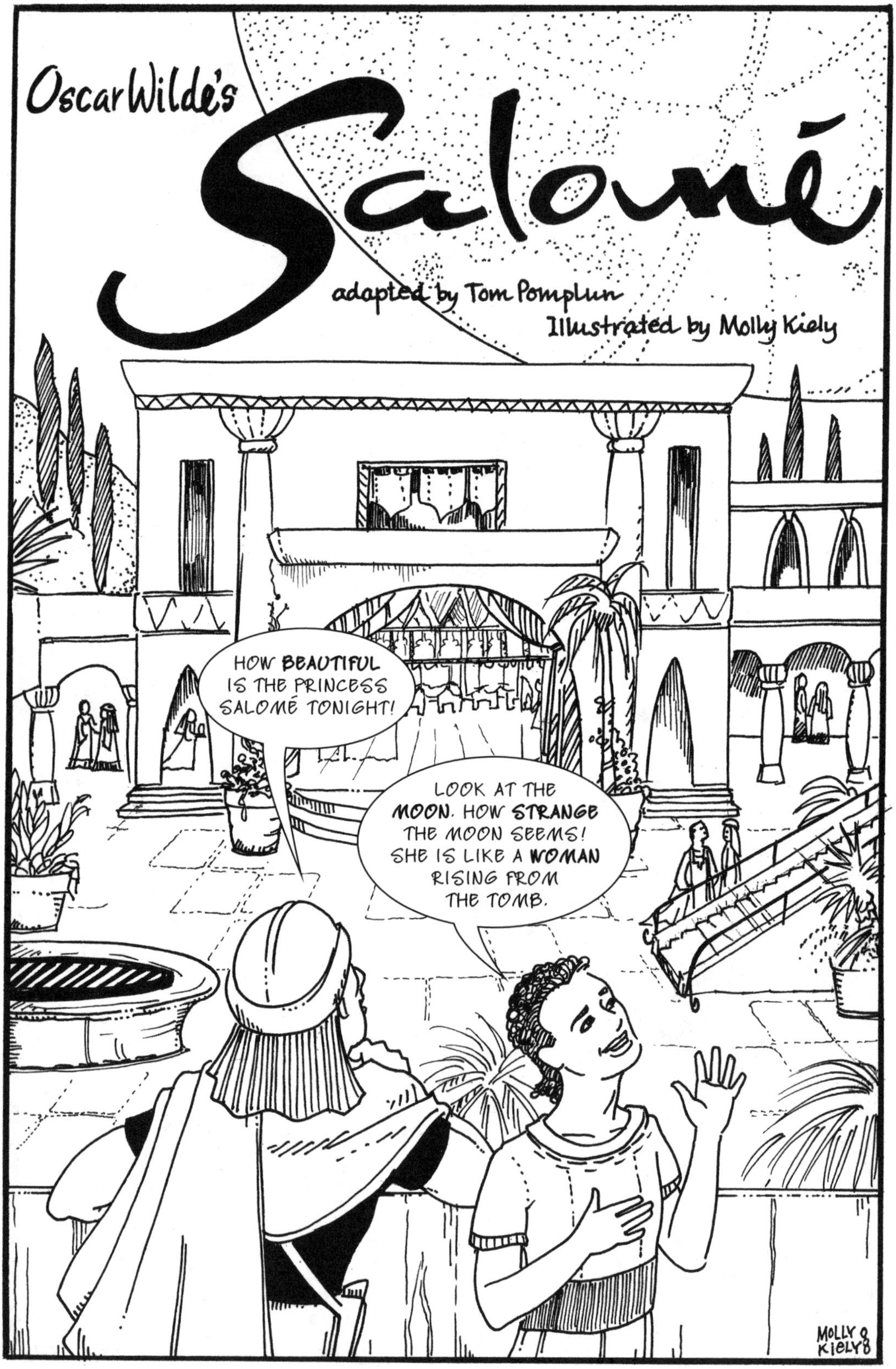
Oscar Wilde's
Salomé
adapted by Tom Pomplun
Illustrated by Molly Kiely
HOW BEAUTIFUL IS THE PRINCESS SALOMÉ TONIGHT!
LOOK AT THE MOON. HOW STRANGE THE MOON SEEMS! SHE IS LIKE A WOMAN RISING FROM THE TOMB.
MOLLY KIELY

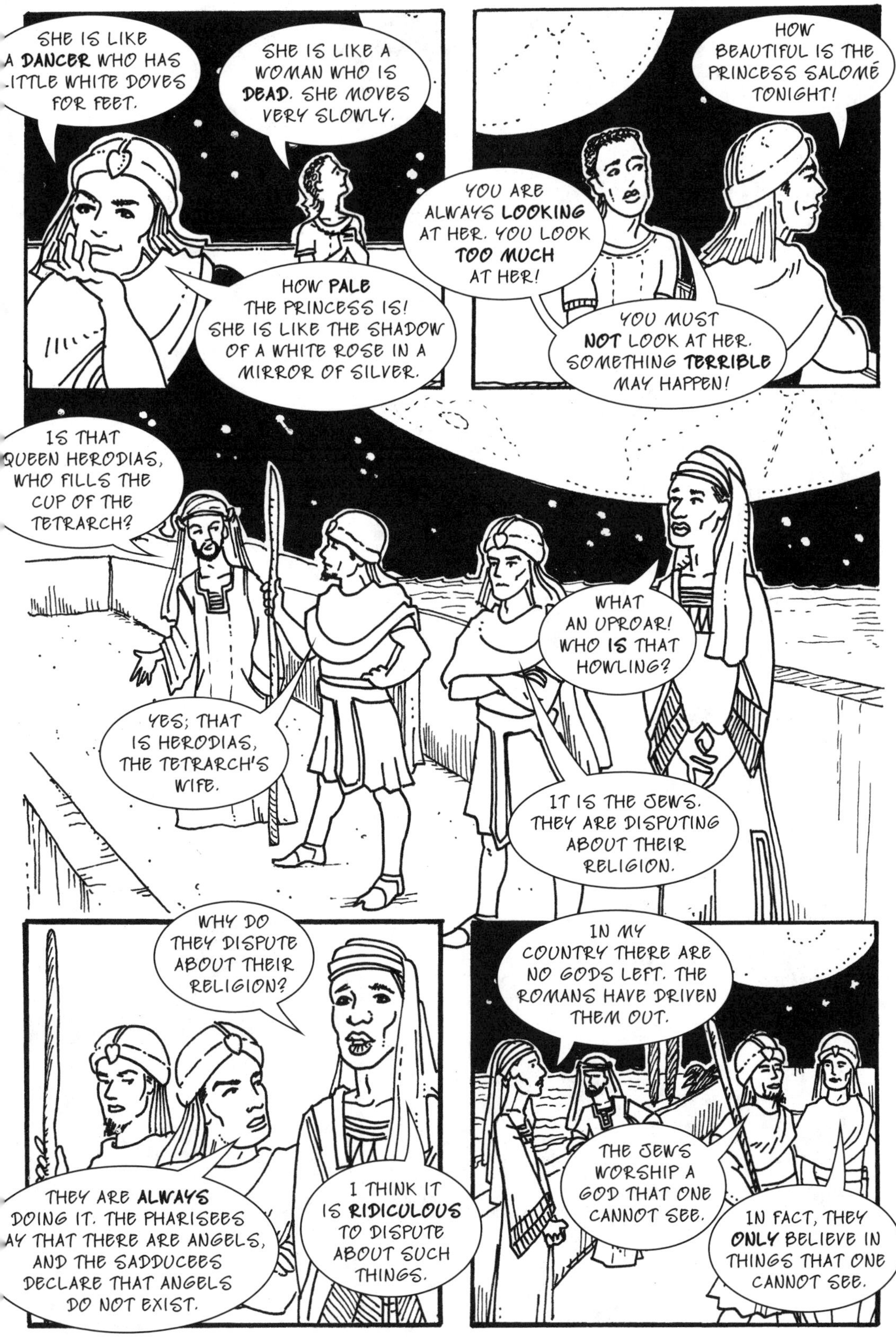

SHE IS LIKE A DANCER WHO HAS ITTLE WHITE DOVES FOR FEET.
SHE IS LIKE A WOMAN WHO IS DEAD. SHE MOVES VERY SLOWLY.
HOW PALE THE PRINCESS IS! SHE IS LIKE THE SHADOW OF A WHITE ROSE IN A MIRROR OF SILVER.
HOW BEAUTIFUL IS THE PRINCESS SALOMÉ TONIGHT!
YOU ARE ALWAYS LOOKING AT HER. YOU LOOK TOO MUCH AT HER!
YOU MUST NOT LOOK AT HER. SOMETHING TERRIBLE MAY HAPPEN!
IS THAT QUEEN HERODIAS, WHO FILLS THE CUP OF THE TETRARCH?
YES; THAT IS HERODIAS, THE TETRARCH'S WIFE.
WHAT AN UPROAR! WHO IS THAT HOWLING?
IT IS THE JEWS. THEY ARE DISPUTING ABOUT THEIR RELIGION.
WHY DO THEY DISPUTE ABOUT THEIR RELIGION?
THEY ARE ALWAYS DOING IT. THE PHARISEES AY THAT THERE ARE ANGELS, AND THE SADDUCEES DECLARE THAT ANGELS DO NOT EXIST.
I THINK IT IS RIDICULOUS TO DISPUTE ABOUT SUCH THINGS.
IN MY COUNTRY THERE ARE NO GODS LEFT. THE ROMANS HAVE DRIVEN THEM OUT.
THE JEWS WORSHIP A GOD THAT ONE CANNOT SEE.
IN FACT, THEY ONLY BELIEVE IN THINGS THAT ONE CANNOT SEE.

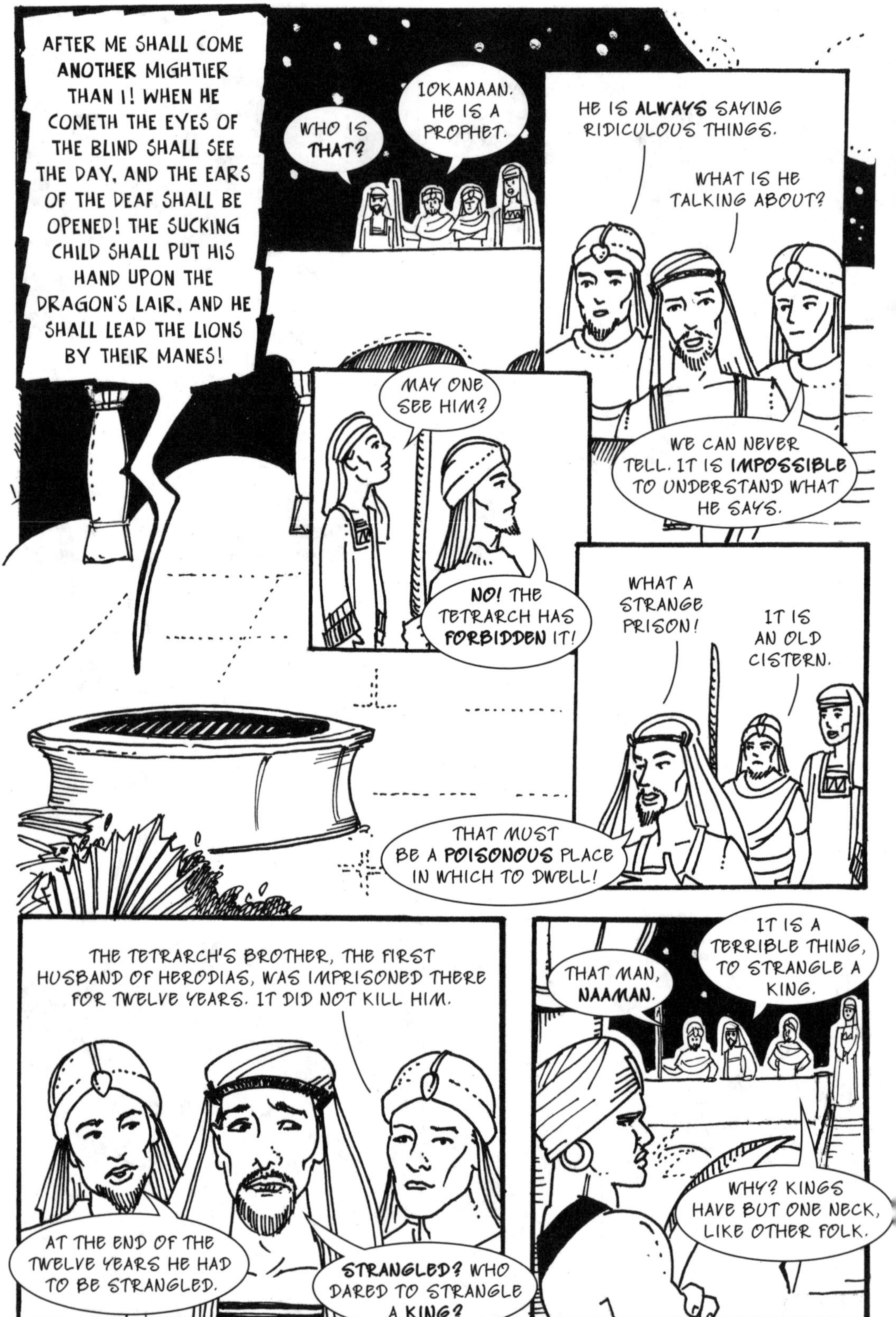
AFTER ME SHALL COME ANOTHER MIGHTIER THAN I! WHEN HE COMETH THE EYES OF THE BLIND SHALL SEE THE DAY, AND THE EARS OF THE DEAF SHALL BE OPENED! THE SUCKING CHILD SHALL PUT HIS HAND UPON THE DRAGON'S LAIR, AND HE SHALL LEAD THE LIONS BY THEIR MANES!
WHO IS THAT?
IOKANAAN. HE IS A PROPHET.
HE IS ALWAYS SAYING RIDICULOUS THINGS.
WHAT IS HE TALKING ABOUT?
WE CAN NEVER TELL. IT IS IMPOSSIBLE TO UNDERSTAND WHAT HE SAYS.
MAY ONE SEE HIM?
NO! THE TETRARCH HAS FORBIDDEN IT!
WHAT A STRANGE PRISON!
IT IS AN OLD CISTERN.
THAT MUST BE A POISONOUS PLACE IN WHICH TO DWELL!
THE TETRARCH'S BROTHER, THE FIRST HUSBAND OF HERODIAS, WAS IMPRISONED THERE FOR TWELVE YEARS. IT DID NOT KILL HIM.
AT THE END OF THE TWELVE YEARS HE HAD TO BE STRANGLED.
STRANGLED? WHO DARED TO STRANGLE A KING?
THAT MAN, NAAMAN.
IT IS A TERRIBLE THING, TO STRANGLE A KING.
WHY? KINGS HAVE BUT ONE NECK, LIKE OTHER FOLK.

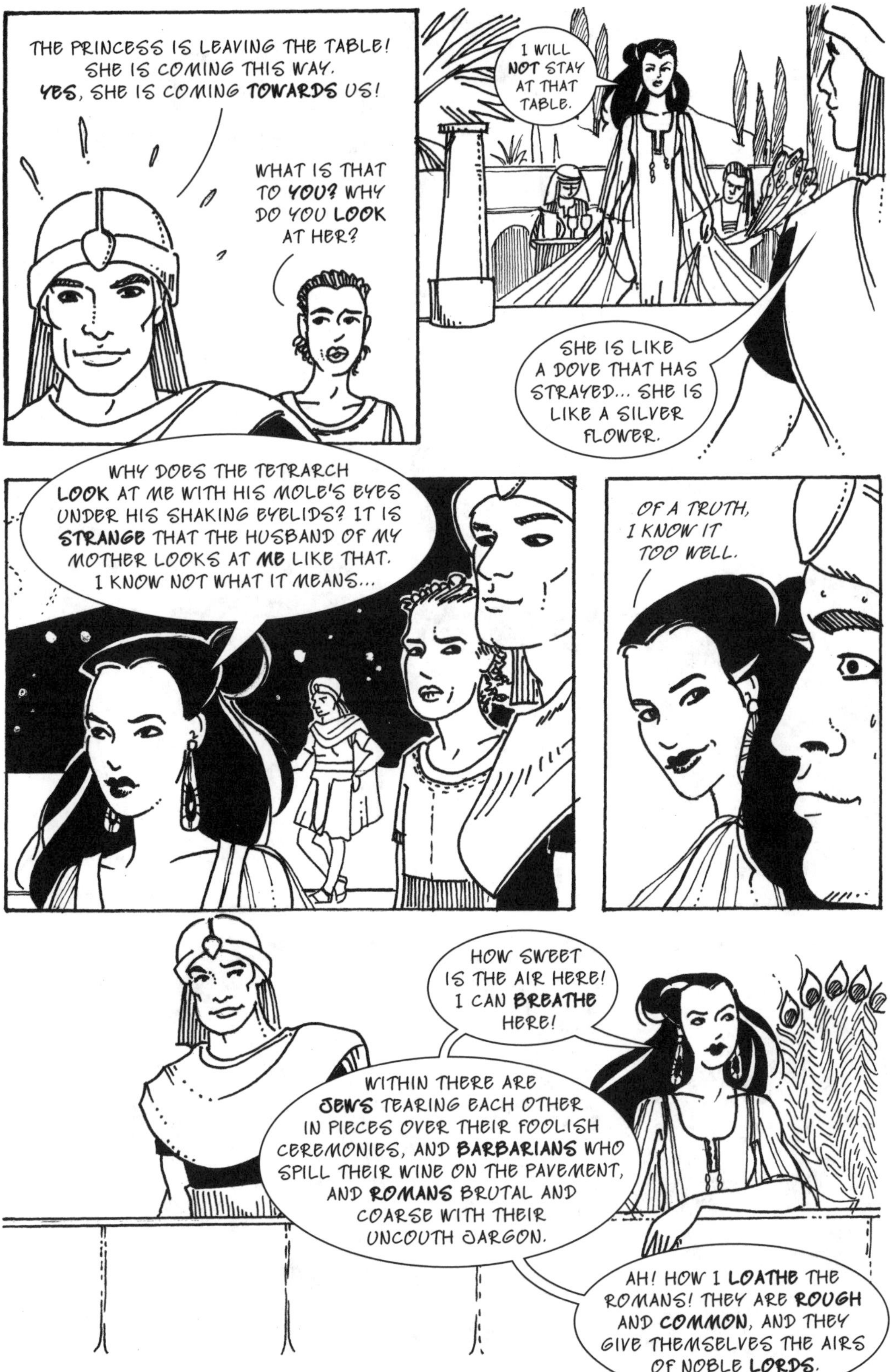
THE PRINCESS IS LEAVING THE TABLE! SHE IS COMING THIS WAY. YES, SHE IS COMING TOWARDS US!
WHAT IS THAT TO YOU? WHY DO YOU LOOK AT HER?
I WILL NOT STAY AT THAT TABLE.
SHE IS LIKE A DOVE THAT HAS STRAYED... SHE IS LIKE A SILVER FLOWER.
WHY DOES THE TETRARCH LOOK AT ME WITH HIS MOLE'S EYES UNDER HIS SHAKING EYELIDS? IT IS STRANGE THAT THE HUSBAND OF MY MOTHER LOOKS AT ME LIKE THAT. I KNOW NOT WHAT IT MEANS...
OF A TRUTH, I KNOW IT TOO WELL.
HOW SWEET IS THE AIR HERE! I CAN BREATHE HERE!
WITHIN THERE ARE JEWS TEARING EACH OTHER IN PIECES OVER THEIR FOOLISH CEREMONIES, AND BARBARIANS WHO SPILL THEIR WINE ON THE PAVEMENT, AND ROMANS BRUTAL AND COARSE WITH THEIR UNCOUTH JARGON.
AH! HOW I LOATHE THE ROMANS! THEY ARE ROUGH AND COMMON, AND THEY GIVE THEMSELVES THE AIRS OF NOBLE LORDS.

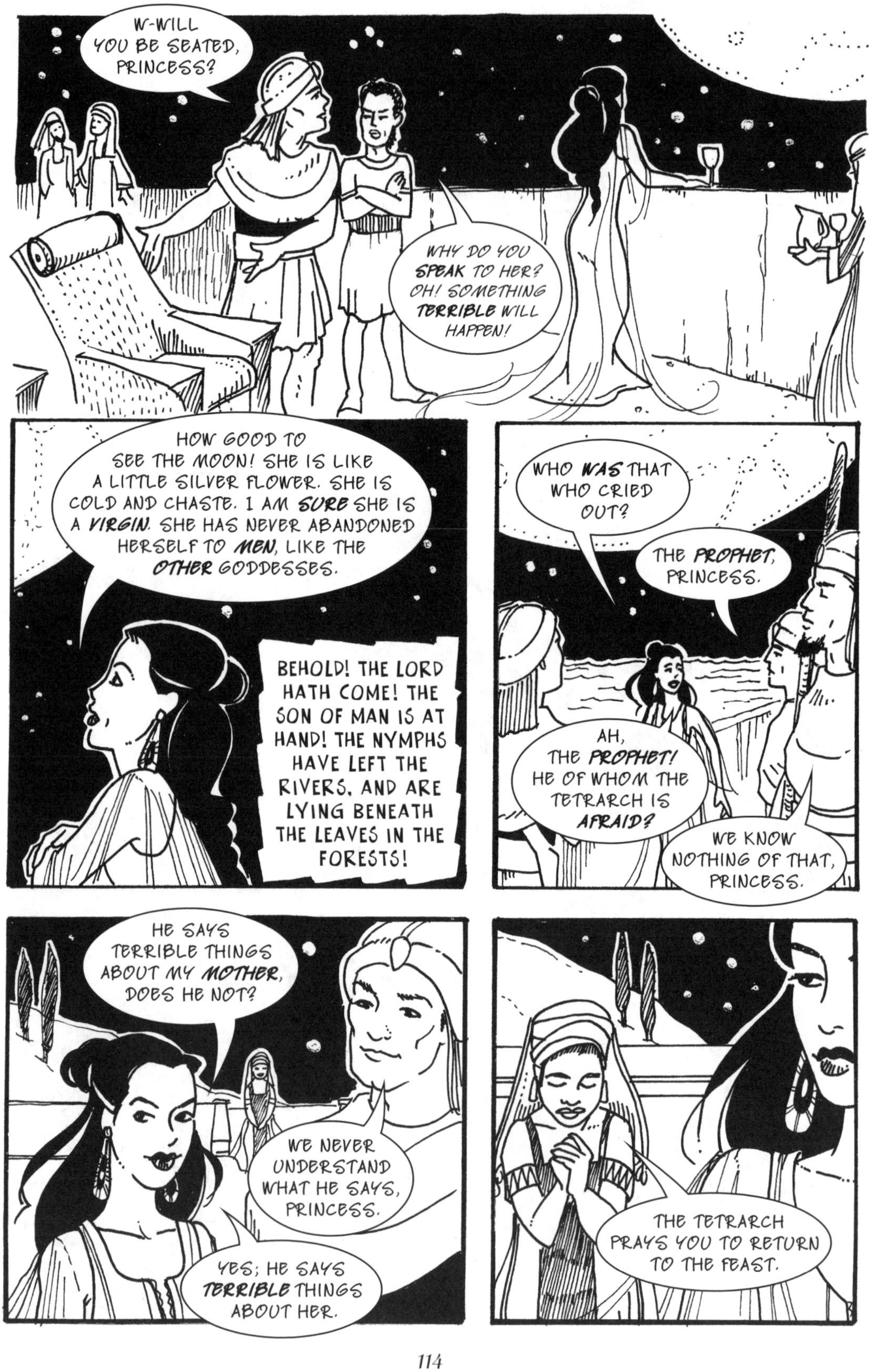
W-WILL YOU BE SEATED, PRINCESS?
WHY DO YOU SPEAK TO HER? OH! SOMETHING TERRIBLE WILL HAPPEN!
HOW GOOD TO SEE THE MOON! SHE IS LIKE A LITTLE SILVER FLOWER. SHE IS COLD AND CHASTE. I AM SURE SHE IS A VIRGIN. SHE HAS NEVER ABANDONED HERSELF TO MEN, LIKE THE OTHER GODDESSES.
BEHOLD! THE LORD HATH COME! THE SON OF MAN IS AT HAND! THE NYMPHS HAVE LEFT THE RIVERS, AND ARE LYING BENEATH THE LEAVES IN THE FORESTS!
WHO WAS THAT WHO CRIED OUT?
THE PROPHET, PRINCESS.
AH, THE PROPHET! HE OF WHOM THE TETRARCH IS AFRAID?
WE KNOW NOTHING OF THAT, PRINCESS.
HE SAYS TERRIBLE THINGS ABOUT MY MOTHER, DOES HE NOT?
WE NEVER UNDERSTAND WHAT HE SAYS, PRINCESS.
YES; HE SAYS TERRIBLE THINGS ABOUT HER.
THE TETRARCH PRAYS YOU TO RETURN TO THE FEAST.

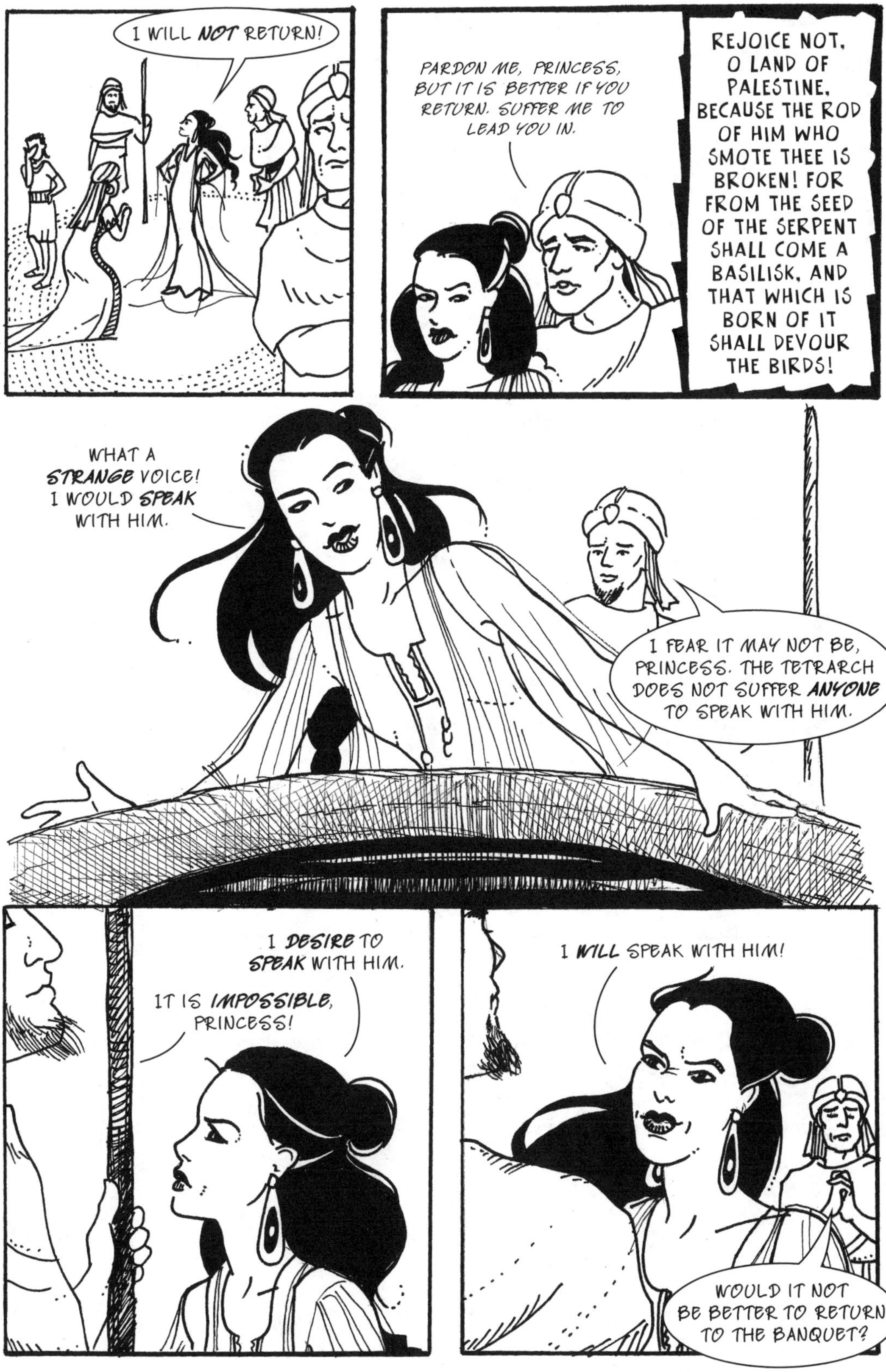
I WILL NOT RETURN!
PARDON ME, PRINCESS, BUT IT IS BETTER IF YOU RETURN. SUFFER ME TO LEAD YOU IN.
REJOICE NOT, O LAND OF PALESTINE, BECAUSE THE ROD OF HIM WHO SMOTE THEE IS BROKEN! FOR FROM THE SEED OF THE SERPENT SHALL COME A BASILISK, AND THAT WHICH IS BORN OF IT SHALL DEVOUR THE BIRDS!
WHAT A STRANGE VOICE! I WOULD SPEAK WITH HIM.
I FEAR IT MAY NOT BE, PRINCESS. THE TETRARCH DOES NOT SUFFER ANYONE TO SPEAK WITH HIM.
I DESIRE TO SPEAK WITH HIM.
IT IS IMPOSSIBLE, PRINCESS!
I WILL SPEAK WITH HIM!
WOULD IT NOT BE BETTER TO RETURN TO THE BANQUET?

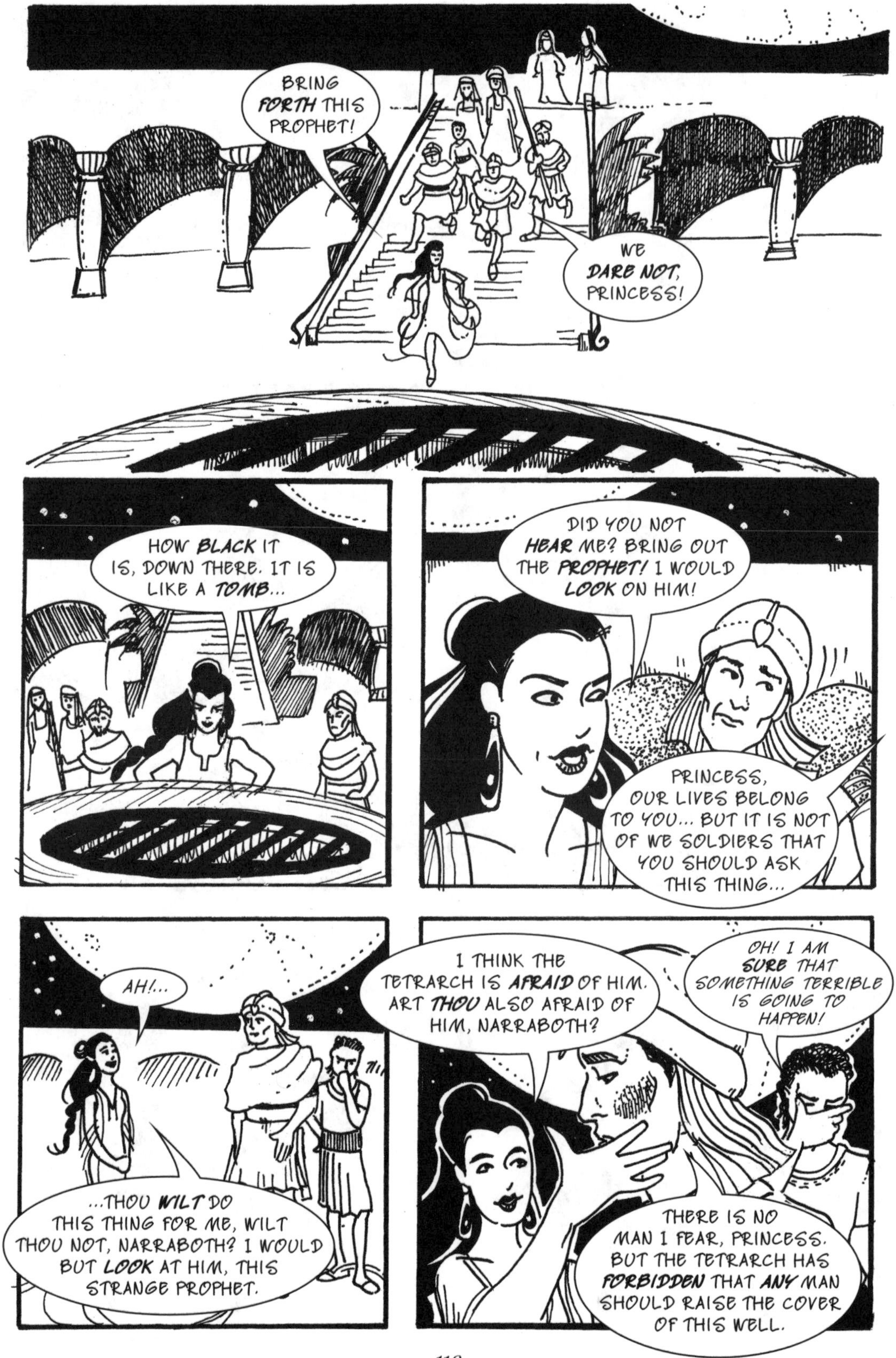
BRING FORTH THIS PROPHET!
WE DARE NOT, PRINCESS!
HOW BLACK IT IS, DOWN THERE. IT IS LIKE A TOMB...
DID YOU NOT HEAR ME? BRING OUT THE PROPHET! I WOULD LOOK ON HIM!
PRINCESS, OUR LIVES BELONG TO YOU... BUT IT IS NOT OF WE SOLDIERS THAT YOU SHOULD ASK THIS THING...
AH!...
...THOU WILT DO THIS THING FOR ME, WILT THOU NOT, NARRABOTH? I WOULD BUT LOOK AT HIM, THIS STRANGE PROPHET.
I THINK THE TETRARCH IS AFRAID OF HIM. ART THOU ALSO AFRAID OF HIM, NARRABOTH?
OH! I AM SURE THAT SOMETHING TERRIBLE IS GOING TO HAPPEN!
THERE IS NO MAN I FEAR, PRINCESS. BUT THE TETRARCH HAS FORBIDDEN THAT ANY MAN SHOULD RAISE THE COVER OF THIS WELL.

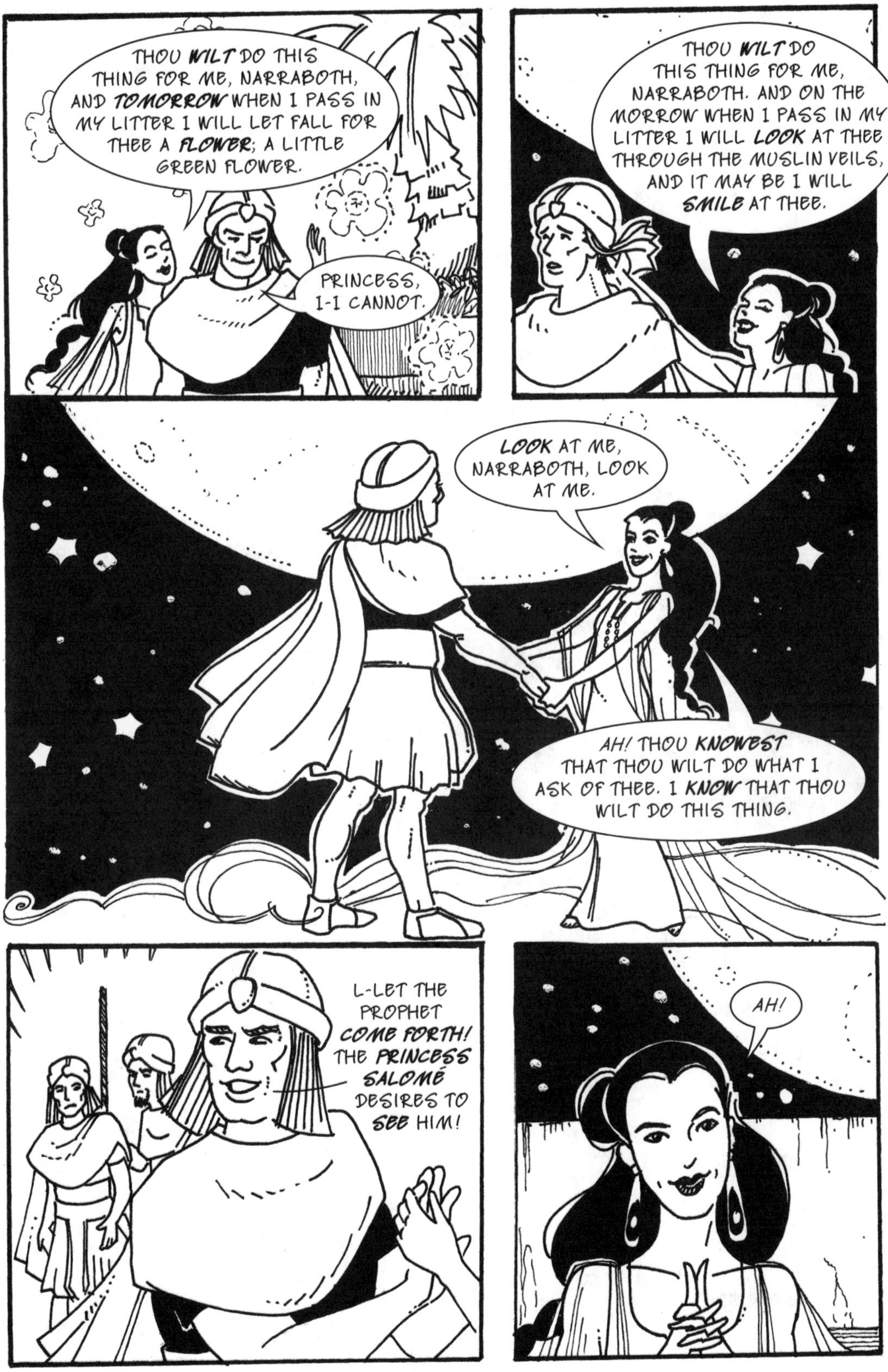
THOU WILT DO THIS THING FOR ME, NARRABOTH, AND TOMORROW WHEN I PASS IN MY LITTER I WILL LET FALL FOR THEE A FLOWER; A LITTLE GREEN FLOWER.
PRINCESS, I-I CANNOT.
THOU WILT DO THIS THING FOR ME, NARRABOTH. AND ON THE MORROW WHEN I PASS IN MY LITTER I WILL LOOK AT THEE THROUGH THE MUSLIN VEILS, AND IT MAY BE I WILL SMILE AT THEE.
LOOK AT ME, NARRABOTH, LOOK AT ME.
AH! THOU KNOWEST THAT THOU WILT DO WHAT I ASK OF THEE. I KNOW THAT THOU WILT DO THIS THING.
L-LET THE PROPHET COME FORTH! THE PRINCESS SALOMÉ DESIRES TO SEE HIM!
AH!

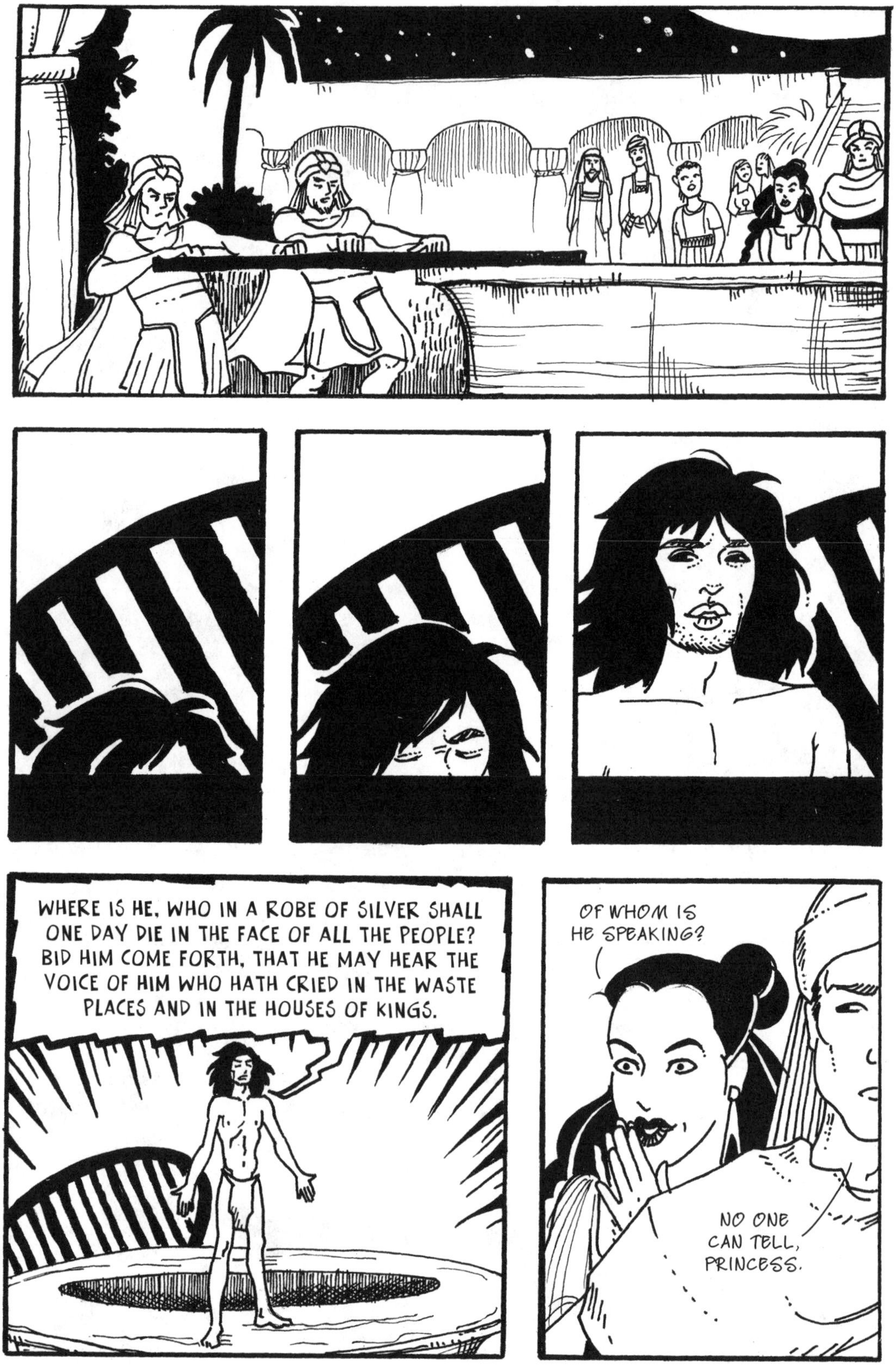
WHERE IS HE, WHO IN A ROBE OF SILVER SHALL ONE DAY DIE IN THE FACE OF ALL THE PEOPLE? BID HIM COME FORTH, THAT HE MAY HEAR THE VOICE OF HIM WHO HATH CRIED IN THE WASTE PLACES AND IN THE HOUSES OF KINGS.
OF WHOM IS HE SPEAKING?
NO ONE CAN TELL, PRINCESS.

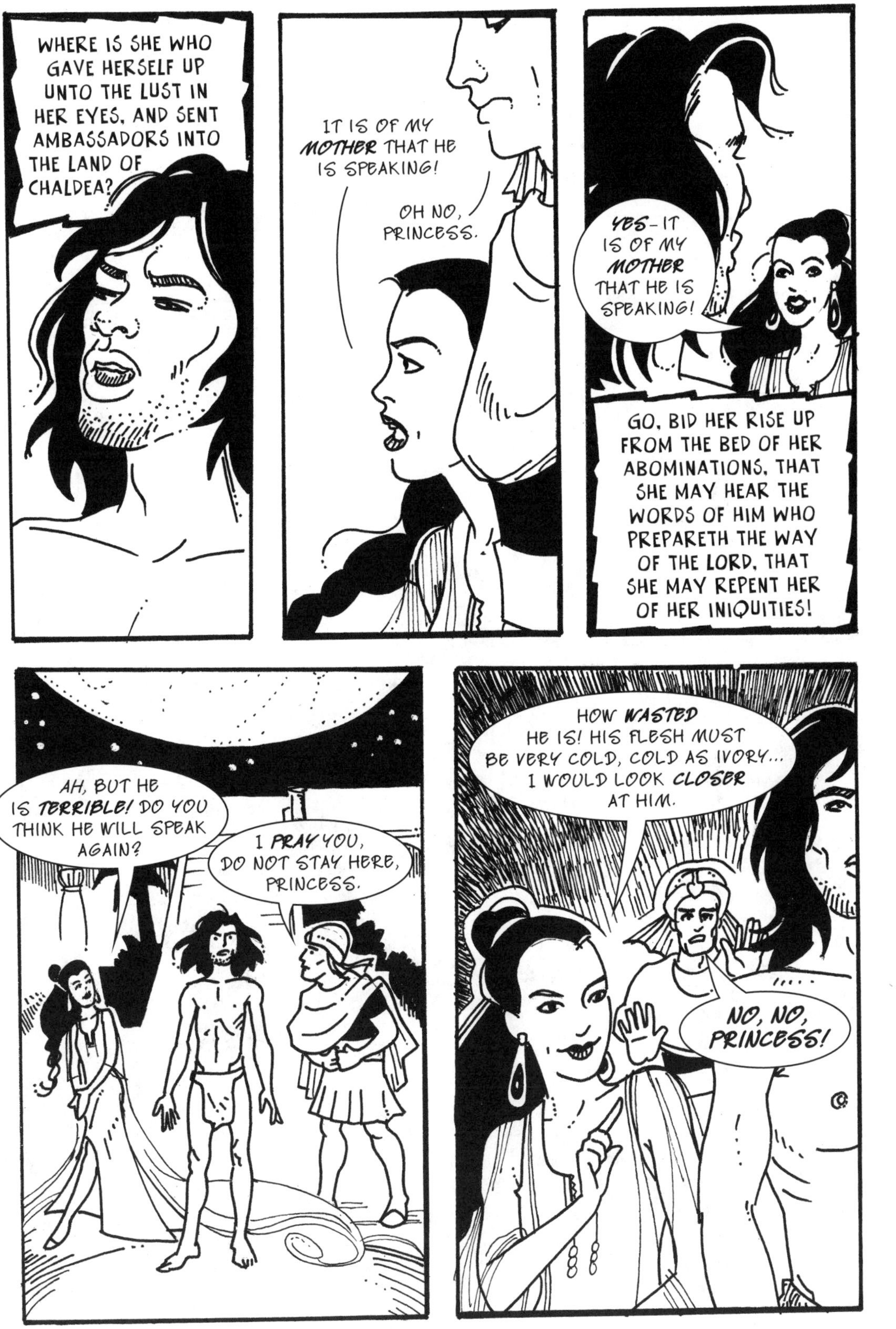
WHERE IS SHE WHO GAVE HERSELF UP UNTO THE LUST IN HER EYES, AND SENT AMBASSADORS INTO THE LAND OF CHALDEA?
IT IS OF MY MOTHER THAT HE IS SPEAKING!
OH NO, PRINCESS.
YES- IT IS OF MY MOTHER THAT HE IS SPEAKING!
GO, BID HER RISE UP FROM THE BED OF HER ABOMINATIONS, THAT SHE MAY HEAR THE WORDS OF HIM WHO PREPARETH THE WAY OF THE LORD, THAT SHE MAY REPENT HER OF HER INIQUITIES!
AH, BUT HE IS TERRIBLE! DO YOU THINK HE WILL SPEAK AGAIN?
I PRAY YOU, DO NOT STAY HERE, PRINCESS.
HOW WASTED HE IS! HIS FLESH MUST BE VERY COLD, COLD AS IVORY... I WOULD LOOK CLOSER AT HIM.
NO, NO, PRINCESS!

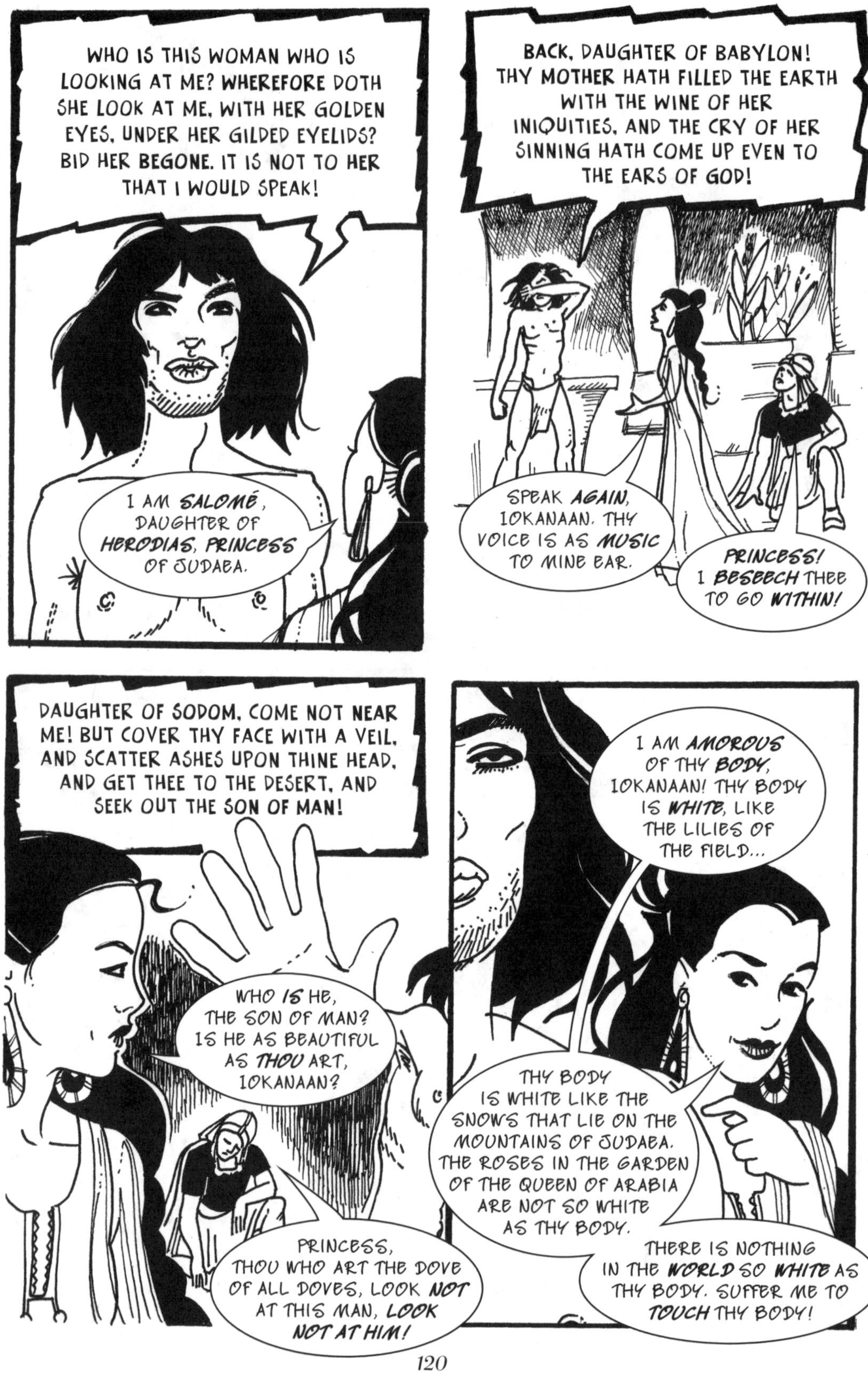
WHO IS THIS WOMAN WHO IS LOOKING AT ME? WHEREFORE DOTH SHE LOOK AT ME, WITH HER GOLDEN EYES, UNDER HER GILDED EYELIDS? BID HER BEGONE. IT IS NOT TO HER THAT I WOULD SPEAK!
I AM SALOMÉ, DAUGHTER OF HERODIAS, PRINCESS OF JUDAEA.
BACK, DAUGHTER OF BABYLON! THY MOTHER HATH FILLED THE EARTH WITH THE WINE OF HER INIQUITIES, AND THE CRY OF HER SINNING HATH COME UP EVEN TO THE EARS OF GOD!
SPEAK AGAIN, IOKANAAN. THY VOICE IS AS MUSIC TO MINE EAR.
PRINCESS! I BESEECH THEE TO GO WITHIN!
DAUGHTER OF SODOM, COME NOT NEAR ME! BUT COVER THY FACE WITH A VEIL, AND SCATTER ASHES UPON THINE HEAD, AND GET THEE TO THE DESERT, AND SEEK OUT THE SON OF MAN!
WHO IS HE, THE SON OF MAN? IS HE AS BEAUTIFUL AS THOU ART, IOKANAAN?
PRINCESS, THOU WHO ART THE DOVE OF ALL DOVES, LOOK NOT AT THIS MAN, LOOK NOT AT HIM!
I AM AMOROUS OF THY BODY, IOKANAAN! THY BODY IS WHITE, LIKE THE LILIES OF THE FIELD...
THY BODY IS WHITE LIKE THE SNOWS THAT LIE ON THE MOUNTAINS OF JUDAEA. THE ROSES IN THE GARDEN OF THE QUEEN OF ARABIA ARE NOT SO WHITE AS THY BODY.
THERE IS NOTHING IN THE WORLD SO WHITE AS THY BODY. SUFFER ME TO TOUCH THY BODY!

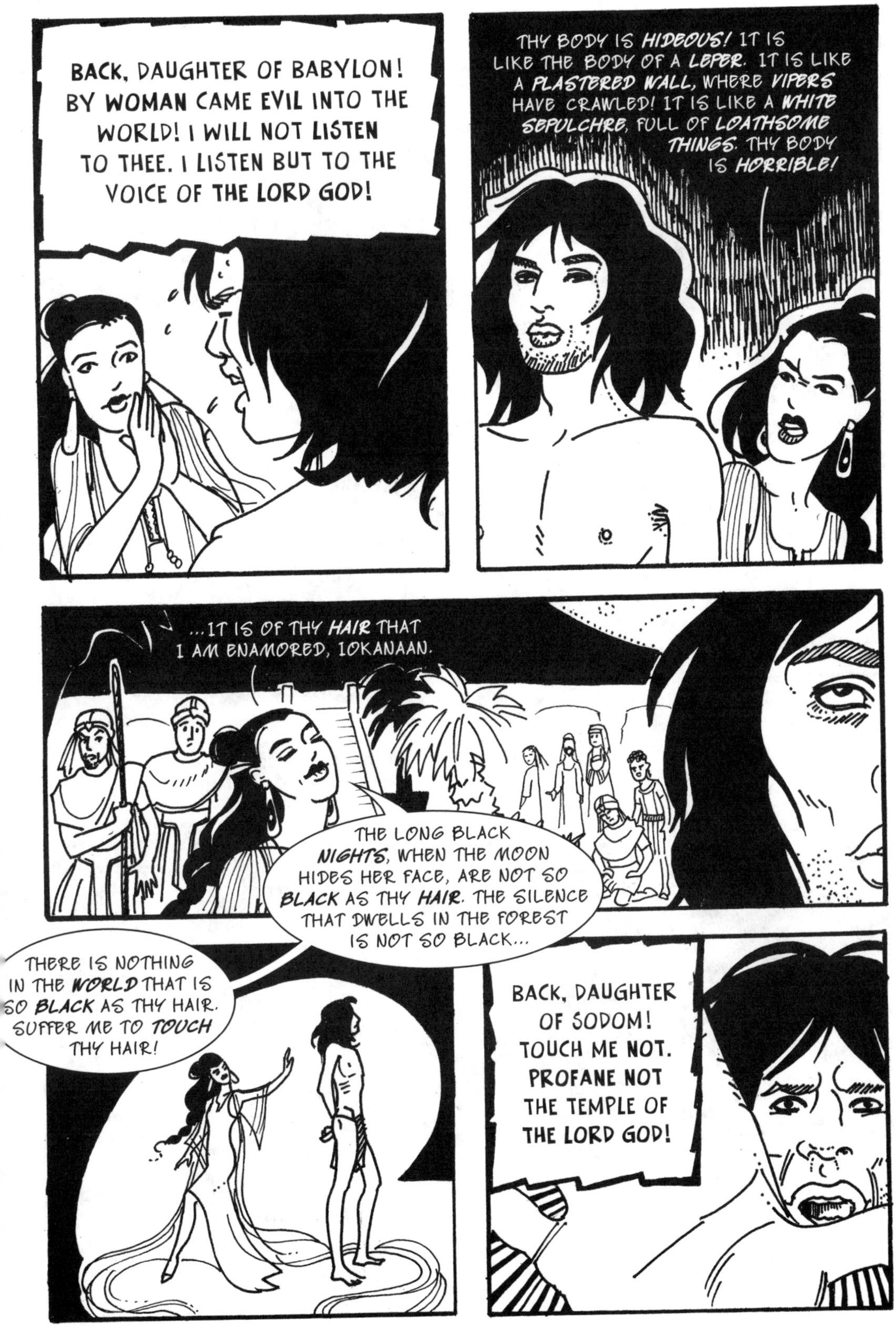
BACK, DAUGHTER OF BABYLON! BY WOMAN CAME EVIL INTO THE WORLD! I WILL NOT LISTEN TO THEE. I LISTEN BUT TO THE VOICE OF THE LORD GOD!
THY BODY IS HIDEOUS! IT IS LIKE THE BODY OF A LEPER. IT IS LIKE A PLASTERED WALL, WHERE VIPERS HAVE CRAWLED! IT IS LIKE A WHITE SEPULCHRE, FULL OF LOATHSOME THINGS. THY BODY IS HORRIBLE!
...IT IS OF THY HAIR THAT I AM ENAMORED, IOKANAAN.
THE LONG BLACK NIGHTS, WHEN THE MOON HIDES HER FACE, ARE NOT SO BLACK AS THY HAIR. THE SILENCE THAT DWELLS IN THE FOREST IS NOT SO BLACK...
THERE IS NOTHING IN THE WORLD THAT IS SO BLACK AS THY HAIR. SUFFER ME TO TOUCH THY HAIR!
BACK, DAUGHTER OF SODOM! TOUCH ME NOT. PROFANE NOT THE TEMPLE OF THE LORD GOD!

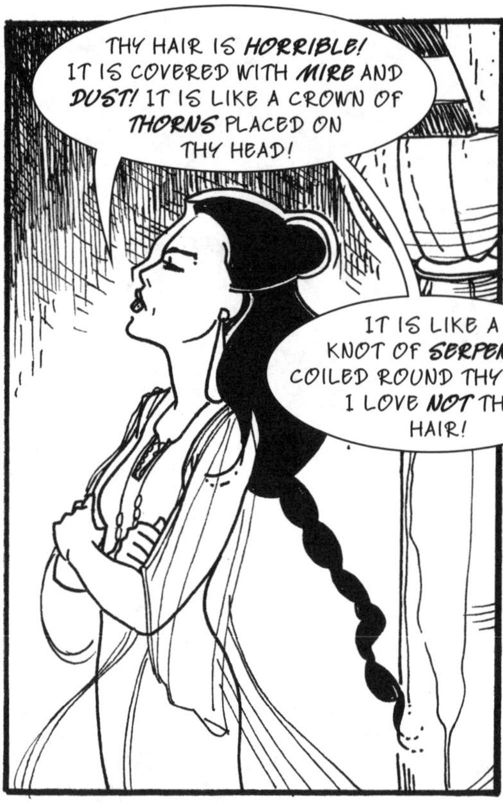
THY HAIR IS HORRIBLE! IT IS COVERED WITH MIRE AND DUST! IT IS LIKE A CROWN OF THORNS PLACED ON THY HEAD!
IT IS LIKE A KNOT OF SERPENTS COILED ROUND THY NECK! I LOVE NOT THY HAIR!

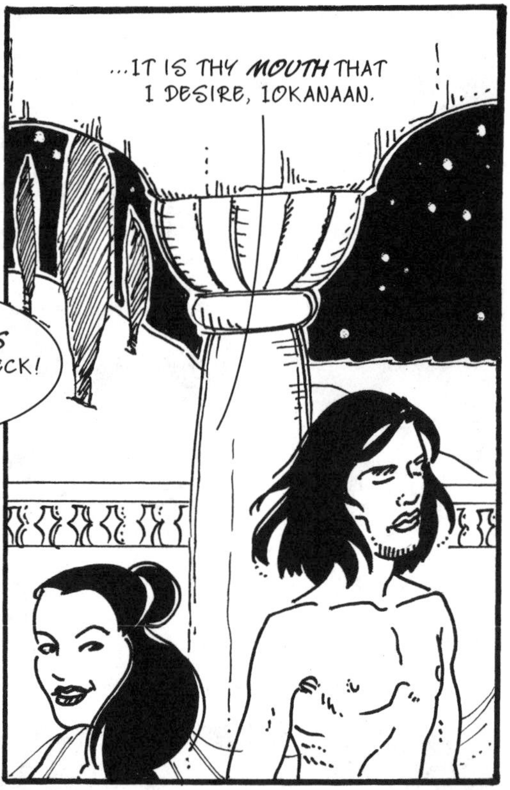
...IT IS THY MOUTH THAT I DESIRE, IOKANAAN.

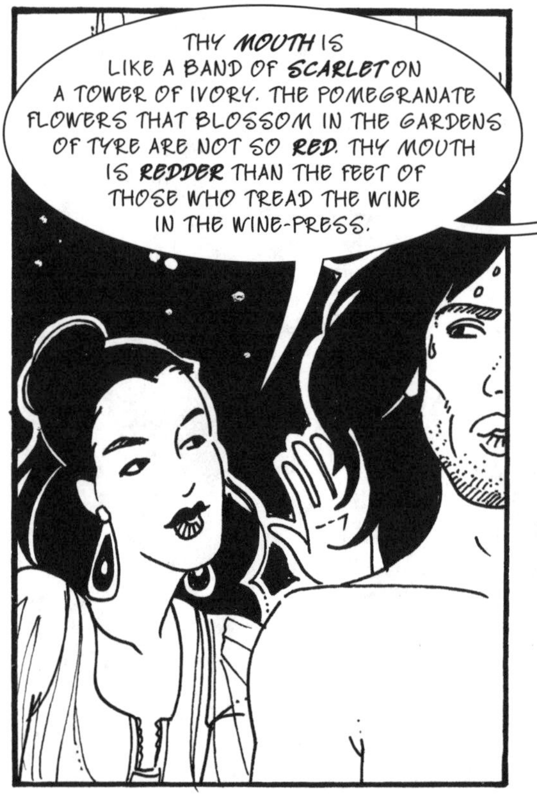
THY MOUTH IS LIKE A BAND OF SCARLET ON A TOWER OF IVORY. THE POMEGRANATE FLOWERS THAT BLOSSOM IN THE GARDENS OF TYRE ARE NOT SO RED. THY MOUTH IS REDDER THAN THE FEET OF THOSE WHO TREAD THE WINE IN THE WINE-PRESS.

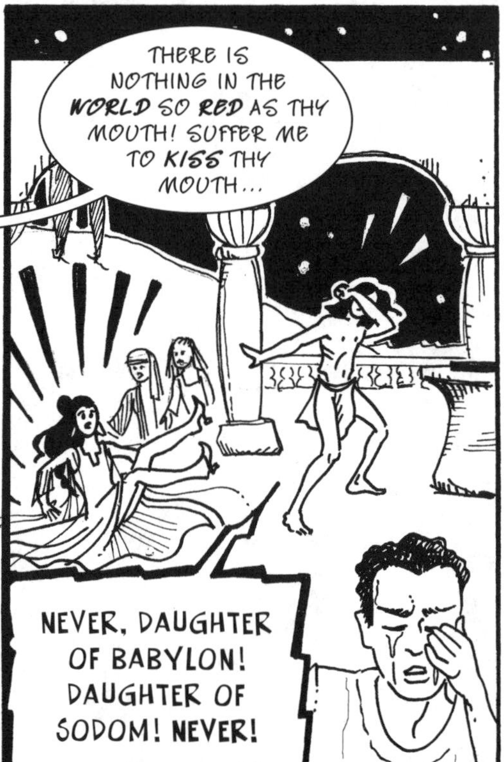
THERE IS NOTHING IN THE WORLD SO RED AS THY MOUTH! SUFFER ME TO KISS THY MOUTH...
NEVER, DAUGHTER OF BABYLON! DAUGHTER OF SODOM! NEVER!

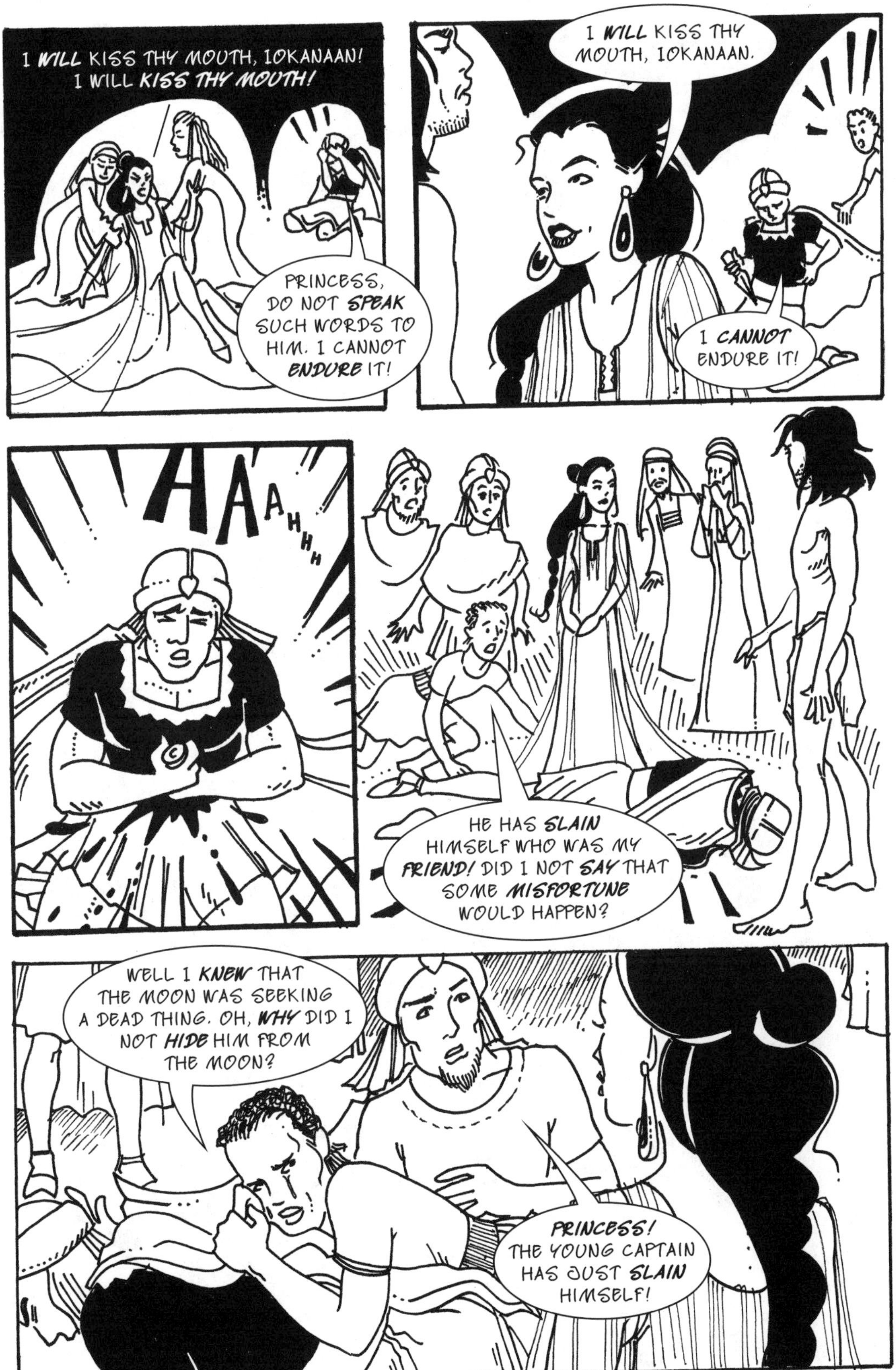
I WILL KISS THY MOUTH, IOKANAAN!
I WILL KISS THY MOUTH!
PRINCESS, DO NOT SPEAK SUCH WORDS TO HIM. I CANNOT ENDURE IT!
I WILL KISS THY MOUTH, IOKANAAN.
I CANNOT ENDURE IT!
HAAAHHH
HE HAS SLAIN HIMSELF WHO WAS MY FRIEND! DID I NOT SAY THAT SOME MISFORTUNE WOULD HAPPEN?
WELL I KNEW THAT THE MOON WAS SEEKING A DEAD THING. OH, WHY DID I NOT HIDE HIM FROM THE MOON?
PRINCESS! THE YOUNG CAPTAIN HAS JUST SLAIN HIMSELF!

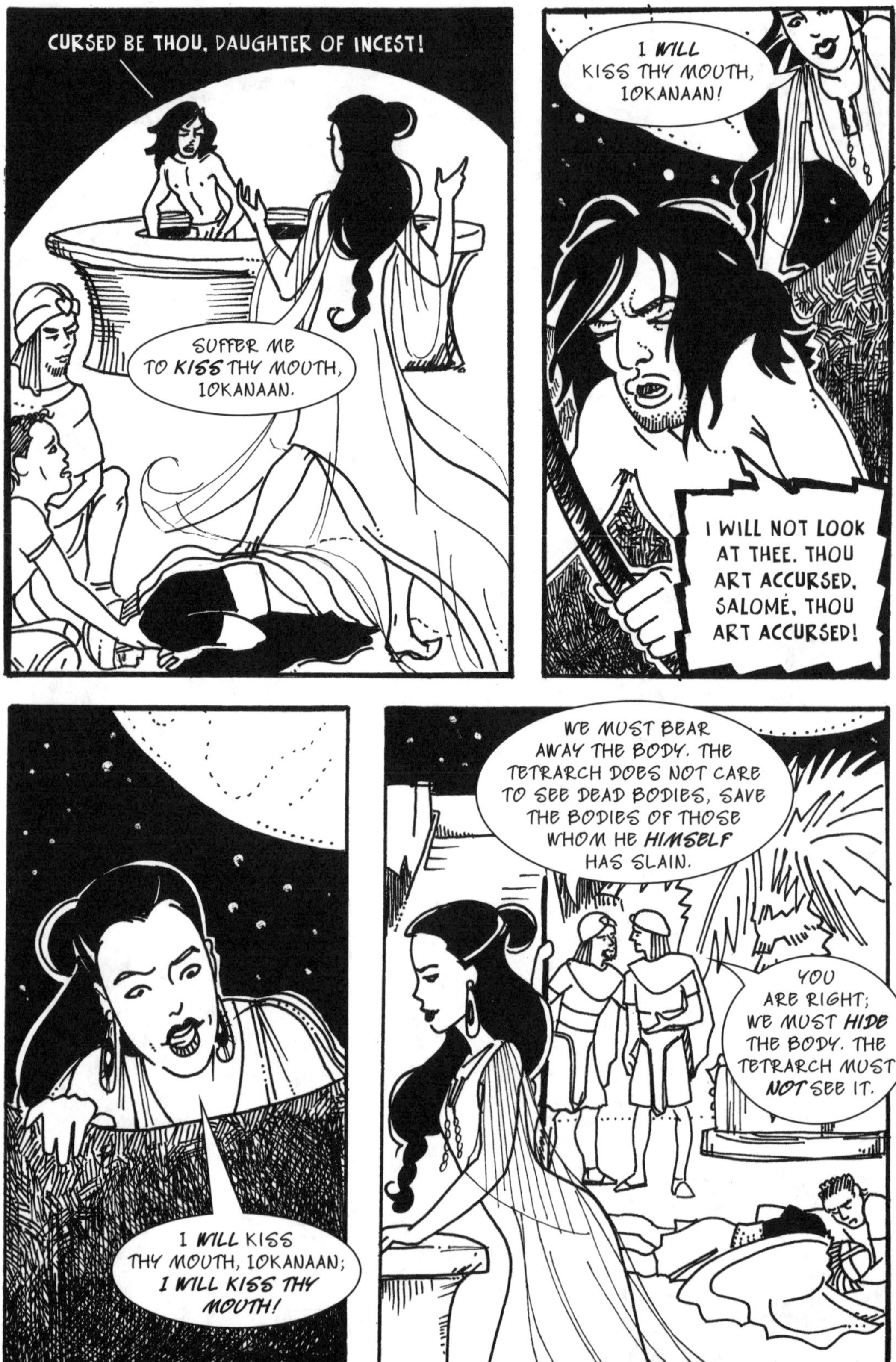
CURSED BE THOU, DAUGHTER OF INCEST!
SUFFER ME TO KISS THY MOUTH, IOKANAAN.
I WILL KISS THY MOUTH, IOKANAAN!
I WILL NOT LOOK AT THEE. THOU ART ACCURSED, SALOMÉ, THOU ART ACCURSED!
I WILL KISS THY MOUTH, IOKANAAN; I WILL KISS THY MOUTH!
WE MUST BEAR AWAY THE BODY. THE TETRARCH DOES NOT CARE TO SEE DEAD BODIES, SAVE THE BODIES OF THOSE WHOM HE HIMSELF HAS SLAIN.
YOU ARE RIGHT; WE MUST HIDE THE BODY. THE TETRARCH MUST NOT SEE IT.

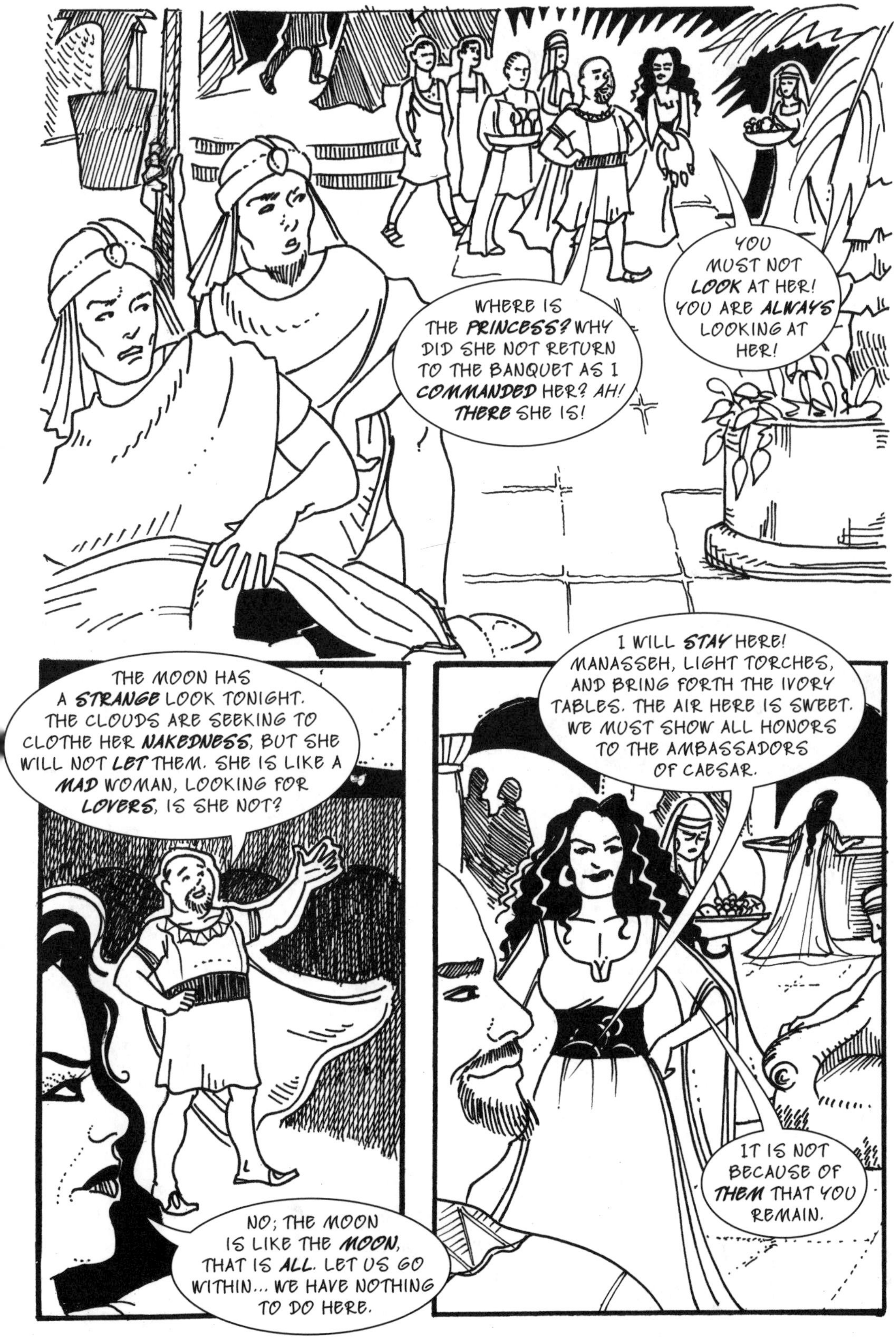
WHERE IS THE PRINCESS? WHY DID SHE NOT RETURN TO THE BANQUET AS I COMMANDED HER? AH! THERE SHE IS!
YOU MUST NOT LOOK AT HER! YOU ARE ALWAYS LOOKING AT HER!
THE MOON HAS A STRANGE LOOK TONIGHT. THE CLOUDS ARE SEEKING TO CLOTHE HER NAKEDNESS, BUT SHE WILL NOT LET THEM. SHE IS LIKE A MAD WOMAN, LOOKING FOR LOVERS, IS SHE NOT?
NO; THE MOON IS LIKE THE MOON, THAT IS ALL. LET US GO WITHIN... WE HAVE NOTHING TO DO HERE.
I WILL STAY HERE! MANASSEH, LIGHT TORCHES, AND BRING FORTH THE IVORY TABLES. THE AIR HERE IS SWEET. WE MUST SHOW ALL HONORS TO THE AMBASSADORS OF CAESAR.
IT IS NOT BECAUSE OF THEM THAT YOU REMAIN.

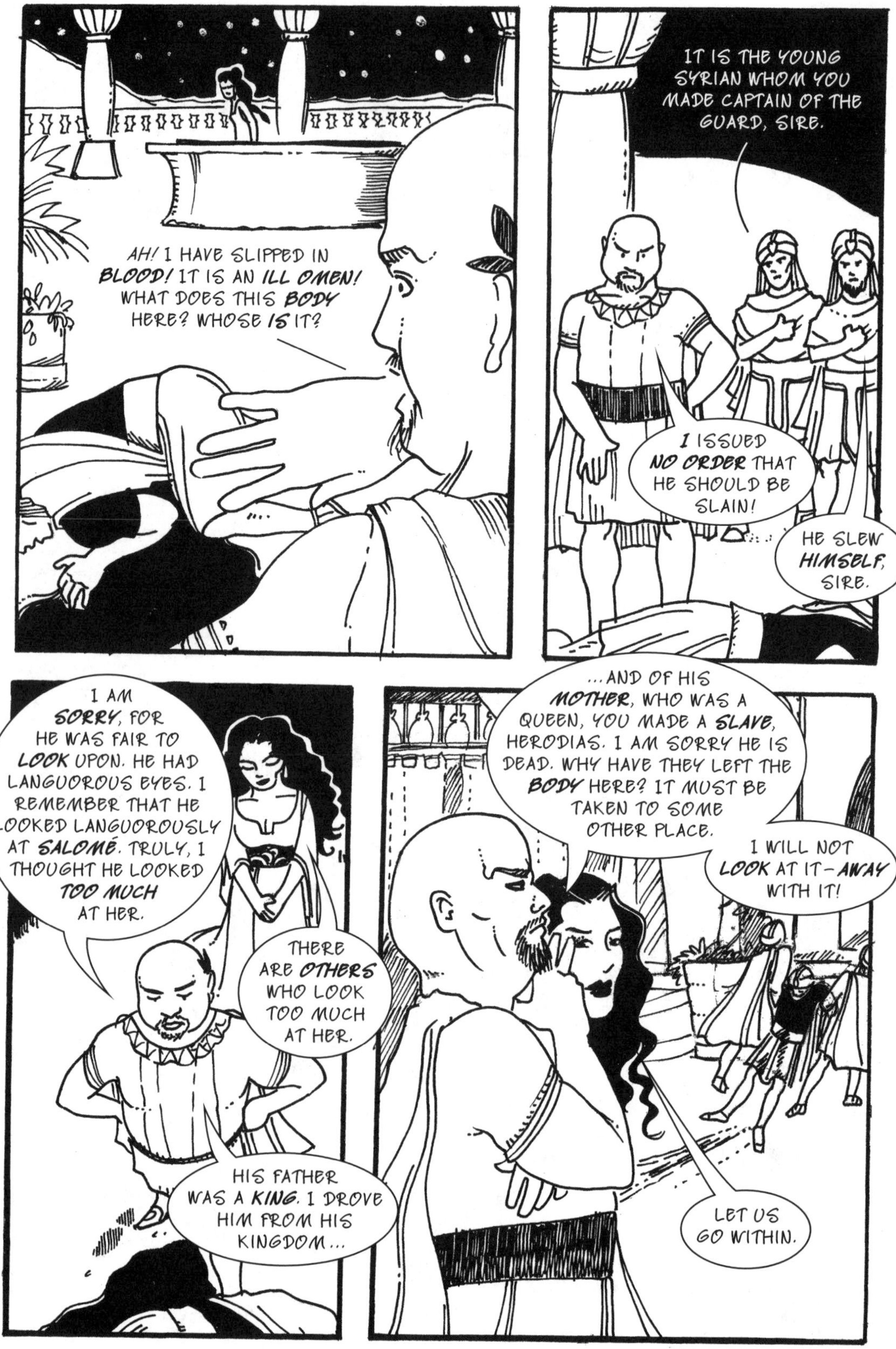
AH! I HAVE SLIPPED IN BLOOD! IT IS AN ILL OMEN! WHAT DOES THIS BODY HERE? WHOSE IS IT?
IT IS THE YOUNG SYRIAN WHOM YOU MADE CAPTAIN OF THE GUARD, SIRE.
I ISSUED NO ORDER THAT HE SHOULD BE SLAIN!
HE SLEW HIMSELF, SIRE.
I AM SORRY, FOR HE WAS FAIR TO LOOK UPON. HE HAD LANGUOROUS EYES. I REMEMBER THAT HE LOOKED LANGUOROUSLY AT SALOMÉ. TRULY, I THOUGHT HE LOOKED TOO MUCH AT HER.
THERE ARE OTHERS WHO LOOK TOO MUCH AT HER.
HIS FATHER WAS A KING. I DROVE HIM FROM HIS KINGDOM...
...AND OF HIS MOTHER, WHO WAS A QUEEN, YOU MADE A SLAVE, HERODIAS. I AM SORRY HE IS DEAD. WHY HAVE THEY LEFT THE BODY HERE? IT MUST BE TAKEN TO SOME OTHER PLACE.
I WILL NOT LOOK AT IT—AWAY WITH IT!
LET US GO WITHIN.

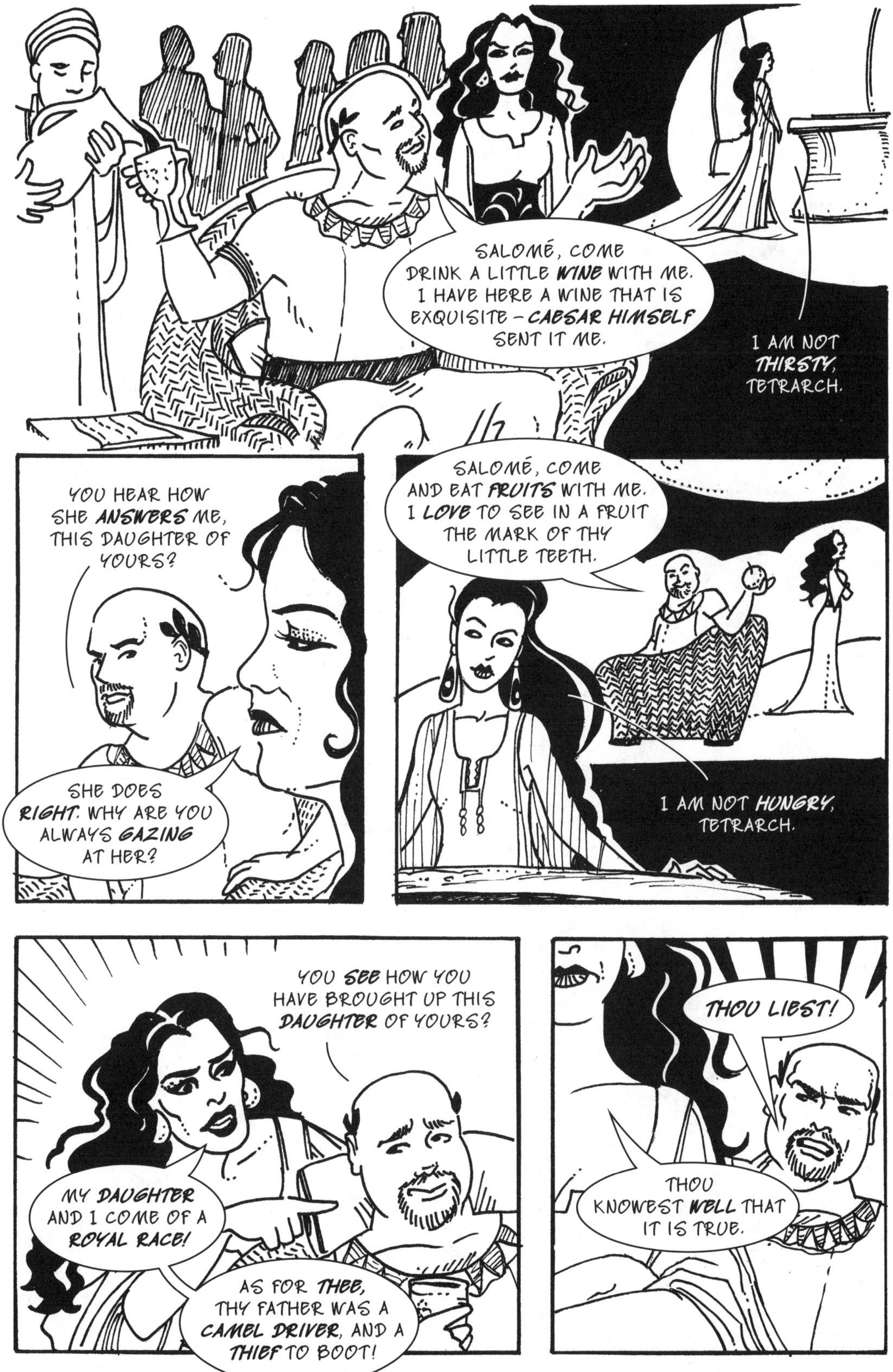
SALOMÉ, COME DRINK A LITTLE WINE WITH ME. I HAVE HERE A WINE THAT IS EXQUISITE – CAESAR HIMSELF SENT IT ME.
I AM NOT THIRSTY, TETRARCH.
YOU HEAR HOW SHE ANSWERS ME, THIS DAUGHTER OF YOURS?
SHE DOES RIGHT. WHY ARE YOU ALWAYS GAZING AT HER?
SALOMÉ, COME AND EAT FRUITS WITH ME. I LOVE TO SEE IN A FRUIT THE MARK OF THY LITTLE TEETH.
I AM NOT HUNGRY, TETRARCH.
YOU SEE HOW YOU HAVE BROUGHT UP THIS DAUGHTER OF YOURS?
MY DAUGHTER AND I COME OF A ROYAL RACE!
AS FOR THEE, THY FATHER WAS A CAMEL DRIVER, AND A THIEF TO BOOT!
THOU LIEST!
THOU KNOWEST WELL THAT IT IS TRUE.

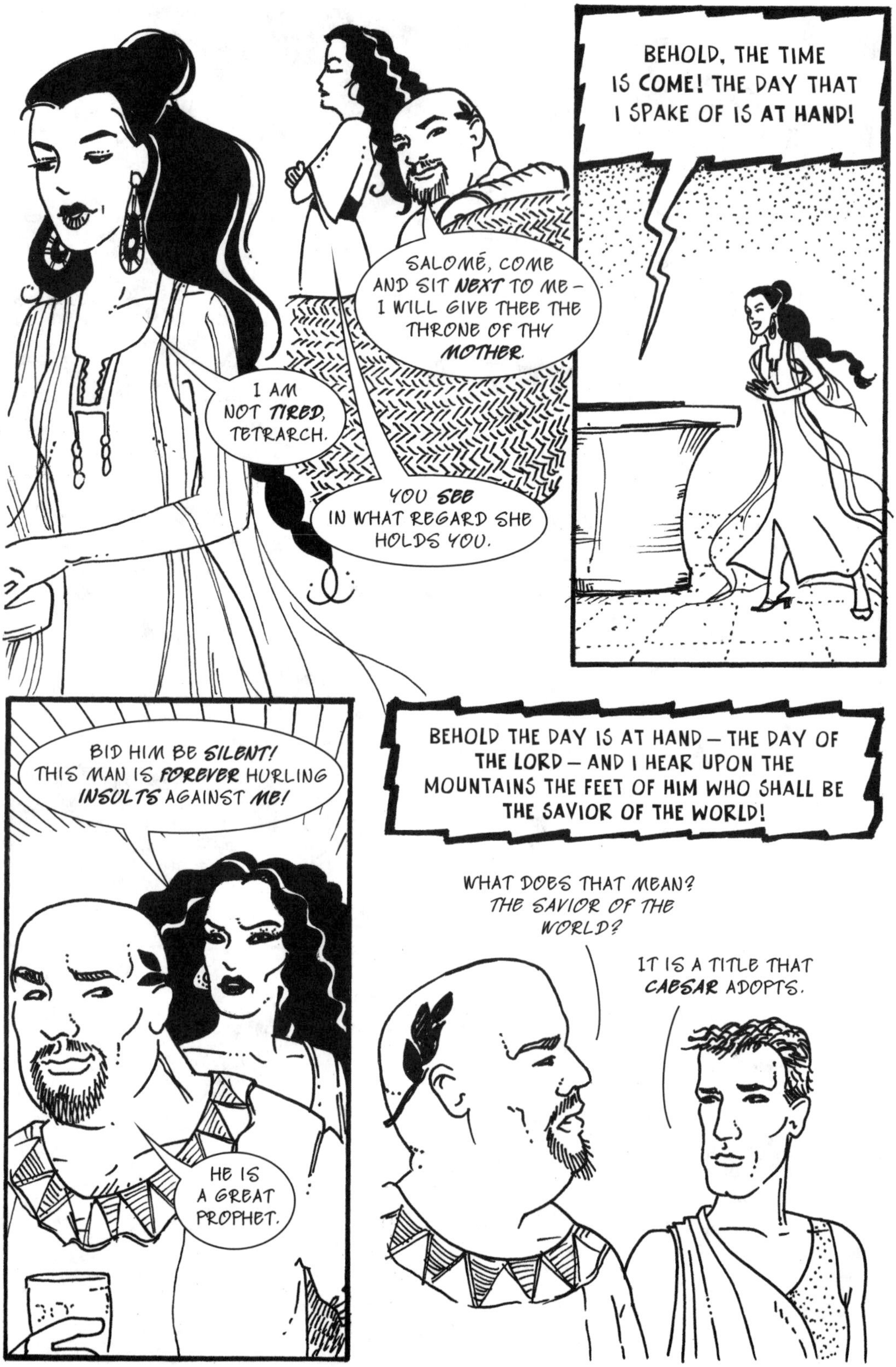
BEHOLD, THE TIME IS COME! THE DAY THAT I SPAKE OF IS AT HAND!
SALOMÉ, COME AND SIT NEXT TO ME — I WILL GIVE THEE THE THRONE OF THY MOTHER.
I AM NOT TIRED, TETRARCH.
YOU SEE IN WHAT REGARD SHE HOLDS YOU.
BEHOLD THE DAY IS AT HAND — THE DAY OF THE LORD — AND I HEAR UPON THE MOUNTAINS THE FEET OF HIM WHO SHALL BE THE SAVIOR OF THE WORLD!
BID HIM BE SILENT! THIS MAN IS FOREVER HURLING INSULTS AGAINST ME!
HE IS A GREAT PROPHET.
WHAT DOES THAT MEAN? THE SAVIOR OF THE WORLD?
IT IS A TITLE THAT CAESAR ADOPTS.

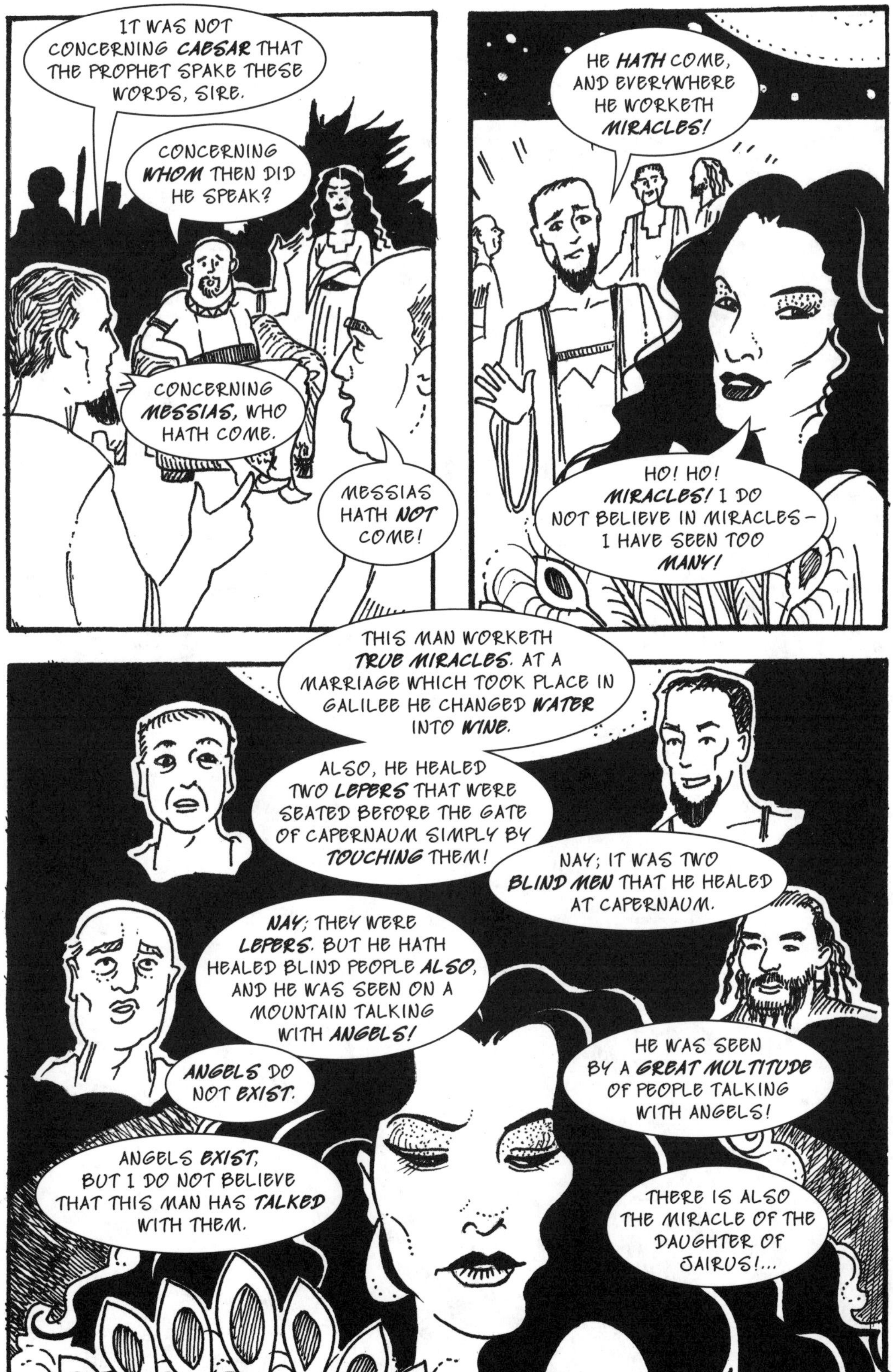
IT WAS NOT CONCERNING CAESAR THAT THE PROPHET SPAKE THESE WORDS, SIRE.
CONCERNING WHOM THEN DID HE SPEAK?
CONCERNING MESSIAS, WHO HATH COME.
MESSIAS HATH NOT COME!
HE HATH COME, AND EVERYWHERE HE WORKETH MIRACLES!
HO! HO! MIRACLES! I DO NOT BELIEVE IN MIRACLES— I HAVE SEEN TOO MANY!
THIS MAN WORKETH TRUE MIRACLES. AT A MARRIAGE WHICH TOOK PLACE IN GALILEE HE CHANGED WATER INTO WINE.
ALSO, HE HEALED TWO LEPERS THAT WERE SEATED BEFORE THE GATE OF CAPERNAUM SIMPLY BY TOUCHING THEM!
NAY; IT WAS TWO BLIND MEN THAT HE HEALED AT CAPERNAUM.
NAY; THEY WERE LEPERS. BUT HE HATH HEALED BLIND PEOPLE ALSO, AND HE WAS SEEN ON A MOUNTAIN TALKING WITH ANGELS!
ANGELS DO NOT EXIST.
HE WAS SEEN BY A GREAT MULTITUDE OF PEOPLE TALKING WITH ANGELS!
ANGELS EXIST, BUT I DO NOT BELIEVE THAT THIS MAN HAS TALKED WITH THEM.
THERE IS ALSO THE MIRACLE OF THE DAUGHTER OF JAIRUS!...

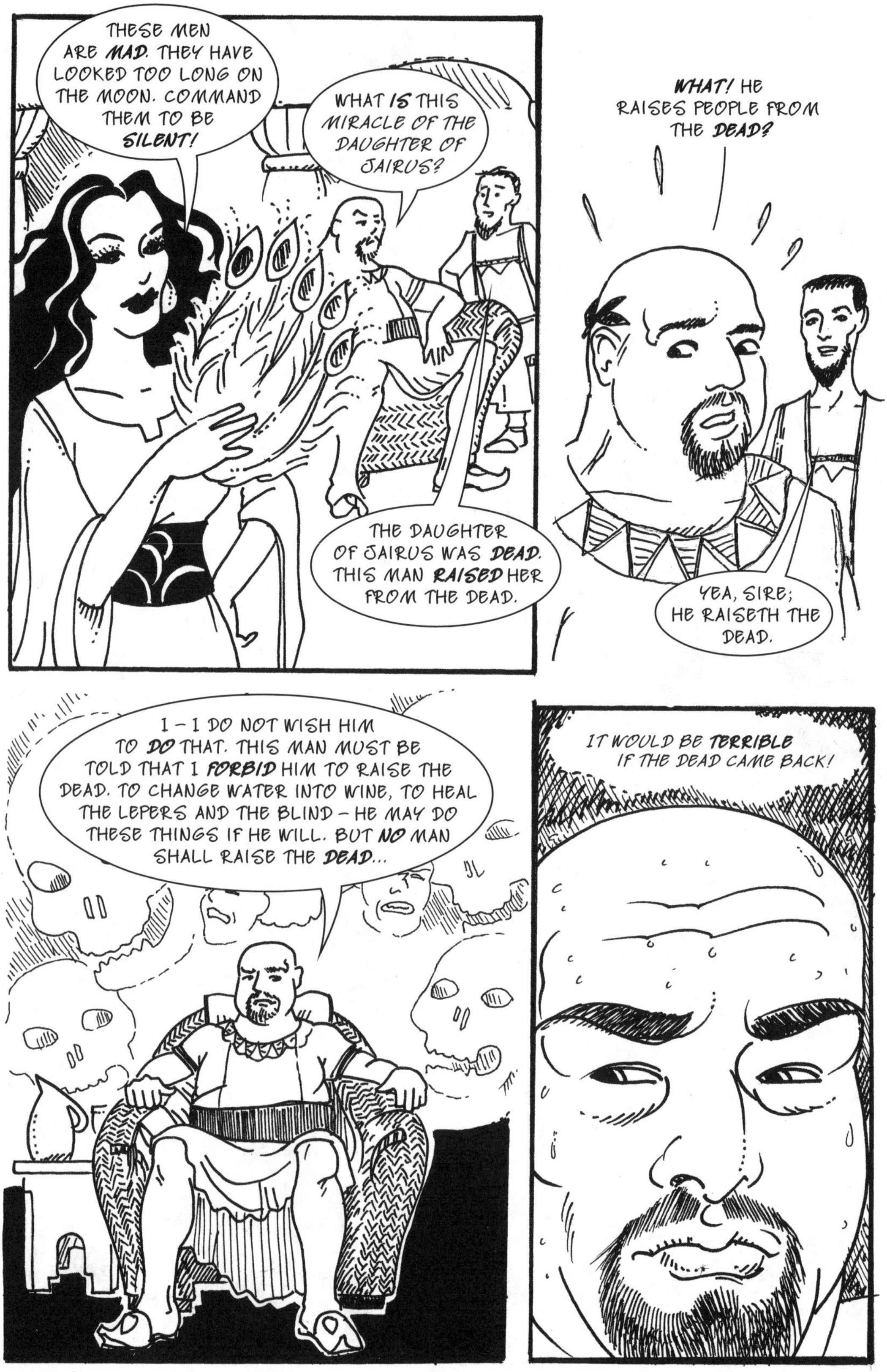
THESE MEN ARE MAD. THEY HAVE LOOKED TOO LONG ON THE MOON. COMMAND THEM TO BE SILENT!
WHAT IS THIS MIRACLE OF THE DAUGHTER OF JAIRUS?
THE DAUGHTER OF JAIRUS WAS DEAD. THIS MAN RAISED HER FROM THE DEAD.
WHAT! HE RAISES PEOPLE FROM THE DEAD?
YEA, SIRE; HE RAISETH THE DEAD.
I — I DO NOT WISH HIM TO DO THAT. THIS MAN MUST BE TOLD THAT I FORBID HIM TO RAISE THE DEAD. TO CHANGE WATER INTO WINE, TO HEAL THE LEPERS AND THE BLIND — HE MAY DO THESE THINGS IF HE WILL. BUT NO MAN SHALL RAISE THE DEAD...
IT WOULD BE TERRIBLE IF THE DEAD CAME BACK!

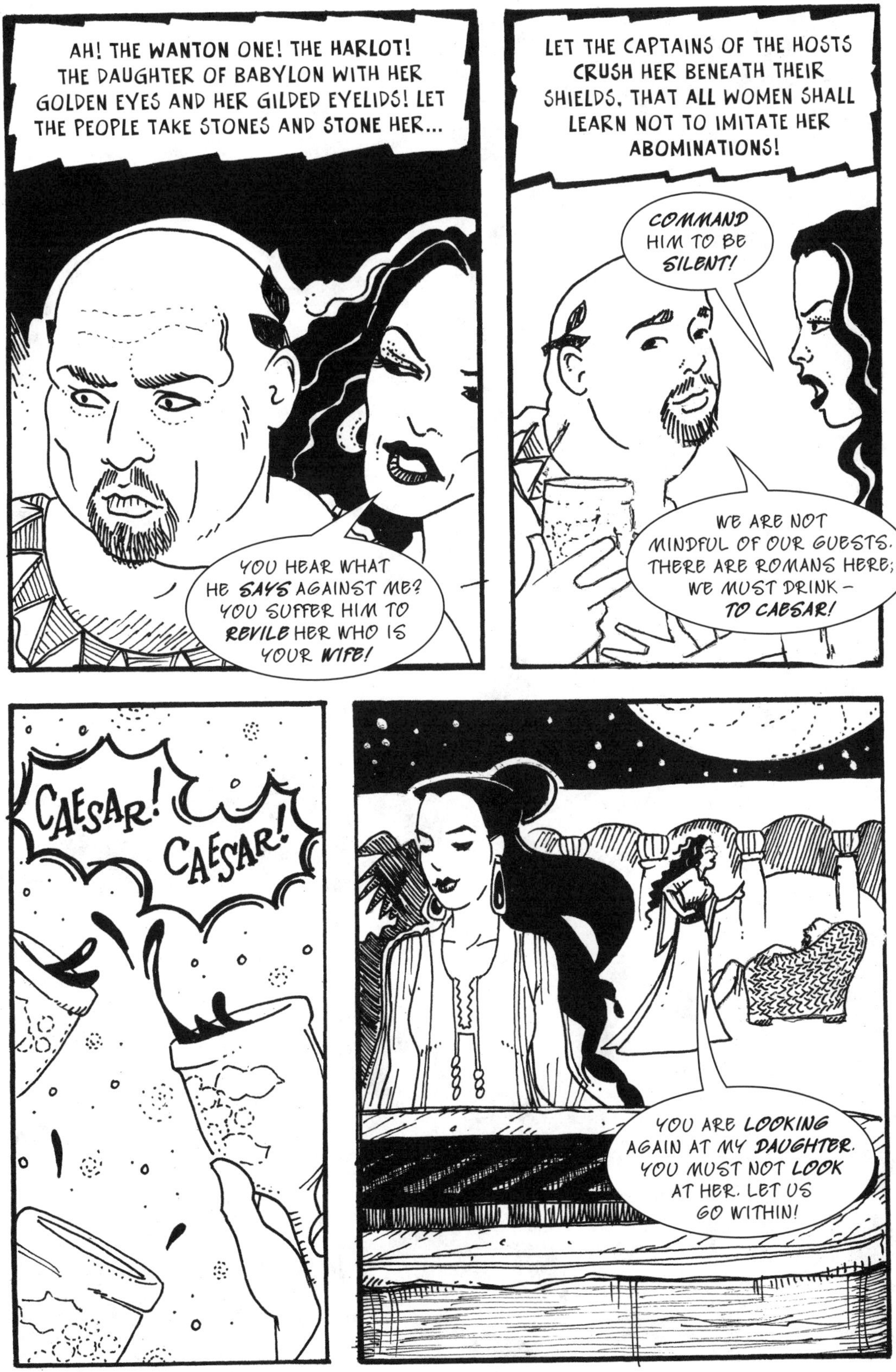
AH! THE WANTON ONE! THE HARLOT! THE DAUGHTER OF BABYLON WITH HER GOLDEN EYES AND HER GILDED EYELIDS! LET THE PEOPLE TAKE STONES AND STONE HER...
YOU HEAR WHAT HE SAYS AGAINST ME? YOU SUFFER HIM TO REVILE HER WHO IS YOUR WIFE!
LET THE CAPTAINS OF THE HOSTS CRUSH HER BENEATH THEIR SHIELDS, THAT ALL WOMEN SHALL LEARN NOT TO IMITATE HER ABOMINATIONS!
COMMAND HIM TO BE SILENT!
WE ARE NOT MINDFUL OF OUR GUESTS. THERE ARE ROMANS HERE; WE MUST DRINK — TO CAESAR!
CAESAR!
CAESAR!
YOU ARE LOOKING AGAIN AT MY DAUGHTER. YOU MUST NOT LOOK AT HER. LET US GO WITHIN!

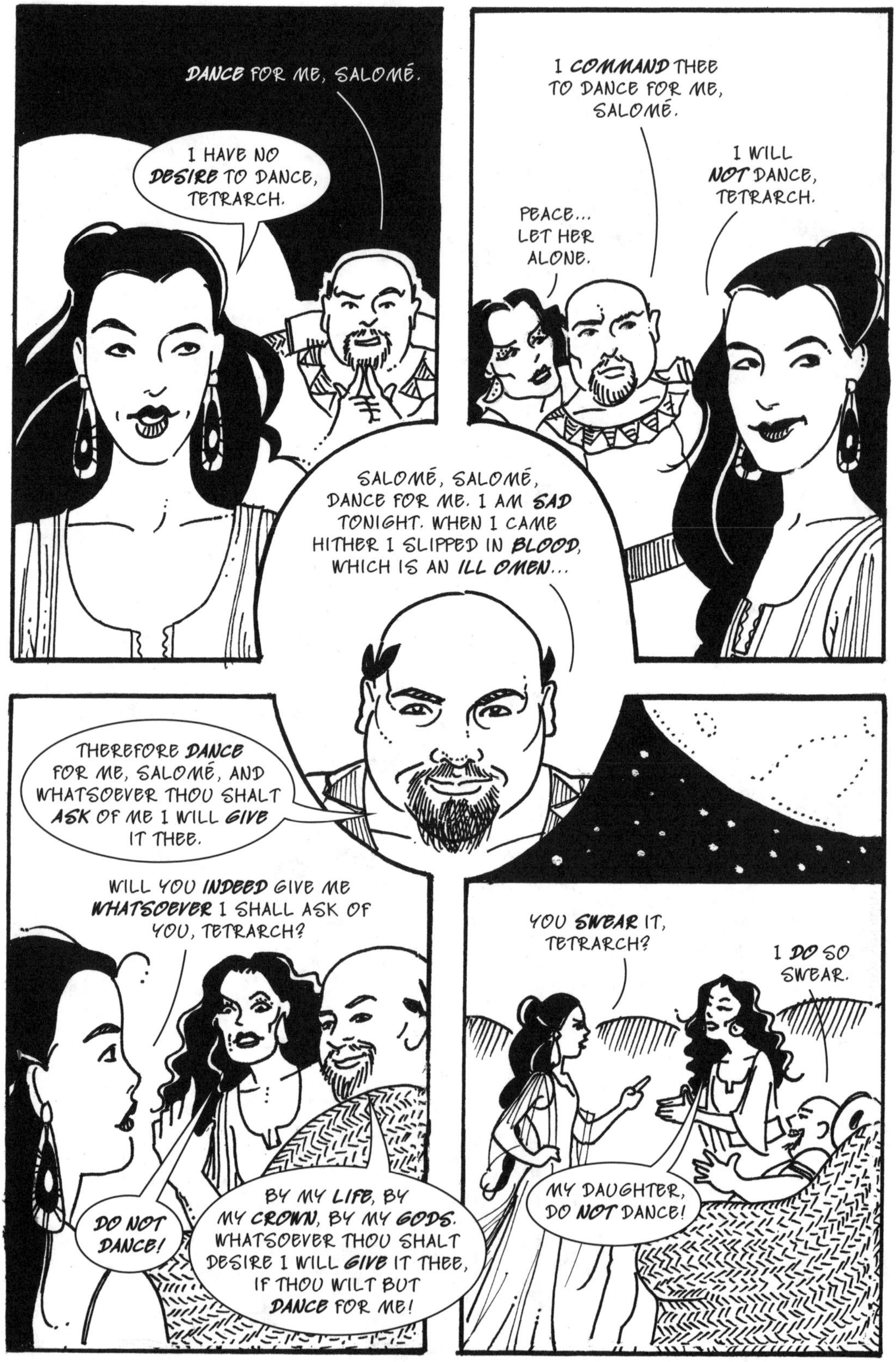
DANCE FOR ME, SALOMÉ.
I HAVE NO DESIRE TO DANCE, TETRARCH.
I COMMAND THEE TO DANCE FOR ME, SALOMÉ.
PEACE... LET HER ALONE.
I WILL NOT DANCE, TETRARCH.
SALOMÉ, SALOMÉ, DANCE FOR ME. I AM SAD TONIGHT. WHEN I CAME HITHER I SLIPPED IN BLOOD, WHICH IS AN ILL OMEN...
THEREFORE DANCE FOR ME, SALOMÉ, AND WHATSOEVER THOU SHALT ASK OF ME I WILL GIVE IT THEE.
WILL YOU INDEED GIVE ME WHATSOEVER I SHALL ASK OF YOU, TETRARCH?
DO NOT DANCE!
BY MY LIFE, BY MY CROWN, BY MY GODS. WHATSOEVER THOU SHALT DESIRE I WILL GIVE IT THEE, IF THOU WILT BUT DANCE FOR ME!
YOU SWEAR IT, TETRARCH?
I DO SO SWEAR.
MY DAUGHTER, DO NOT DANCE!

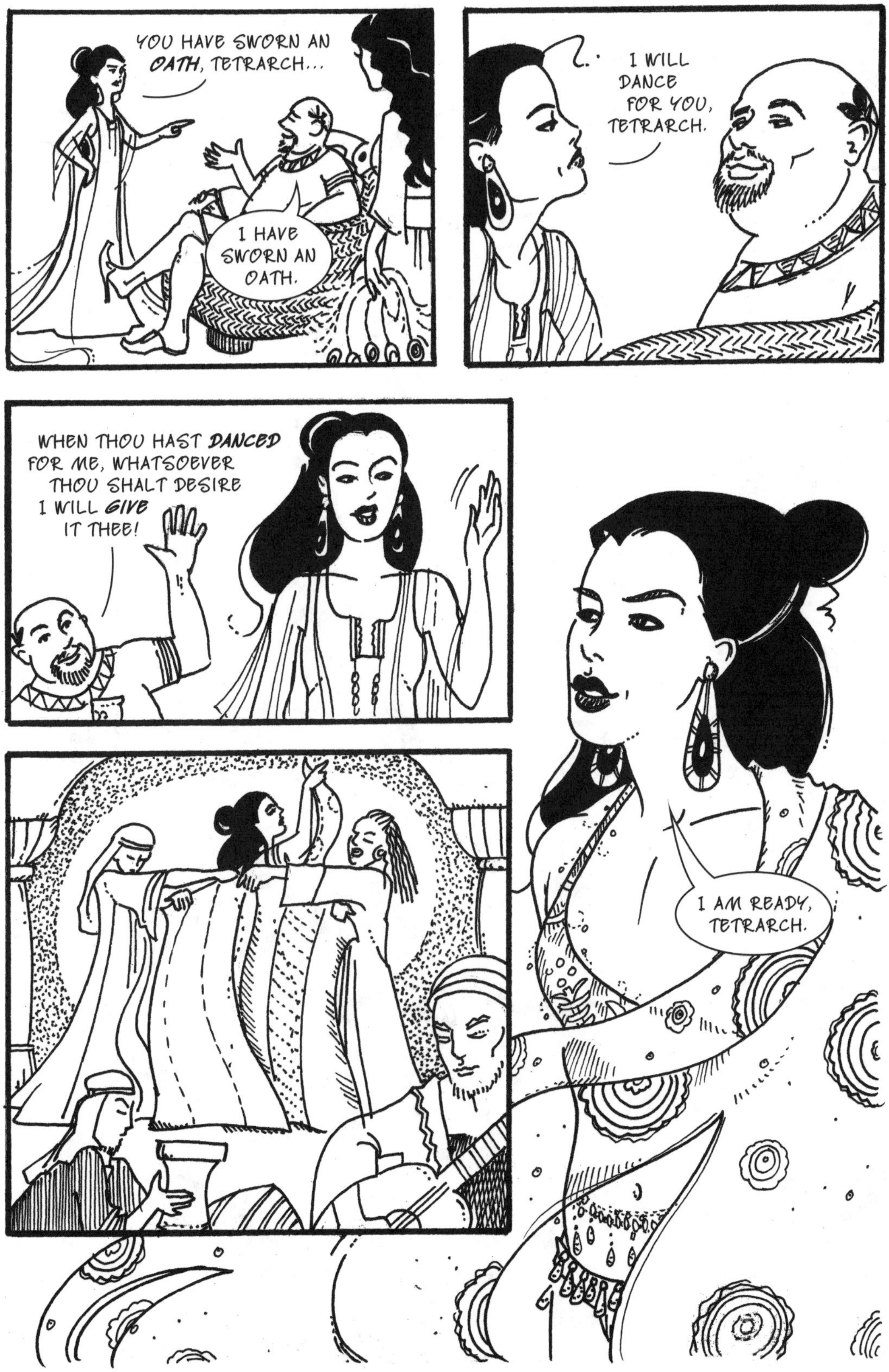
YOU HAVE SWORN AN OATH, TETRARCH...
I HAVE SWORN AN OATH.
I WILL DANCE FOR YOU, TETRARCH.
WHEN THOU HAST DANCED FOR ME, WHATSOEVER THOU SHALT DESIRE I WILL GIVE IT THEE!
I AM READY, TETRARCH.

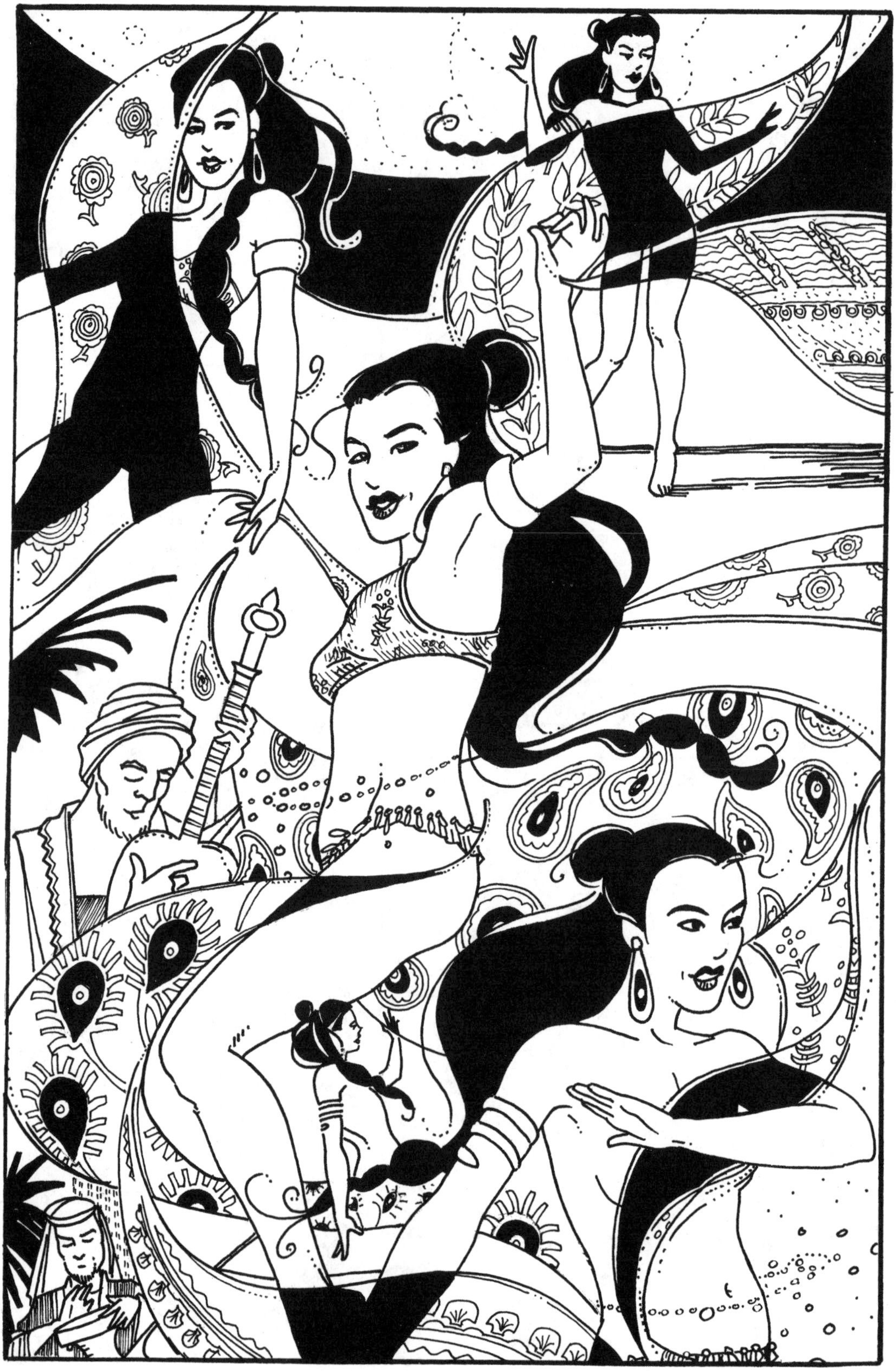

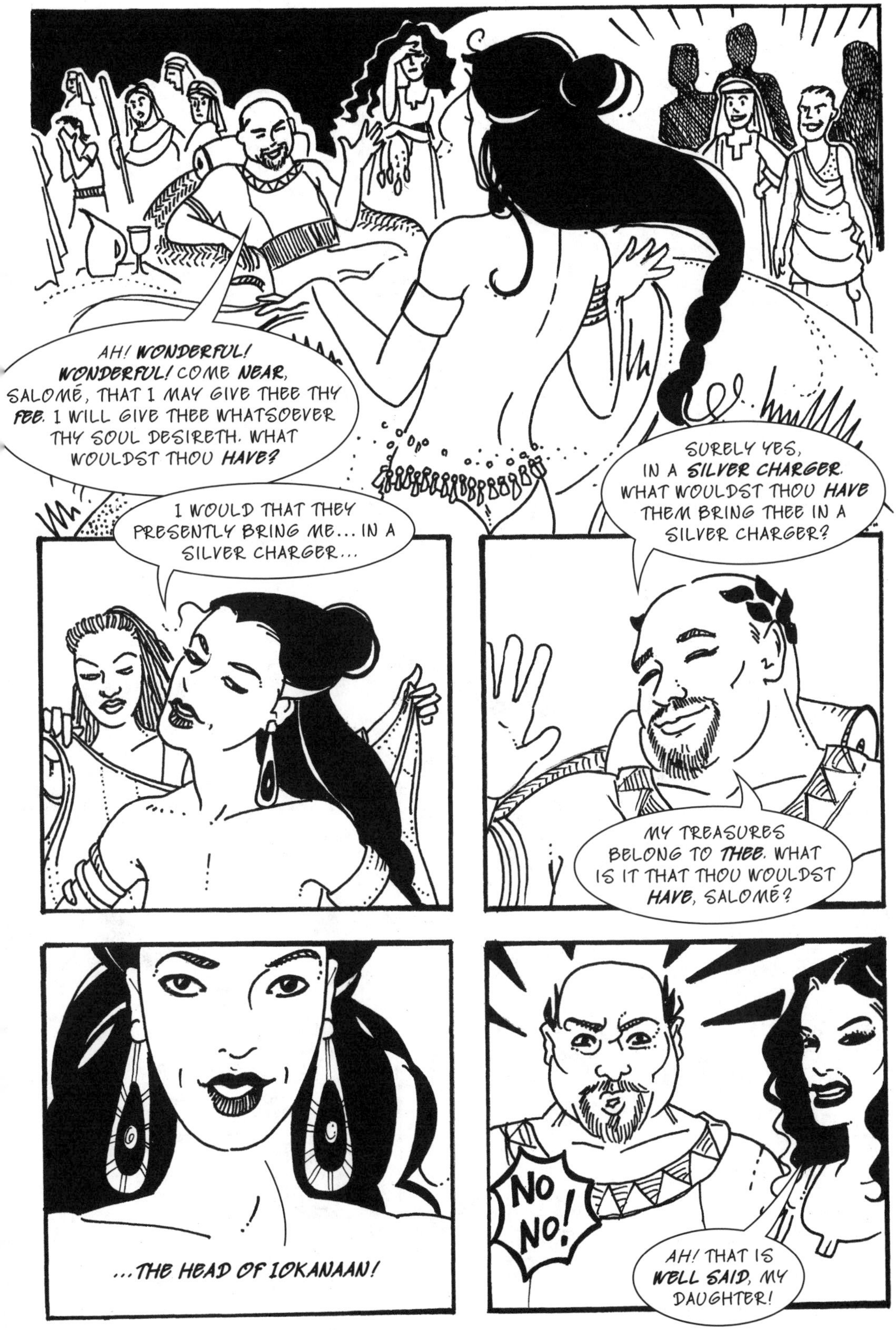
AH! WONDERFUL! WONDERFUL! COME NEAR, SALOMÉ, THAT I MAY GIVE THEE THY FEE. I WILL GIVE THEE WHATSOEVER THY SOUL DESIRETH. WHAT WOULDST THOU HAVE?
I WOULD THAT THEY PRESENTLY BRING ME... IN A SILVER CHARGER...
SURELY YES, IN A SILVER CHARGER. WHAT WOULDST THOU HAVE THEM BRING THEE IN A SILVER CHARGER?
MY TREASURES BELONG TO THEE. WHAT IS IT THAT THOU WOULDST HAVE, SALOMÉ?
...THE HEAD OF IOKANAAN!
NO NO!
AH! THAT IS WELL SAID, MY DAUGHTER!

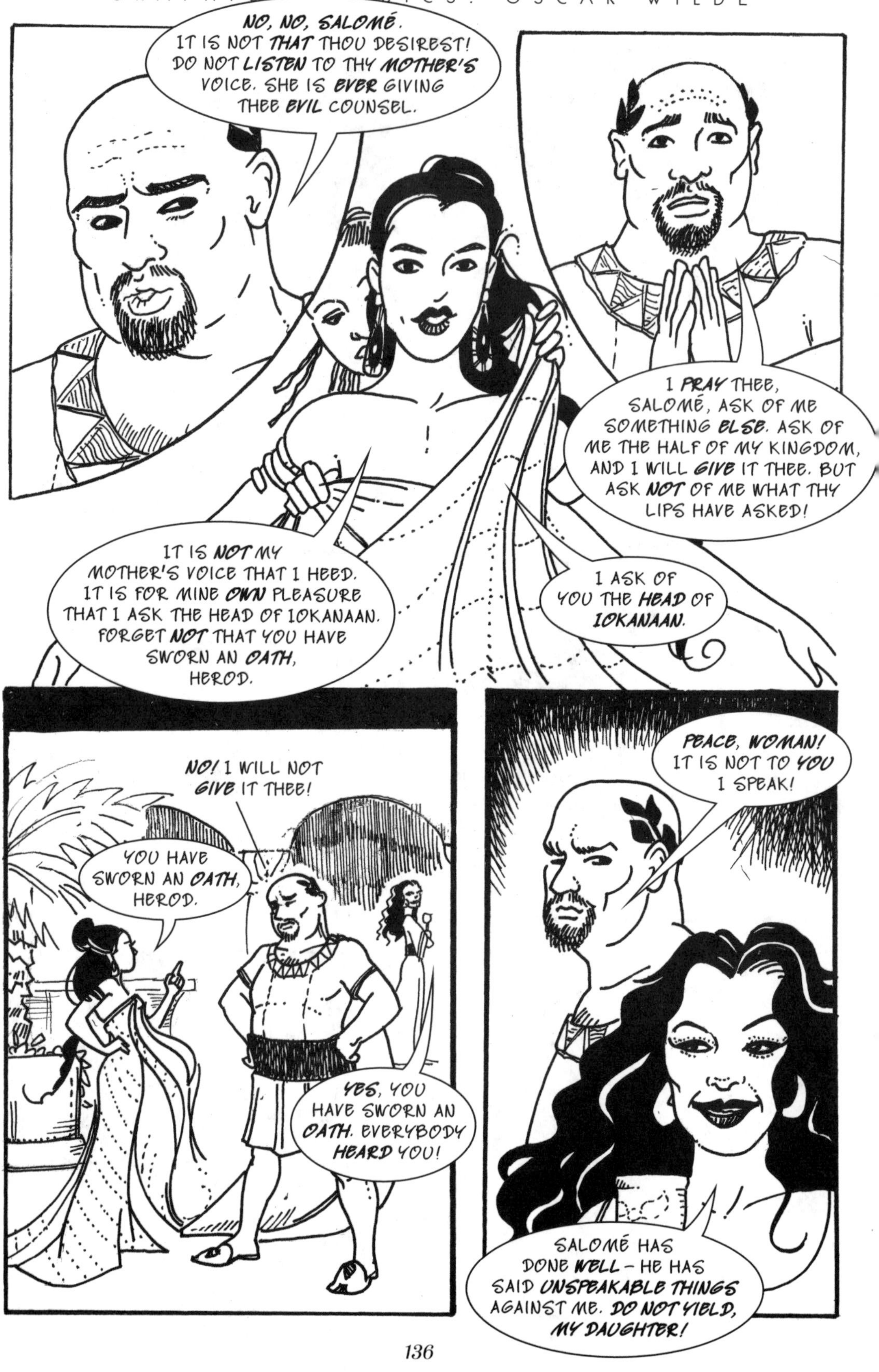
NO, NO, SALOMÉ. IT IS NOT THAT THOU DESIREST! DO NOT LISTEN TO THY MOTHER'S VOICE. SHE IS EVER GIVING THEE EVIL COUNSEL.
IT IS NOT MY MOTHER'S VOICE THAT I HEED. IT IS FOR MINE OWN PLEASURE THAT I ASK THE HEAD OF IOKANAAN. FORGET NOT THAT YOU HAVE SWORN AN OATH, HEROD.
I PRAY THEE, SALOMÉ, ASK OF ME SOMETHING ELSE. ASK OF ME THE HALF OF MY KINGDOM, AND I WILL GIVE IT THEE. BUT ASK NOT OF ME WHAT THY LIPS HAVE ASKED!
I ASK OF YOU THE HEAD OF IOKANAAN.
NO! I WILL NOT GIVE IT THEE!
YOU HAVE SWORN AN OATH, HEROD.
YES, YOU HAVE SWORN AN OATH. EVERYBODY HEARD YOU!
PEACE, WOMAN! IT IS NOT TO YOU I SPEAK!
SALOMÉ HAS DONE WELL – HE HAS SAID UNSPEAKABLE THINGS AGAINST ME. DO NOT YIELD, MY DAUGHTER!

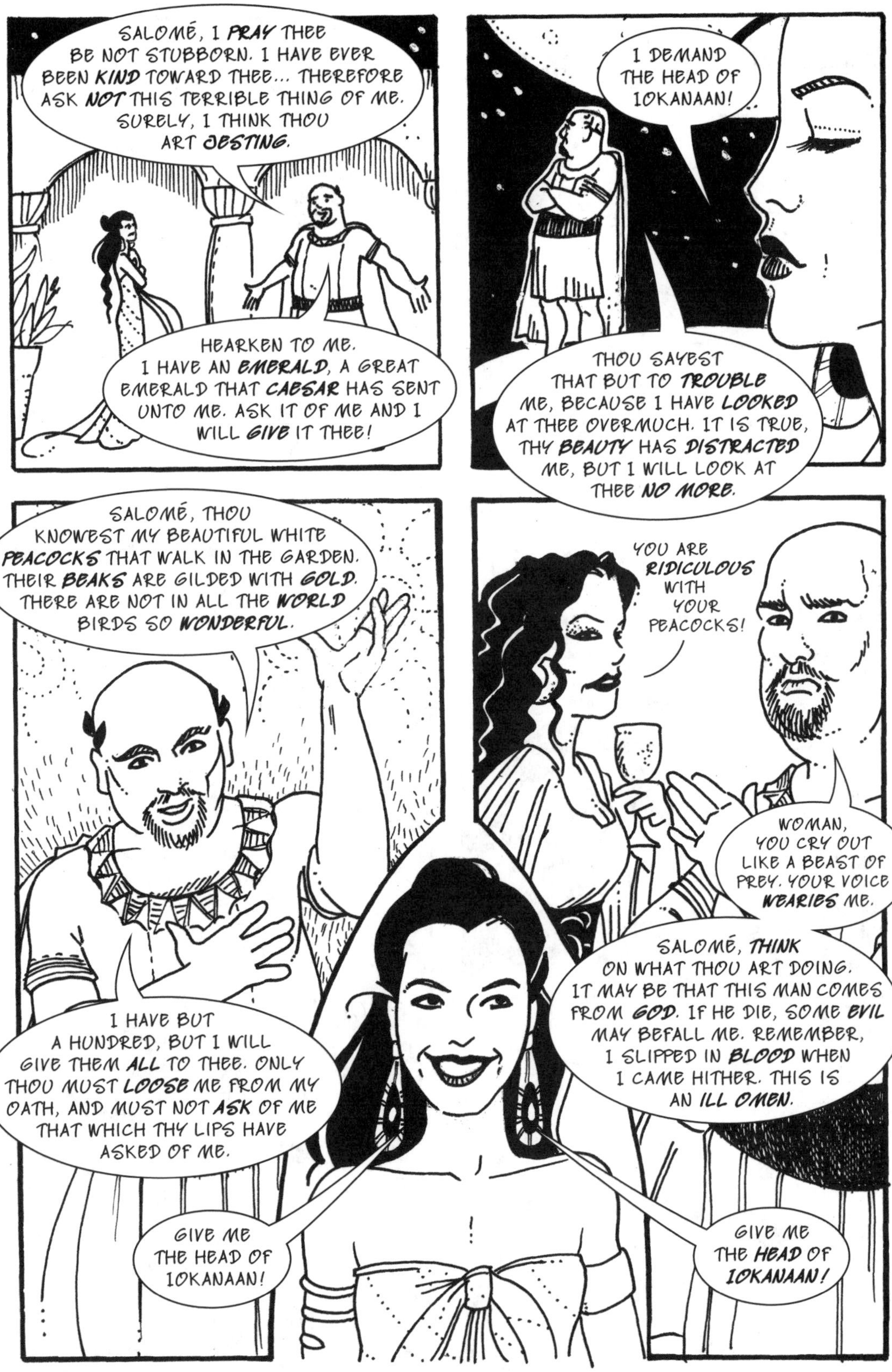
SALOMÉ, I PRAY THEE BE NOT STUBBORN. I HAVE EVER BEEN KIND TOWARD THEE... THEREFORE ASK NOT THIS TERRIBLE THING OF ME. SURELY, I THINK THOU ART JESTING.
HEARKEN TO ME. I HAVE AN EMERALD, A GREAT EMERALD THAT CAESAR HAS SENT UNTO ME. ASK IT OF ME AND I WILL GIVE IT THEE!
I DEMAND THE HEAD OF IOKANAAN!
THOU SAYEST THAT BUT TO TROUBLE ME, BECAUSE I HAVE LOOKED AT THEE OVERMUCH. IT IS TRUE, THY BEAUTY HAS DISTRACTED ME, BUT I WILL LOOK AT THEE NO MORE.
SALOMÉ, THOU KNOWEST MY BEAUTIFUL WHITE PEACOCKS THAT WALK IN THE GARDEN. THEIR BEAKS ARE GILDED WITH GOLD. THERE ARE NOT IN ALL THE WORLD BIRDS SO WONDERFUL.
I HAVE BUT A HUNDRED, BUT I WILL GIVE THEM ALL TO THEE. ONLY THOU MUST LOOSE ME FROM MY OATH, AND MUST NOT ASK OF ME THAT WHICH THY LIPS HAVE ASKED OF ME.
YOU ARE RIDICULOUS WITH YOUR PEACOCKS!
WOMAN, YOU CRY OUT LIKE A BEAST OF PREY. YOUR VOICE WEARIES ME.
SALOMÉ, THINK ON WHAT THOU ART DOING. IT MAY BE THAT THIS MAN COMES FROM GOD. IF HE DIE, SOME EVIL MAY BEFALL ME. REMEMBER, I SLIPPED IN BLOOD WHEN I CAME HITHER. THIS IS AN ILL OMEN.
GIVE ME THE HEAD OF IOKANAAN!
GIVE ME THE HEAD OF IOKANAAN!

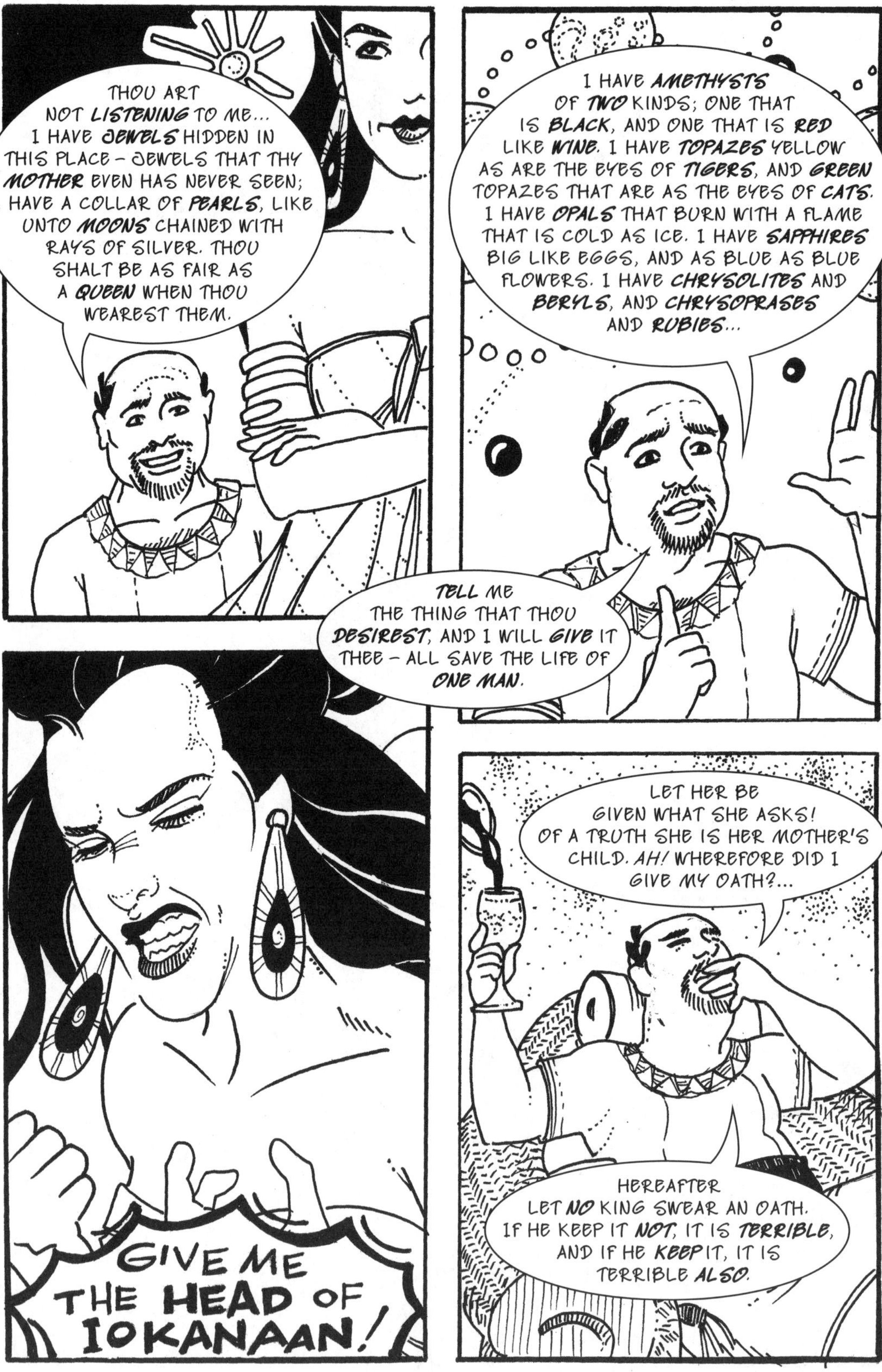
THOU ART NOT LISTENING TO ME... I HAVE JEWELS HIDDEN IN THIS PLACE – JEWELS THAT THY MOTHER EVEN HAS NEVER SEEN; I HAVE A COLLAR OF PEARLS, LIKE UNTO MOONS CHAINED WITH RAYS OF SILVER. THOU SHALT BE AS FAIR AS A QUEEN WHEN THOU WEAREST THEM.
I HAVE AMETHYSTS OF TWO KINDS; ONE THAT IS BLACK, AND ONE THAT IS RED LIKE WINE. I HAVE TOPAZES YELLOW AS ARE THE EYES OF TIGERS, AND GREEN TOPAZES THAT ARE AS THE EYES OF CATS. I HAVE OPALS THAT BURN WITH A FLAME THAT IS COLD AS ICE. I HAVE SAPPHIRES BIG LIKE EGGS, AND AS BLUE AS BLUE FLOWERS. I HAVE CHRYSOLITES AND BERYLS, AND CHRYSOPRASES AND RUBIES...
TELL ME THE THING THAT THOU DESIREST, AND I WILL GIVE IT THEE – ALL SAVE THE LIFE OF ONE MAN.
GIVE ME THE HEAD OF IOKANAAN!
LET HER BE GIVEN WHAT SHE ASKS! OF A TRUTH SHE IS HER MOTHER'S CHILD. AH! WHEREFORE DID I GIVE MY OATH?...
HEREAFTER LET NO KING SWEAR AN OATH. IF HE KEEP IT NOT, IT IS TERRIBLE, AND IF HE KEEP IT, IT IS TERRIBLE ALSO.

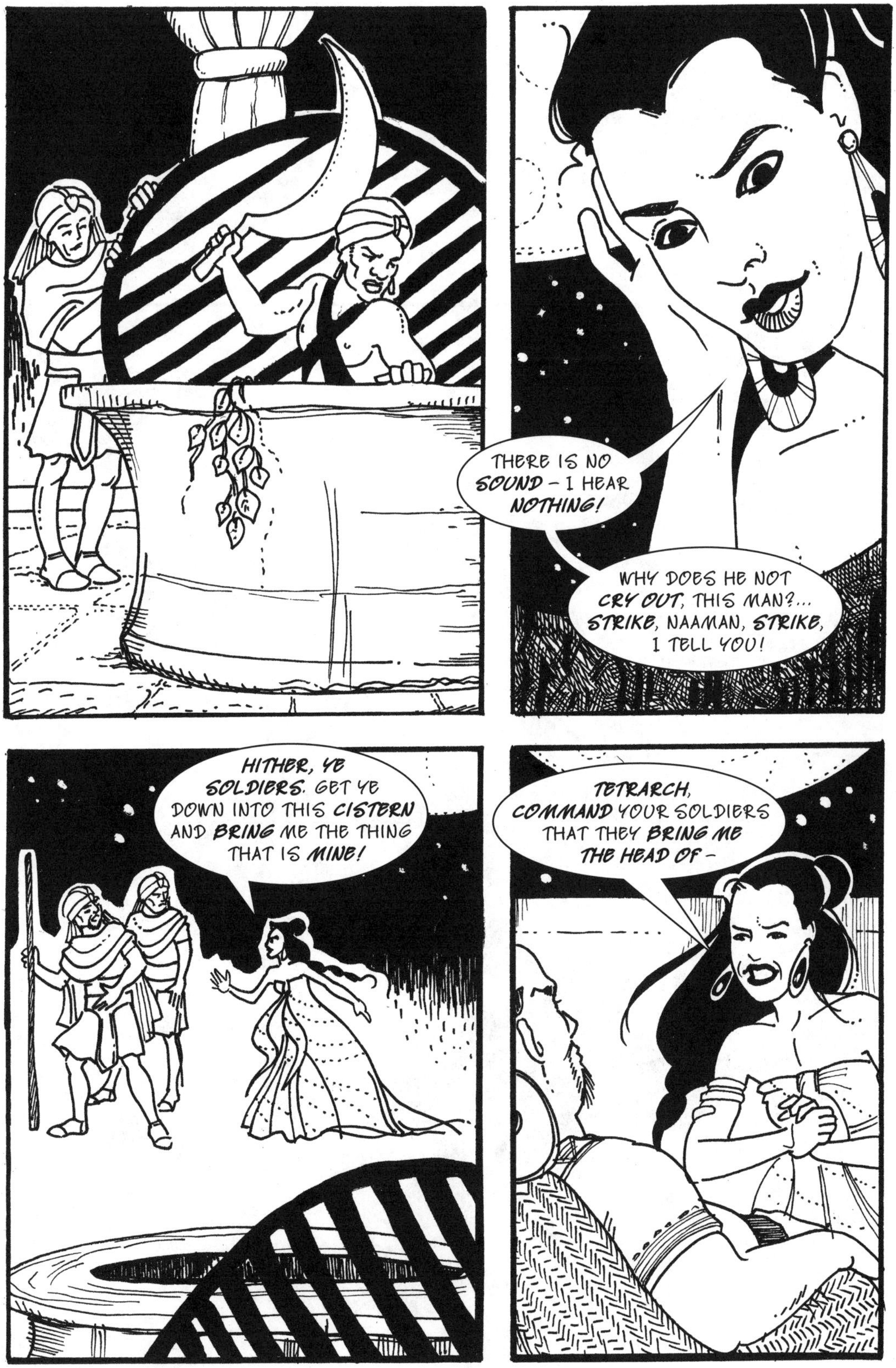
THERE IS NO SOUND – I HEAR NOTHING!
WHY DOES HE NOT CRY OUT, THIS MAN?... STRIKE, NAAMAN, STRIKE, I TELL YOU!
HITHER, YE SOLDIERS. GET YE DOWN INTO THIS CISTERN AND BRING ME THE THING THAT IS MINE!
TETRARCH, COMMAND YOUR SOLDIERS THAT THEY BRING ME THE HEAD OF –

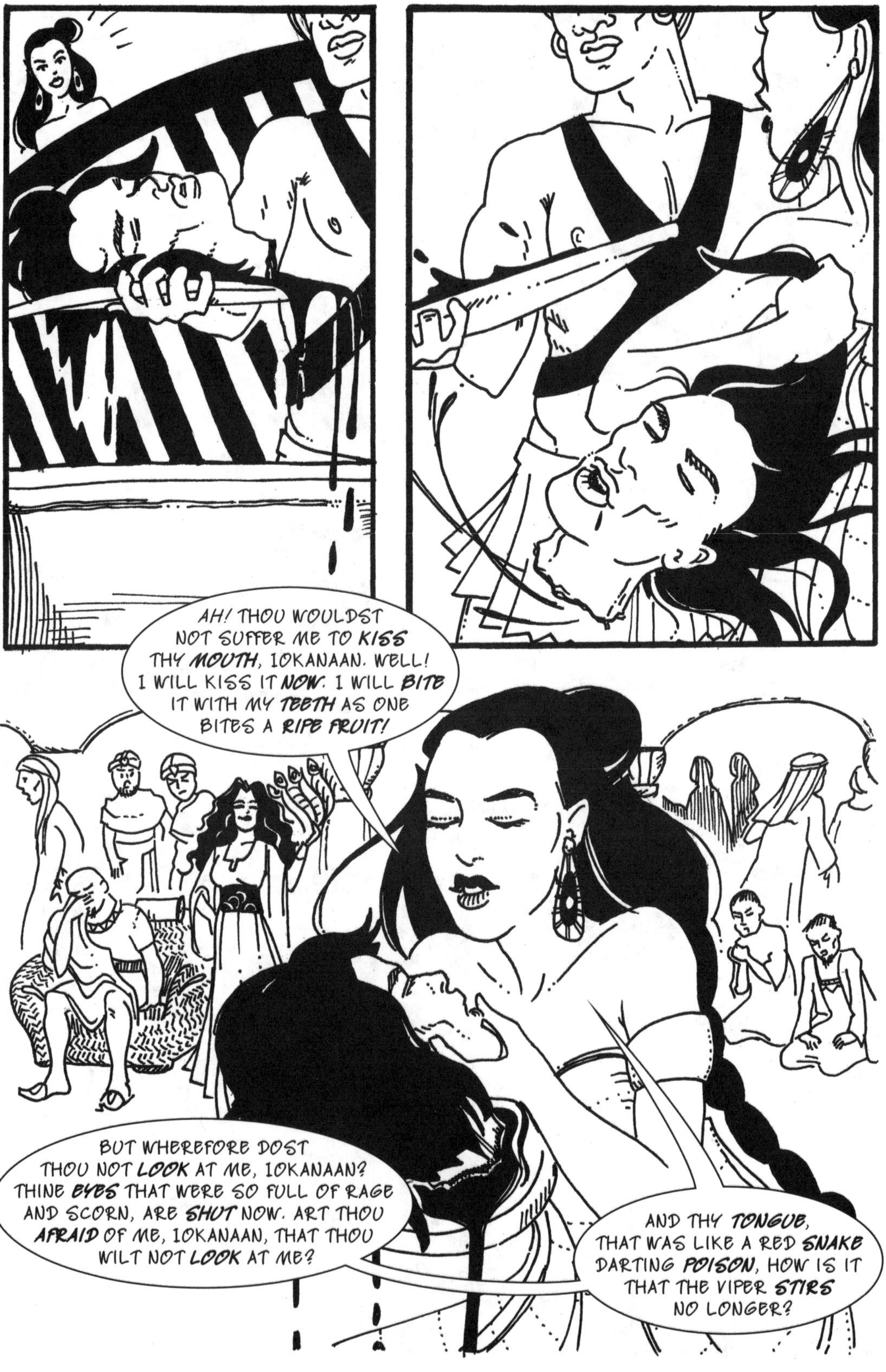
AH! THOU WOULDST NOT SUFFER ME TO KISS THY MOUTH, IOKANAAN. WELL! I WILL KISS IT NOW. I WILL BITE IT WITH MY TEETH AS ONE BITES A RIPE FRUIT!
BUT WHEREFORE DOST THOU NOT LOOK AT ME, IOKANAAN? THINE EYES THAT WERE SO FULL OF RAGE AND SCORN, ARE SHUT NOW. ART THOU AFRAID OF ME, IOKANAAN, THAT THOU WILT NOT LOOK AT ME?
AND THY TONGUE, THAT WAS LIKE A RED SNAKE DARTING POISON, HOW IS IT THAT THE VIPER STIRS NO LONGER?

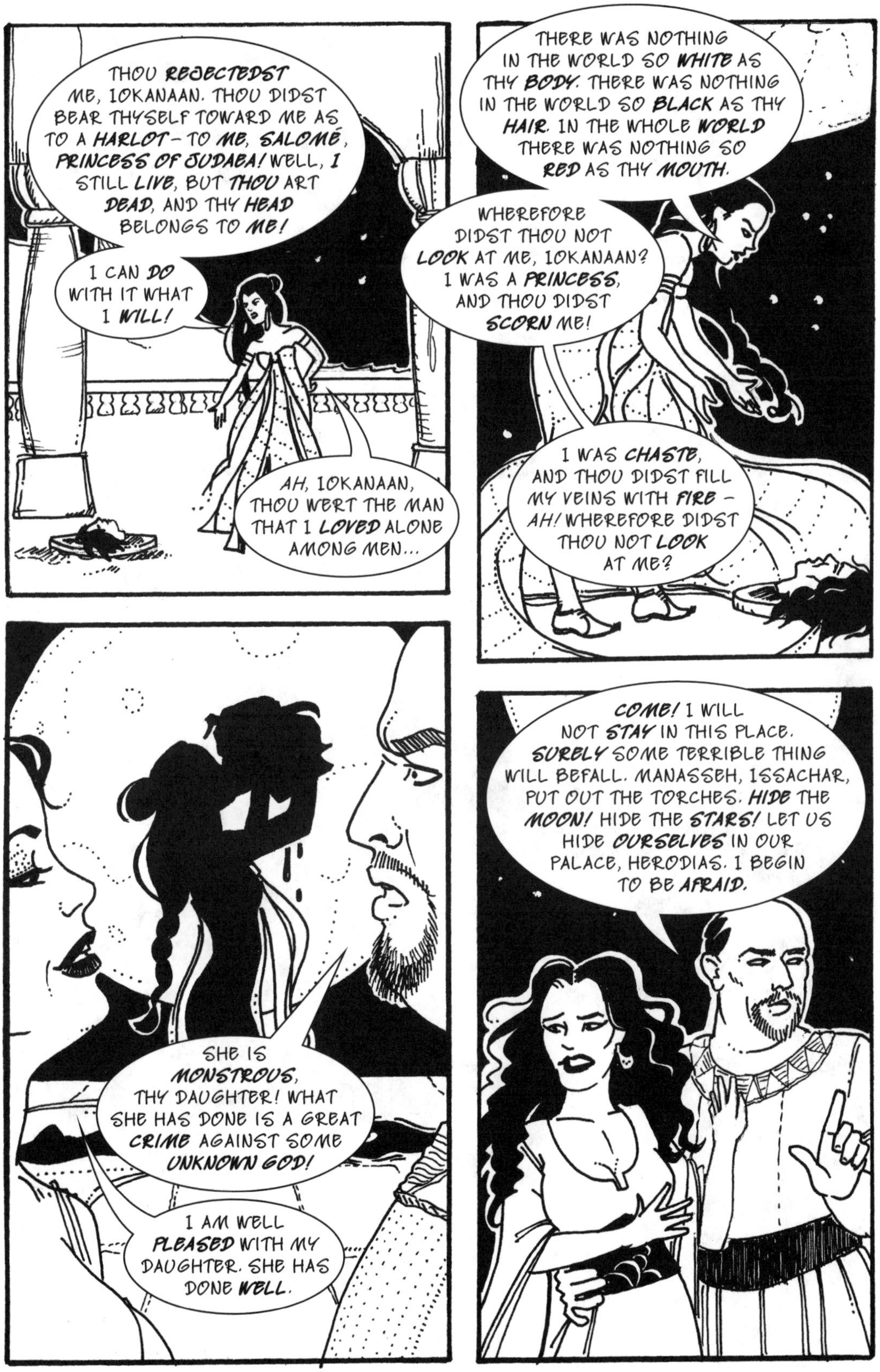
THOU REJECTEDST ME, IOKANAAN. THOU DIDST BEAR THYSELF TOWARD ME AS TO A HARLOT – TO ME, SALOMÉ, PRINCESS OF JUDAEA! WELL, I STILL LIVE, BUT THOU ART DEAD, AND THY HEAD BELONGS TO ME!
I CAN DO WITH IT WHAT I WILL!
AH, IOKANAAN, THOU WERT THE MAN THAT I LOVED ALONE AMONG MEN...
THERE WAS NOTHING IN THE WORLD SO WHITE AS THY BODY. THERE WAS NOTHING IN THE WORLD SO BLACK AS THY HAIR. IN THE WHOLE WORLD THERE WAS NOTHING SO RED AS THY MOUTH.
WHEREFORE DIDST THOU NOT LOOK AT ME, IOKANAAN? I WAS A PRINCESS, AND THOU DIDST SCORN ME!
I WAS CHASTE, AND THOU DIDST FILL MY VEINS WITH FIRE – AH! WHEREFORE DIDST THOU NOT LOOK AT ME?
SHE IS MONSTROUS, THY DAUGHTER! WHAT SHE HAS DONE IS A GREAT CRIME AGAINST SOME UNKNOWN GOD!
I AM WELL PLEASED WITH MY DAUGHTER. SHE HAS DONE WELL.
COME! I WILL NOT STAY IN THIS PLACE. SURELY SOME TERRIBLE THING WILL BEFALL. MANASSEH, ISSACHAR, PUT OUT THE TORCHES. HIDE THE MOON! HIDE THE STARS! LET US HIDE OURSELVES IN OUR PALACE, HERODIAS. I BEGIN TO BE AFRAID.

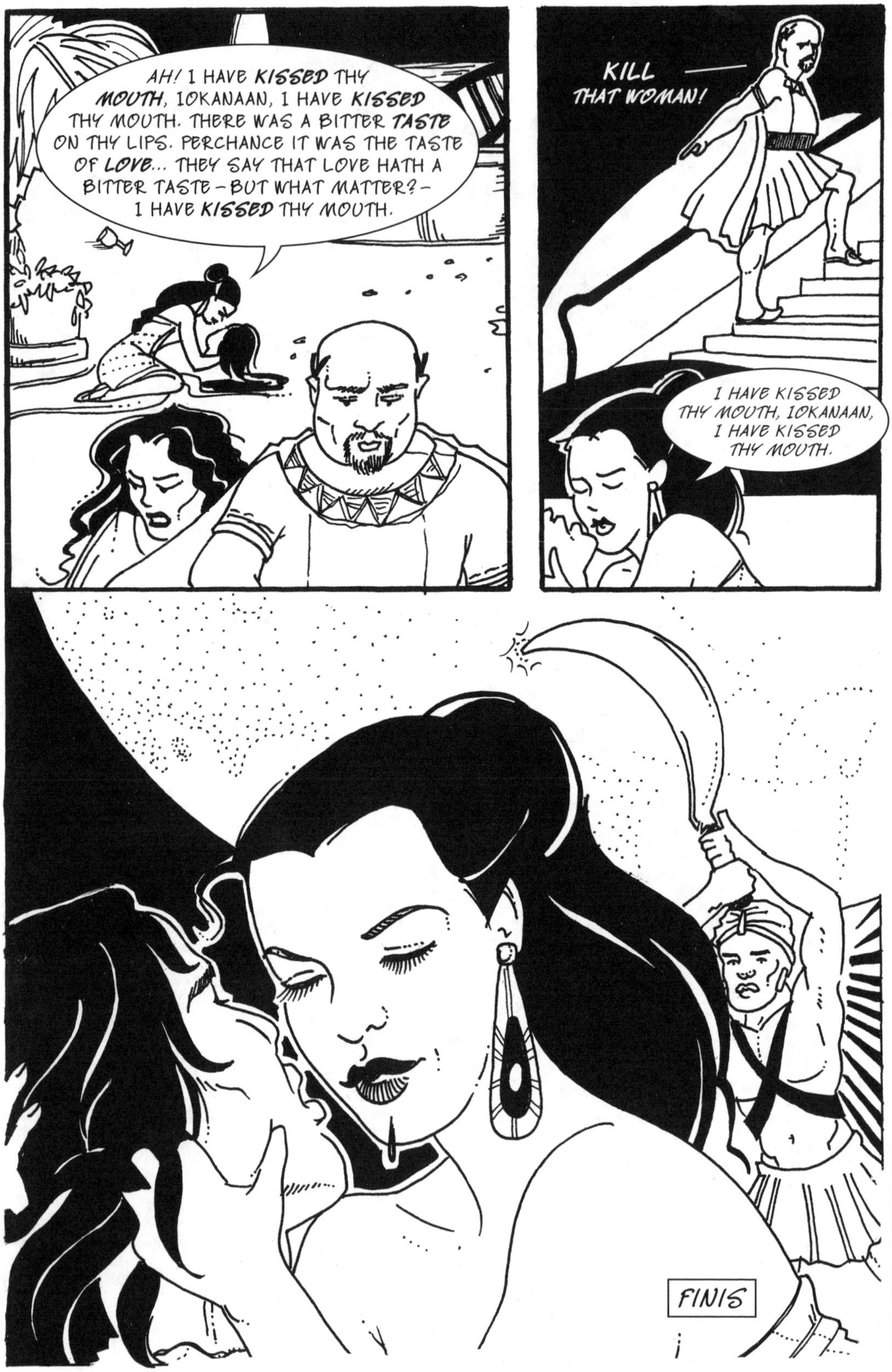
AH! I HAVE KISSED THY MOUTH, IOKANAAN, I HAVE KISSED THY MOUTH. THERE WAS A BITTER TASTE ON THY LIPS. PERCHANCE IT WAS THE TASTE OF LOVE... THEY SAY THAT LOVE HATH A BITTER TASTE — BUT WHAT MATTER? — I HAVE KISSED THY MOUTH.
KILL THAT WOMAN!
I HAVE KISSED THY MOUTH, IOKANAAN, I HAVE KISSED THY MOUTH.
FINIS

OSCAR WILDE

Born in Dublin, Ireland in 1854, Wilde studied at Trinity College before leaving Ireland for Oxford University. His first volume of poetry, *Patience*, was published in 1881, followed by a play, *The Duchess of Padua*, two years later. He became a famous celebrity as a poet, playwright, and wit, but his works did not find wide recognition until the publication of a book of stories for his children, *The Happy Prince and Other Tales*, in 1888. His most famous work, and his only novel, was *The Picture of Dorian Gray*, which was published in an American magazine in 1890 to a storm of controversy over its homoerotic themes and its attacks on hypocrisy in England. Wilde wrote numerous short stories, including *The Canterville Ghost* (1887) and *Lord Arthur Savile's Crime* (1891). His first publicly performed play, *Lady Windermere's Fan*, opened in February 1892. Its success prompted him to continue to write for the theater, and subsequent plays included *A Woman of No Importance* (1893), *An Ideal Husband* (1895) and *The Importance of Being Earnest* (1895). These plays continue to be performed today, and have been translated to films. *Salomé* was adapted to an opera by Richard Strauss in 1905. Oscar Wilde was a married man, but he had affairs with many men, including a young aristocrat named Lord Alfred Douglas, who translated *Salomé*, originally written in French, into English in 1894. Douglas' father, the Marquess of Queensberry, publicly denounced Wilde. He was tried for "gross indecency" and sentenced to two years hard labor in prison. On his release, he was a penniless, dejected man and he soon died in Paris, aged 46. Of his post-prison writings, the best is his poem *The Ballad of Reading Gaol*.

MOLLY KIELY (pages 1, 110, back cover)

Molly Kiely is a Canadian artist best known for her *Diary of a Dominatrix* comics series and the graphic novels *That Kind of Girl* and *Tecopa Jane*, all published by Fantagraphics. Molly currently lives in Tucson, Arizona, where she does art and chases her toddler, Perla, around the house. She maintains a journal at www.mollykiely.com and her artwork can be seen at www.tecopajane.com.

Molly's work also appears in
Gothic Classics: Graphic Classics Volume Fourteen

LANCE TOOKS (page 2)

As an animator for fifteen years, as well as a comics artist, Lance Tooks' work has appeared in more than a hundred television commercials, films and music videos. He has self-published the comics *Divided by Infinity Danger Funnies* and *Muthafucka*. His stories have appeared in *Zuzu*, *Shade*, *Vibe*, *Girltalk*, *World War 3 Illustrated*, *Floaters*, *Pure Friction* and the Italian magazine *Lupo Alberto*. He also illustrated *The Black Panthers for Beginners*, written by Herb Boyd. Lance's first graphic novel, *Narcissa*, was named one of the best books of 2002 by *Publisher's Weekly*, and he has recently completed his *Lucifer's Garden of Verses* series for NBM ComicsLit. In 2004 Lance moved from his native New York to Madrid, Spain, where he married and has recently finished a Spanish translation of *Narcissa*.

His stories appear in
Graphic Classics: Edgar Allan Poe
Graphic Classics: Ambrose Bierce
Graphic Classics: Mark Twain
Graphic Classics: Robert Louis Stevenson
Fantasy Classics: Graphic Classics Volume Fourteen

STEPHEN SILVER (page 3)

A self-taught artist, Stephen says he first aspired to be a professional when at the age of six he found an artist's sketchbook lying in his back yard. He began his career by drawing caricatures at amusement parks and then went on to establish his own illustration and caricature company called Silvertoons in 1992. In 1996 he was hired as a graphic designer for No Fear, the clothing company, and in 1997 he joined Warner Brothers Television Animation as a character designer. Silver has been working in the animation industry ever since. He has done animation and character design for Disney Television, Nickelodeon, and Sony Feature Animation on shows including *Clerks*, *Kim Possible*, and *Danny Phantom*. He continues to operate Silvertoons (www.silvertoons.com) and also teaches character design full-time with an online class at www.schoolism.com.

ALEX BURROWS (page 4)

Journalist and writer Alex Burrows lives in Oxfordshire and works in London as Managing Editor for *Classic Rock* magazine. His publishing career began with *Arnie*, a comics and punk rock zine co-published with artist Simon Gane. *The Picture Of Dorian Gray* is his third adaptation for *Graphics Classics*. "It was the most challenging but also the most rewarding adaptation I've worked on so far. But having to edit Wilde's legendary wordplay felt criminal at times — trying to shoehorn in as much dialogue as possible whilst still giving Lisa's beautiful artwork room to breathe was tortuous."

Alex is currently working on stories by Louisa May Alcott and Charles Dickens for upcoming volumes. His previous adaptations appear in
Graphic Classics: H.P. Lovecraft
Graphic Classics: Special Edition

LISA K. WEBER (page 4, cover)

Lisa K. Weber is an artist currently residing in Brooklyn, New York, having graduated from Parsons School of Design in 2000 with a BFA in Illustration. Her whimsically twisted characters and illustrations have appeared in various print, animation, and design projects including work for clients *Scholastic*, *Cricket Magazine*, Children's Television Workshop, and many others. Her work will be featured in a series of young reader's books, called *The Sisters Eight*, to be published by Houghton Mifflin in early 2009. She has also participated in exhibitions in New York and Philadelphia. To see more of her art, visit www.creatureco.com.

Lisa has provided comics and illustrations for
Graphic Classics: Edgar Allan Poe
Graphic Classics: H.P. Lovecraft
Graphic Classics: Ambrose Bierce
Graphic Classics: Mark Twain
Graphic Classics: O. Henry
Gothic Classics: Graphic Classics Volume Fourteen

ANTONELLA CAPUTO *(page 50)*

Antonella was born and raised in Rome, Italy, and now lives in Lancaster, England. She has been an architect, archaeologist, art restorer, photographer, calligrapher, interior designer, theater designer, actress and theater director. Her first published work was *Casa Montesi,* a fortnightly comic strip that appeared in the national magazine *Il Giornalino*. She has since written comedies for children and scripts for comics and magazines in the U.K., Europe and the U.S.

Antonella works with Nick Miller as the writing half of Team Sputnik, and has collaborated with Nick and other artists in
Graphic Classics: Edgar Allan Poe
Graphic Classics: Arthur Conan Doyle
Graphic Classics: H.G. Wells
Graphic Classics: Jack London
Graphic Classics: Ambrose Bierce
Graphic Classics: Mark Twain
Graphic Classics: O. Henry
Graphic Classics: Rafael Sabatini
Horror Classics: Graphic Classics Volume Ten
Adventure Classics: Graphic Classics Volume Twelve
Gothic Classics: Graphic Classics Volume Fourteen
Fantasy Classics: Graphic Classics Volume Fifteen
Graphic Classics: Special Edition

NICK MILLER *(page 50)*

Nick grew up in the depths of rural England, and now lives in Lancaster with his partner, Antonella Caputo. The son of two artists, he learned to draw at an early age. After leaving art school he worked as a graphic designer before switching to cartooning and illustration full-time in the early '90s. Since then his work has appeared in many comics and magazines in the U.K., U.S. and Europe, as well as in comic anthologies, websites and in advertising. His weekly comic strip, *The Really Heavy Greatcoat*, can be seen online at www.lancasterukonline.net. He works as part of Team Sputnik with Antonella Caputo, and also independently with other writers including John Freeman, Tony Husband, Mark Rogers and Tim Quinn.

Nick's stories have appeared in
Graphic Classics: Arthur Conan Doyle
Graphic Classics: H.G. Wells
Graphic Classics: Jack London
Graphic Classics: Ambrose Bierce
Graphic Classics: Mark Twain
Horror Classics: Graphic Classics Volume Ten
Adventure Classics: Graphic Classics Volume Twelve

RICH RAINEY *(page 80)*

A ghostwriter who also writes about ghosts, Rich Rainey's nonfiction books include *Phantom Forces* (a history of warfare and the occult), *Haunted History*, and *The Monster Factory*, a book about classic horror writers and the real-life incidents that inspired their fiction. He's written over thirty adventure and science fiction novels and also created *The Protector* series about a modern day D'Artagnan in New York City. His short fiction has appeared in literary and mystery magazines, and numerous anthologies, including *Best Detective Stories of the Year*. In the comics field he created *Flesh Crawlers* for Kitchen Sink, *Antrax: One Nation Underground* for Caliber, and has written for *The Punisher* and Neil Gaiman's *Lady Justice*. He recently scripted an adaptation of H.G. Wells' *The War of the Worlds* for *Science Fiction Classics*.

Rich also adapted stories for
Graphic Classics: H.P. Lovecraft
Graphic Classics: Bram Stoker

STAN SHAW *(page 80)*

Stan Shaw (drawstanley.com) illustrates for various clients all over the country including *The Village Voice, Esquire, Slate,* Starbucks, The Seattle Mariners, Nintendo, Rhino Records, Microsoft, R.E.I., B.E.T., P.O.V., DC Comics, ABCNEWS.com, Wizards of The Coast, The Flying Karamazov Brothers, *Amazing Stories, Vibe* and *Willamette Week*. In addition to practicing illustration, he teaches it at Cornish School of the Arts, School of Visual Concepts and Pacific Lutheran University. He is now part of a group of artists advising on an illustration textbook.

Stan can be reached at drawstanley@harbornet.com. He has illustrated stories in
Graphic Classics: Edgar Allan Poe
Graphic Classics: Ambrose Bierce
Graphic Classics: O. Henry
Graphic Classics: Rafael Sabatini

TOM POMPLUN

The designer, editor and publisher of *Graphic Classics*, Tom has a background in both fine and commercial art and a lifelong interest in comics. He designed and produced *Rosebud*, a journal of fiction, poetry and illustration, from 1993 to 2003, and in 2001 he founded *Graphic Classics*. Tom is currently working on *Science Fiction Classics,* scheduled for June 2009 release. The book will feature a new comics adaptation of *The War of the Worlds* by Rich Rainey and *Graphic Classics* newcomer Micah Farritor, plus stories by Jules Verne, Stanley Weinbaum, Lord Dunsany, E.M. Forster and Arthur Conan Doyle, with art by Brad Teare, Johnny Ryan, George Sellas, Roger Langridge and Ellen Lindner (in her *GC* début) plus a stunning cover by Micah Farritor.

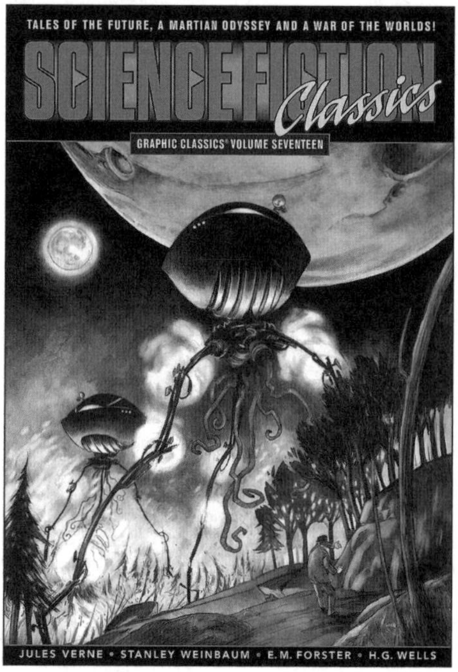
TALES OF THE FUTURE, A MARTIAN ODYSSEY AND A WAR OF THE WORLDS!
SCIENCE FICTION Classics
GRAPHIC CLASSICS® VOLUME SEVENTEEN
JULES VERNE • STANLEY WEINBAUM • E.M. FORSTER • H.G. WELLS